John Wesley's Social Ethics

Praxis and Principles

John Wesley's Social Ethics

Praxis and Principles

Manfred Marquardt

Translated by John E. Steely and
W. Stephen Gunter

ABINGDON PRESS
Nashville

JOHN WESLEY'S SOCIAL ETHICS: PRAXIS AND PRINCIPLES

Copyright © 1992 by Abingdon Press

This book is printed on recycled, acid-free paper.

Library of Congress Cataloging-in-Publication Data

MARQUARDT, MANFRED.
    [Praxis und Prinzipien der Sozialethik John Wesleys. English]
    John Wesley's social ethics : praxis and principles / Manfred Marquardt; translated by John E. Steely and W. Stephen Gunter.
        p.   cm.
    Translation of: Praxis und Prinzipien der Sozialethik John Wesleys.
    Includes bibliographical references and index.
    ISBN 0-687-20494-1 (alk. paper)
    1. Wesley, John, 1703-1791. 2. Social ethics—History—18th century. I. Title.
BX8495.W5M28713   1991
241'.047092—dc20   91-42505
                                                                        CIP

Translation from the German with permission of Vandenhoeck & Ruprecht, Göttingen. © Vandenhoeck & Ruprecht in Göttingen.

MANUFACTURED IN THE UNITED STATES OF AMERICA

CONTENTS

Translator's Preface...9

Foreword to the English Edition.....................................11

Foreword to the Original German Edition.........................13

Introduction..15

PART A:
THE MAJOR AREAS OF WESLEY'S SOCIAL PRAXIS...............17

Chapter I: The Social Work of the Early
Oxford Methodists.......................................19

1. The Misery of the Lower Classes............................19
2. Christian Philanthropy..21
3. The Social Activity of the Early Oxford Methodists............23

Chapter II: Wesley's and the Methodist Societies'
Aid to the Poor.......................................27

1. Practical Measures for Aid to the Poor....................27
2. The Altered Attitude Toward the Poor.....................30
3. The Methodist Societies as Fields of Social Probation..........33

**Chapter III: John Wesley's Contribution
to Economic Ethics**.. 35

1. The Economic Responsibility of the Individual.................... 35

2. Methodism and the Capitalist Spirit........................ 41

3. The Economic Responsibility of Society......................... 43

**Chapter IV: The Educational and Training Work
of Wesley and His Colleagues**............................ 49

1. English Schools in the Eighteenth Century...................... 49

2. Methodist Schools and Sunday Schools...................... 51

3. Adult Education in Methodism............................ 55

4. Education and Training in the Context of Wesley's
Theological Ethic.. 60

Chapter V: John Wesley's Battle Against Slavery...................... 67

1. Slavery and the Slave Trade in Eighteenth-Century
England and Its Colonies...................................... 67

2. The Churches' Attitude Toward Slavery.................... 68

3. The Beginning of the Battle Against Slavery.................. 70

4. John Wesley's Attitude Toward Slavery.................... 70

Chapter VI: Concern for Prisoners and Prison Reform............... 77

1. The English Penal System in the Eighteenth Century........... 77

2. Wesley's Aid to Prisoners.................................. 81

**PART B:
THE PRINCIPLES OF WESLEY'S SOCIAL ETHICS**.................. 87

Chapter VII: Presuppositions of Wesley's Social Ethics.............. 89

1. Prevenient Grace.. 89

2. Renewing Grace.. 95

Chapter VIII: Standards for Social Ethics.............................. 103

    1. Love of God and Neighbor................................ 103

    2. The Divine Commandments................................110

    3. Examples.. 113

    4. Personal Insights....................................116

Chapter IX: Aims of Wesley's Social Ethics............................119

    1. The Renewal of the Individual........................... 119

    2. The Renewal of Society................................ 123

Chapter X: Concluding Observations.. 133

    1. The Weaknesses of Wesley's Social Ethics.......................... 133

    2. The Strengths of Wesley's Social Ethics........................... 135

Abbreviations...139

Notes.. 141

Bibliography.. 191

Index..201

To my teachers
who remained
students, and
to my students
who still teach me

TRANSLATOR'S PREFACE

The late Dr. John Steely, who was well known and highly regarded for his abilities as a scholar and translator, began the work of translating this volume several years ago. When the publisher approached me about taking up the project that had been left incomplete by Dr. Steely's untimely death and seeing it to publication, I was very flattered.

Professor Manfred Marquardt is known to many of us who are actively involved in the theological enterprise in the tradition of John Wesley. The publication of this volume in English will make his important work accessible to a much broader public, an honor richly deserved.

Although the present work is now several years old, its appearance in English is very timely. For most of the twentieth century, the Methodist tradition has been keenly interested in the social dimensions of the gospel. Recently a revival of interest in integrating social and ethical theory with praxis and theological presuppositions has set the stage for a fresh look at one who, within the limitations of his century, succeeded to a remarkable degree in achieving just such an integration.

Professor Marquardt recognizes and points out many of Wesley's limitations in these areas, but he also reminds us through his analysis of the Wesley corpus that John Wesley worked on several fronts simultaneously with considerable skill. Even those of us who have "lived with" Wesley for several years (perhaps us most of all) are not willing to make Wesley the final authority on any subject, but the leader of the early Methodist movement remains for us still a rich resource, as well as a vivid example. This essay on the principles and praxis of Wesley's ethic will open new doors of insight to many readers.

W. Stephen Gunter
Bethany, Oklahoma
July, 1991

9

FOREWORD TO THE ENGLISH EDITION

This book was first published some fifteen years ago for a German-speaking public in continental Europe; a second edition appeared in 1986. Its aim was two-fold: to provide an interpretation of Wesley's theology, and to demonstrate the interdependence of his social praxis with his ethical principles (both explicit and implicit); and to inform European Methodists, who live in a minority situation with all its attendant problems, as well as the members of other (majority) churches who have an interest in Wesleyan theology, about an essential aspect of their inheritance from the founder of Methodism.

The approach to Wesley taken here is primarily theological, although I have also attempted to be historically accurate. However my intention was not purely academic in nature. By taking seriously Wesley's understanding of the Christian faith and its implications, I have been concerned to discover how his way of practicing and reflecting on Christian ethics could help in finding solutions for pressing contemporary social problems. At the same time, I have tried to maintain a critical stance toward the founder of Methodism, who (I assume) would not have expected anything less.

Since a more intensive dialogue between German-speaking and English-speaking Methodists has begun in recent years, I am particularly pleased that an English translation of this work can now be published. Several outstanding and well-known Methodist theologians in the English-speaking world (e.g., Thomas A. Langford, James Logan, John Walsh, and Henry Rack) have used the German edition in their own academic work, and have recommended it to others who were able to read German. With the publication of this English edition, the language barrier is overcome, making the work more widely accessible.

I am grateful to David Steinmetz of the Labyrinth Press, who took the first steps toward an English edition, and to Rex D. Matthews of Abingdon Press, who has seen it through to publication. The translators, John Steely, who unfortunately died before finishing his work, and W. Stephen Gunter, who completed the translation, have done a superb job. I regret that it has not been possible, for reasons of time, to alter the references to Wesley's writings to correspond to the new critical edition of *The Works of John Wesley* now being published by Abingdon Press.

Wesley studies in continental Europe during the last fifteen years have dealt mostly with historical and theological themes (i.e., the "Wesleyan quadrilateral," justification and sanctification, assurance, the church, liturgy and sacraments, the holiness movement, and so on). No other major treatments of Wesley's ethic have appeared in German. Recent English publications in this area, e.g., Leon O. Hynson, *To Reform the Nation: Theological Foundations of Wesley's Ethics* (1984), and L. D. Hulley, *To Be and To Do: Exploring Wesley's Thought on Ethical Behaviour* (1988), take a different approach to Wesley's theology and have a different focus, but are mainly complementary to, rather than in conflict with, my interpretation.

This work, therefore, continues to be a standard treatment of Wesley's social ethics, and I am very pleased by its appearance in English. My hope is that it will help to foster among "the people called Methodists"—ministers and lay persons, professors and students—a vivid understanding of Wesley's singular contribution to Christian social ethics, and will thus contribute to a renewal of his responsible discipleship in our time.

Manfred Marquardt
Reutlingen
Summer 1991

FOREWORD TO THE ORIGINAL
GERMAN EDITION

Under the title "Praxis and Prinzipien sozialer Verantwortung. Eine Studie zur Sozialethik John Wesleys," this work was presented as an inaugural dissertation to the Theological Faculty of Christian-Albrechts University in Kiel in the winter semester of 1974-75. It has been slightly revised for publication, particularly by reduction of quotations from Wesley, which in the original version had been given in the original English and then translated into German. The indication of where these materials may be found will provide for the reader of the present work the possibility of checking the sources.

I am happy to express my thanks to the following: to Dr. E. Wölfel for his counsel, and in many other respects to the Systematic Theology Society of Kiel under the leadership of Dr. H. J. Birkner, Dr. W. Härle, E. Wölfel, and Dr. E. Herms for encouragement and critical questions; to the Northwest German Annual Conference of my church for a temporary leave of absence; to Dr. M. Schmidt and his colleagues for their acceptance of this work for publication in their series "Kirche und Konfession"; and to Bishop C. E. Sommer and the University of Kiel for helping to underwrite the cost of printing as well as for a stipend for graduate study. For their help in securing literature that rarely is easily accessible in Germany, I thank E. Baass (Bodenwerder), Dr. K. Bockmühl (Bettingen), Dozent K. Dahn (Bauschlott), D. M. Davin (Oxford), Director E. P. Sheeby (New York), Director K. Steckel, D. D. (Reutlingen), Dozent P. Wüthrich (Reutlingen), and Dr. W. Wittwer (Kiel), as well as my colleagues R. Gebhardt (Zürich), Dr. J. C. Bowmer (London), K. Kumm (Frankfurt/M), K. H. Grüneke (Los Angeles), H. Robbe (London), B. Schwabe (Essen), and K. H. Voigt (Bremen). I thank Superintendent V. Schneeberger for permission to look at his manuscript before its publication. My wife has given up many hours of our time together and has prepared the manuscript with great care. I am indebted to her most of all.

INTRODUCTION

After an incalculable flood of literature about the founder of Methodism had already appeared in Anglo-Saxon countries over the span of two centuries, interest in John Wesley on the European continent has increased in the recent past. Yet it could be said of most of the books and other written assessments, even up to the present time, that partisanship, in veneration or rejection, has clouded the vision and produced an abundance of contradictory pictures. Only during the past two generations have people begun to concern themselves critically with Wesley, his theology, and his life's work.[1] Several monographs have explored his anthropology and his individual ethics.[2] Others concern themselves, from historical and sociological perspectives, with his social work and the significance of the Methodist Societies and Class-meetings for English society.[3] The first one to examine the connection between theology and social activity in a more precise and profound fashion is V. Schneeberger, in his dissertation "Theologische Wurzeln des sozialen Akzents bei John Wesley."[4] Schneeberger posed the question "whether there is a direct connection between Wesley's theological proclamation and his social work," and ended his study precisely where "a study of ethics in John Wesley should begin."[5]

The present study, on the other hand, is concerned with working out some of the essential elements of the interdependence between Wesley's social activity and his theory of social ethics, interpreting these elements in their own terms, and making critical inquiry into them. In that a combination of historical and systematic method appears best suited to the topic as proposed, in the first part of the work some exemplary areas of social work are briefly presented and analyzed. In the second part, the principles that underlie them are traced out and are placed in a larger context.

THE MAJOR AREAS OF WESLEY'S SOCIAL PRAXIS

CHAPTER I

THE SOCIAL WORK OF THE EARLY OXFORD METHODISTS

Anyone wanting to achieve an overview of the amazing breadth of Wesley's social activity[1] must become seriously concerned with his individual actions, and place them in the broader perspective of social responsibility. The student of John Wesley's life work must remember that it belongs almost entirely to the pre-revolutionary epoch of recent European history. The early socialists' activity was beginning while Wesley's activity was coming to an end. The first phase of what can be properly labeled as the English labor movement began just after Wesley had died.[2] The intensity of the class conflicts that followed, and their effect on society at large and the church's work in particular, tend to obscure our vision of Wesley's theological achievement and cloud our recognition that Wesley was very much a product of his historical context. It is important to outline the social situation of the lower classes of English society in the mid-eighteenth century.

1. THE MISERY OF THE LOWER CLASSES

At the beginning of the eighteenth century, the not insignificant number of poor varied from one part of England to another and from year to year, depending on the harvest. The rather considerable middle class included skilled workers and craftsmen; this changed, however, with the beginning of the Industrial Revolution. Even the Marxist historian Jürgen Kuczynski characterizes the period up to 1760 favorably in comparison with what was to follow: "The polarization process—that is, the division of the populace into a great mass of people becoming poorer and poorer, ever more wretched, and a small minority of very rich people—was, in comparison with the time of the Industrial Revolution, still in the beginning stages of development."[3] Nevertheless,

19

the cottagers and the poor already formed the largest stratum of the populace.[4] During the eighteenth century their number increased considerably. Most lacked any schooling or vocational training. Most no longer lived in their home communities, but in newly developed industrial areas or slum districts at the cities' edge. Hence they had lost their privileges of economic support and were no longer accessible to the ecclesiastical arrangement that was oriented to traditional parochial structures. They survived as crowded masses in living conditions that were catastrophic even for that time. Without any medical care, the high mortality rate was offset only by the even higher birthrate.[5]

This increasing wretchedness of large segments of the population would reach its peak in the nineteenth century. Its causes lay above all in the dispossession of the rural population, incipient industrialization, the rigid attitude of public social agencies, and the traditional attitude of property owners.

The rural population became dispossessed due to the enclosure of communal lands, the expropriation of fallow land, and the consolidation of farms and fields. Parliament had provided the legal preconditions for all of the above. The almost exclusive beneficiaries of this development were the property owners, whose strong investment power and modernized agricultural methods took away the very foundation of existence from the no-longer-competitive small farmers, freeholders, and part-time farmers. After 1760, this process rapidly increased, produced a growing number of unemployed persons, and thereby depressed industrial wages.[6] The invention of the steam engine and other laborsaving devices only heightened unemployment. The wool industry machine work replaced the handwork once carried out in innumerable small household businesses.[7] Independent craftsmen, like the peasants before them, fell into the insecure fate of dependence upon wages.

Until well into the nineteenth century, public measures regarding the poor[8] were oriented to the almost unaltered poor-laws of the Elizabethan era, which can be summed up thus:

> All persons able to work must be compelled to work when they are found unemployed, the youth among them placed in apprenticeship. The handicapped and the sick are cared for at public cost in poorhouses, where they too are to work insofar as they are able. The cost of their maintenance and of the maintenance of people capable of work who are being punished in houses of correction for begging is the responsibility of the respective places of birth, which also must bear the cost of this care for the poor.[9]

This law left unresolved in ever-increasing gravity the social problems of the eighteenth century that arose out of poverty. This should be attributed not only to the apathy of the appropriate authorities,[10] but also to the requirement that the poor seek help in their birthplace,[11] and to the population movements that necessarily occurred as a result of economic changes.[12] Partial responsibility also belongs to the traditional English attitude that poverty itself is a fault, to be borne as a stigma of divine punishment.[13] A fixed scale of religiously grounded values supported the static character of a segmented society. The property owners' egotism was so great that their charitable activities and humanitarian gifts were frequently exercises of religious obligation rather than actual help directed toward bringing about change for the needy.[14] Because criminal acts resulting from poverty were better known than the misery of the poor, indignation tended to replace sympathy.[15]

But conservatism was not limited to property owners. Even the poor were not inclined to a different attitude toward the state, society, and the economy, an attitude that would have been better suited to the new realities.[16] But when the exploitation of workers, increasing unemployment, inhumane working conditions (especially of miners, women, and children), and low wages were joined by lack of food and extraordinary brutality by employers, local demonstrations arose and the mob's wrath occasionally led to violence. Instead of doing away with the evils that had caused such justifiable protests, the authorities interpreted every disturbance of public order as an attack on traditional privileges. Thus they usually had military forces intervene, smash the demonstration, and impose severe punishment upon the instigators.[17]

The wealthy were generally concerned with securing property and enhancing income. In spite of the many efforts of individuals and of some philanthropic societies, neither state nor church could comprehend or relieve the increasingly urgent and sizable problem of poverty. The basic motive behind all public and private measures was to maintain the existing order.

2. CHRISTIAN PHILANTHROPY

Historians' judgments of England's ecclesiastical circumstances at the beginning of the eighteenth century are unequivocally negative: "The feasts of the Church were ignored; daily worship was neglected; buildings were allowed to fall into disrepair; and Holy Communion was observed infrequently. Bishops and clergy had become indolent and worldly. They neglected their spiritual duties."[18] Newly developed residential districts in the spreading cities particularly suffered from a lack of pastoral care. The existing churchmanship of the Anglican Christians, and to some extent of the Dissenters, resembled only an external morality.[19]

This was not true of the "religious societies" that had arisen near the end of the seventeenth century under the initiative of Anton Horneck and Richard Smithies. They were mainly concerned with personal conversations in small circles and lives lived in accordance with strict rules. Their ecclesiastical affiliation was high-church Anglican—prayers from the Book of Common Prayer and regular celebration of Communion defined their religious activity. These societies spread, especially among younger people, from London outward into other cities. In keeping with other contemporary philanthropic efforts, the societies undertook social tasks as well: financially supporting poor people, caring for prisoners, and visiting the sick and those in hospitals and workhouses.[20] The scope of their influence is very difficult to define. The societies admitted only Anglicans, no Dissenters; they focused on liturgical and devotional practices; their basic motif, to which even social work was entirely subordinate, was holiness, in the sense of ecclesiastical-ascetic piety. Nevertheless, these societies clearly contrast with an inactive state church and a society that almost totally denied the burning needs of its poor.

Two societies in particular developed and grew beyond the narrow circle of a local club: the Society for Promoting Christian Knowledge (SPCK, founded in 1698) and the Society for the Propagation of the Gospel (SPG, founded in 1701). The SPCK aspired "to provide schools in London where children not normally within the reach of the Church could receive catechism; to print good books for the poor; and to promote religion in the American plantations, by means, mostly, of suitable literature."[21] The SPG especially emphasized church care for English citizens in the colonies and evangelizing the natives.

An indeterminate number of individual initiatives accompanied these institutional activities. Particularly influential were Jeremy Taylor and William Law, who worked to eliminate moral and social evils and alleviate the plight of the poor. The overall picture of English society in this period remained extremely tense. A predominant majority of conservative property owners, who were concerned only with preserving their privileges, stood opposed to the poor, who were almost apathetically dependent and needy. Even the minority of groups and individuals who exerted themselves greatly were not able to overcome the wretchedness of those whose life they were striving to improve. Prejudice for the traditional structures obscured their vision of poverty's evil causes. The very character of their piety meant that ultimately even their devoted care for the poor was only the means of their own sanctification.

3. THE SOCIAL ACTIVITY OF THE EARLY OXFORD METHODISTS

The social activity of the Oxford "Holy Club," of which John Wesley had become the leader, should be viewed in this context of other religious societies.[22] Here Wesley was first confronted with the challenge for social work and recognized it to be an essential, inseparable part of the Christian life.

The Practical Social Work of the Club Members

Three theological students, including John's younger brother Charles, had formed a small circle "for the study of the classics and of the New Testament and for the cultivation of piety."[23] They desired to provide mutual assistance in study and in their Christian lives.

John, their senior or superior in several respects, joined them and became their leader. They read books for edification, especially those of Thomas à Kempis, Jeremy Taylor, and William Law. Employing formulated questions, they regularly examined their personal lives in thought, word, and deed, including the content and carrying out of their plans. Without exception they were faithful members of the Anglican church, intending to encourage the better fulfillment of its rules and ordinances in the lives of other students also. However, this very concern—and later, their social activity—met with resistance, sometimes expressed in ridicule or irritation among their fellow students and teachers, only a few of whom approved or understood.

The Oxford circle undertook a task costly in time and money: social work in the city. Again, it was not John Wesley who provided the stimulus for this undertaking, but a younger member of the circle; however, it was Wesley who took up the initiative and gave direction. This social undertaking survived even after John's departure for Georgia until the Holy Club was entirely dissolved. The students' involvement appeared essentially at four points: in the two city prisons in Oxford, among poor families, in the workhouse, and in a school for underprivileged children. With approval of the appropriate ecclesiastical and civil officials in Oxford, the Wesleys and their friends regularly visited the two prisons, assumed responsibility for preaching and pastoral care to the prisoners, and occasionally provided financial support to help prisoners begin a new occupation.

An especially serious distress arose in deprived families in which the mother or the father became ill. When the student circle undertook their care, they visited the family at least once each week, secured medicines and clothing, taught the children, and explained Christian doctrines to the entire family. They offered similar support to the community's workhouse residents. Monies were supplied by a fund of regular or occasional contributions of friends and supplemented by the young men themselves. They saved money by denying themselves the typical student pleasures and stylish clothing, and later by fasting.

The scope of this small group's social activity is best indicated by the school for poor children, probably established by John Wesley himself. As a teacher he apparently felt strongly the inadequacy of the children's sporadic instruction. John secured and paid a teacher, inspected the children's instruction and handwork, and taught them biblical stories, prayers, and truths of the Christian faith. For years some twenty children from poor families were given an education they would otherwise have been denied.

Religious Motivation for Social Work

Why did these young men do all this despite personal sacrifice and the high price of hostility? We gain accurate information from John Wesley himself. During the discussions about the Holy Club, John had formulated for both friends and adversaries a series of questions, differing from earlier lists, related particularly to charitable activity. Some of them read as follows:

I. Whether it does not concern all men of all conditions to imitate him as much as they can, "who went about doing good"?

Whether all Christians are not concerned in that command, "While we have time, let us do good to all men"?

Whether we shall not be happy hereafter the more good we do now?

Whether we can be happy at all hereafter unless we have, according to our power, "fed the hungry, clothed the naked, visited those that are sick and in prison"; and made all these actions subservient to a higher purpose, even the saving of souls from death?

Whether it be not our bounden duty always to remember that He did more for us than we can do for him, who assures us, "Inasmuch as ye have done it to one of the least of these my brethren, ye have done it unto me"? . . .

III. Whether, upon these considerations above-mentioned we may not try to do good to those that are hungry, naked, or sick? In particular whether if we know any necessitous family, we may not give them a little food, clothes, or physic as they want?

Whether we may not give them, if they can read, a Bible, Common Prayer Book, or "Whole Duty of Man" [a devotional book by Richard Allestree, London, 1659]?

Other needs would be guidance for understanding this literature, for prayer, and for church attendance, as well as assistance in clothing and teaching the children. And, "Lastly: Whether, upon the considerations above-mentioned, we may not try to do good to those who are in prison?"[24]

In light of these questions the society's motives appear to have been on the one hand, imitation of Jesus and fulfillment of his commandments, and on the other, striving for blessedness through commitment to the higher goal of the salvation of souls. Obedience to Christ's undisputed authority was connected with the worthy goal of one's own blessedness.

A letter of Wesley's from July, 1731 echoes a similar religious eudaemonism: "I was made to be happy: to be happy I must love God; in proportion to my love of whom my happiness must increase."[25] The shape of this love became visible in Jesus and has been transmitted in the New Testament in exemplary fashion. Accordingly, the Bible is understood primarily as an ethical norm; Christ, the apostles, and the first Christians are the examples one should emulate.[26] Christians can attain blessedness in this life by carefully fulfilling the commandments given to them.

Before Wesley departed for Georgia to work as a pastor to the colonists and a missionary to the Indians, he stated his motivation: "My main motive, to which all others are subordinate, is the hope of saving my own soul."[27] However, this motivation may be in tension with another: his orientation to God's will. Wesley had rejected his father's request that he succeed him as pastor in Epworth. Wesley explained that his only reason was the glory of God, most fully realized by a way of life "whereby we can most promote holiness in ourselves and in others."[28] Sanctification is God's will, most thoroughly fulfilled by obeying the commandment of love. Loving God and one's neighbors is the Christian's highest obligation; failing to fulfill this obligation blocks the way to happiness. Love for God commands first place.[29]

Aside from the Wesley brothers and George Whitefield, the members of the Oxford student circle played no role in later Methodist work. Most of them became "ordinary, unremarkable ministers."[30] John Wesley, however, throughout his life remained active in social issues. Wesley's activity gained a new foundation when justification by faith alone became the basis of his life and work.[31] The work at Oxford had its continuing significance primarily in the fact that it kept Wesley from being diverted into a monastic or ascetic style of piety[32] and permanently stamped upon him the duty of practical love of neighbor. The demise of the Oxford circle made evident to Wesley the necessity of a more reliable foundation than works-righteousness.[33] In his encounters with Luther's theology and the Moravians,[34] Wesley discovered this foundation in justification by faith as a personal experience giving the assurance of salvation.

CHAPTER II

WESLEY'S AND THE METHODIST SOCIETIES' AID TO THE POOR

The Methodist movement began as evangelism, proclaiming the gospel of God's justifying grace to an unchurched audience drawn largely from the lower classes. After some twenty years of evangelism, Wesley wrote in his journal:

> It is well a few of the rich and noble are called. Oh, that God would increase their number! But I should rejoice (were it the will of God) if it were done by the ministry of others. If I must choose, I should still (as I have done hitherto) preach the gospel to the poor.[1]

Wesley was one of the first not only to see the poor as recipients of alms and objects of charitable care, but also to set forth the genuinely Christian duty to eliminate their wretchedness. This work, of course, was within Wesley's limits as a layman in political and social science in the pre-revolutionary eighteenth century and an Anglican loyal to the king. The fact remains basically undisputed that Wesley nevertheless exerted a preeminently positive influence in English social history. The nature of that influence and Wesley's theological justification of it should be distinguished from his practical activity and from his theoretical statements on other topics.

1. PRACTICAL MEASURES FOR AID TO THE POOR

Wesley undertook various measures to relieve the poor—some independently, some in concert with other groups such as the religious societies, and some of his own design. These efforts were prompted by his own perception of the misery he encountered in his numerous travels and visits to families, factories, workhouses, hospitals, and prisons. These actions consisted of measures toward self-help and charitable deeds to relieve distress. Understandably in such a young, numerically small movement, these were at first limited. The earliest and most widely practiced aid for the poor was the weekly "class meeting" conducted by the class leader, with the aid of the members of the fellowship assigned to him.[2] After careful consultation among administrators expressly chosen for this task, the collective contributions were distributed to the needy,[3] partly in cash, partly in clothing, foodstuffs, fuel, or medicine. In extraordinary distress from poor harvests, severe winter weather, or other unexpected circumstances, special collections were solicited to bring substantial relief, or Wesley himself traveled to plead for the needed funds.[4] The amounts collected, often reaching more than one hundred pounds, may be compared with Wesley's ability to meet his own needs with twenty-eight pounds per year,[5] and the fact that the majority of Methodists were not among the propertied class.[6]

Of course, Wesley knew that to occasionally supply the poor with the most sorely needed foodstuffs did not permanently deliver them from dire need. But the financial means raised in response to Wesley's preaching and pointed appeals provided the economic basis for most of his social undertakings. Repeatedly Wesley stirred the public conscience through appeals in sermons, conversations, and the press.

Alongside the provision of foodstuffs and clothing, Wesley introduced an additional assistance in London and Bristol in 1746-47: medical care for the poor. The hygienic conditions in many residences were catastrophic, medical care was utterly inadequate, nutrition was often poor, and knowledge about healthly living and caring for the sick was minimal. In addition, the widespread use of poor quality alcoholic beverages weakened the body's power of resistance.[7] Numerous poor were not able to secure medicine or the aid of a physician; others fell into the hands of quacks.[8] Even the Methodists' regular, well-organized ministry of visiting the sick[9] was insufficient.

A more extensive "desperate" step was required once Wesley decided all other possibilities of help appeared fruitless:[10] he himself dispensed medicine and treated simple illnesses. At Oxford, Wesley had attended medical lectures, preparing himself in case there were no physicians in the Georgia colony. Now he secured the advice of a pharmacist and an experienced physician, and he referred the more serious cases to the medical specialists.[11] Using some quite "modern" methods, always without payment, Wesley was able to aid some hundreds of people within a few months.[12] Most of them did not belong to any of the Methodist societies.

This important activity of free medical care continued, even outside the sphere of the Methodists' work.[13] Wesley's efforts also pioneered medical care for a broader strata of the English population and the establishment of free "dispensaries" (pharmacies/clinics).[14] Moreover, he provided many with self-help for problems of proper nourishment and hygiene, treatment of illnesses, and care of the sick with his manual *Primitive Physic*, which appeared in its thirty-second edition in 1828.[15]

Wesley introduced two other measures that realistically encouraged the poor in their oppressive and seemingly insuperable poverty: a loan fund and a system for finding jobs. Interest-free loans could be secured up to three months from a "loan fund," to the basic capital of which Wesley had contributed from his own savings. The loan amount was first limited to twenty shillings, but later raised to five pounds.[16] Within one year the limited starting capital of barely thirty pounds provided assistance for more than 250 persons, rescuing them from lenders demanding extortionate interest that would have compounded their distress.[17] In 1767, the loan fund was increased to 120 pounds, and the number of borrowers multiplied. The financial dealings, from which Wesley received no profit, were handled by administrators from the very outset.

Even more important than providing loans was finding jobs, to which Wesley constantly devoted himself. He recognized unemployment as one of the chief causes of widespread poverty. Because he was frequently unable to place unemployed persons in firms, he arranged the initiation of work projects as often as possible. The first of these projects was carried out in the newly erected London meetinghouse, a former cannon foundry. During the winter, twelve persons were engaged in processing cotton, and later, women were also employed in knitting.[18] How many received such assistance or how long this project continued is not known, but we do know that Wesley suffered public suspicion and accusations about it.[19]

Wesley's most important contribution improving the poor's quality of life lay neither in these individual projects (however exemplary), nor in his extremely beneficial comprehensive educational efforts. Instead, it lay in the changed consciousness that this now nortorious preacher began to engender both among the affected poor and the higher strata of English society.

2. THE ALTERED ATTITUDE TOWARD THE POOR

A chief impediment to long-range social improvement lay in the view of poverty as a self-incurred fate or a stigma of divine punishment. Through discrimination and social isolation this view only intensified the misery of material need. This attitude was firmly rooted in the traditional and religiously exalted perspective. Neither the property holders, who wished to preserve the existing order, nor the poor, whose apathy confirmed their wretchedness, considered the necessity or possibility of fundamentally altering the existing social structures. Even John Wesley did not contemplate this. His activities, however, contributed to the climate in which class opposition in England did not escalate, as in other countries, to revolution.[20] The social climate in England during Wesley's lifetime and immediately following his death facilitated urgently needed social reforms.

What preconditions put Wesley in a position to dissociate himself from the attitudes regarded as valid in his day and to arouse, first in the Methodist fellowships and then in other groups, a new attitude toward the socially disadvantaged?

Analysis of the Causes of Poverty

Wesley's social impetus arose essentially from a precise knowledge of contemporary attitudes toward poverty and the plight of the English poor. In contrast to the contemporary charitable practice of anonymously transmitting gifts through specific persons or institutions, Wesley emphasized personal contact with those who needed help. Wesley wanted to see with his own eyes what they needed,[21] and he demanded that those active in the social work of his fellowship must deliver help to the poor, not merely send it.[22] To him, the gulf between the strata of society appeared too great for the wealthier people to know the gravity of the poor's actual situation.

Wesley saw, too, that the charity many used to relieve their social obligations only perpetuated the conditions this charity was actually supposed to eliminate.[23] According to Wesley, many people consciously avoided opportunities to become better informed: "And then they plead their voluntary ignorance as an excuse for their hardness of heart."[24] Often they were not even aware whether their money and gifts were misused, as was frequently the case.[25] Hardness of heart and ignorance were the two "inner" causes of the rise and continuation of the grievous social conditions among the English people. If these causes were to be lessened and ultimately eliminated, then not just *enlightenment*, but especially *compassion*[26] growing out of love for one's neighbor, would be necessary. One could not exist without the other; Wesley insisted on both.

According to Wesley, poverty's actual basis lies neither in an inscrutable divine decree nor in the unworthiness of those affected by it. Instead, poverty can be traced to clearly recognizable causes. In a frequently preached sermon[27] Wesley made eminently clear to his hearers what it meant to provide for a family on minimum wage. They not only had to eat their bread in the sweat of their faces, often they even had no bread:

> Is it not worse for one, after a hard day's labour, to come back to a poor, cold, dirty, uncomfortable lodging, and to find there not even the food which is needful to repair his wasted strength? . . . . Is it not worse to seek bread day by day and find none? Perhaps to find the comfort also of five or six children crying for what he has not to give![28]

By no means could Wesley regard the alleged laziness of many poor folk as the major cause of their plight. Instead, because of weakness, illness, or joblessness due to excess available labor, it was precisely those who appeared to be lazy who became even more helplessly wretched. Labeling as "wickedly, devilishly false" the widespread accusation that "they are poor only because they are idle," Wesley added, "If you saw these things with your own eyes [i.e., what I have seen] could you lay out money in ornaments or superfluities?"[29]

Wesley's own observations, dating from the Oxford Holy Club, exposed prejudices of that sort for what they were. These observations positioned Wesley to form his own well-founded judgment, a necessary precondition for concrete ethical action and thought. In the majority of cases, unemployment was simply undeserved.[30] Those affected should not be blamed for something that had its cause in other factors. For this reason, others must provide help for them. This conclusion bestows a special ethical rank to the knowledge of causes. Wesley and the Methodists felt themselves ethically obligated to render such assistance.

But Wesley did not simply inform his hearers and readers about these immediate causes of poverty. He also used the occasion to deal with other economic questions. His 1772 polemic "On the Present Scarcity of Provisions" provides a splendid example. Making use of his own

31

observations and the economic information available to him, Wesley tried to uncover empirically verifiable and demonstrable causes of the existing widespread poverty.[31]

This more objective methodology made previous solutions appear either inadequate or ineffective and facilitated attempts to thoroughly investigate social grievances by correcting the traditional, customary conceptions of order. It also helped to alter the attitude toward the poor so that a solution to the social question became realistic for the first time. The fact that Wesley and his friends were only partially able to surpass the limits of merely charitable aid is not surprising. Wesley's basically conservative attitude allowed him to move forward only a step at a time, and the limited personal and financial resources available to him from the very outset restricted comprehensive implementation of his proposals for improvement. But he saw the evil, attacked it,[32] and thus contributed to a change in the public consciousness. He also initiated a series of helping measures that provided a validating testimony to his preaching.

The Activity of Unrestricted Love for One's Neighbor

Despite many hindrances, early Methodism produced astounding social achievements. This should be attributed not only to Wesley's serious investigation of the causes of social injustice, but above all to his preaching God's love for all persons—an emphasis which lent to this movement of awakening its great impetus for ministry. According to Wesley, true Christianity consists not in a formal, lifeless "religion," such as he observed so often in his time, but in "the love of God and of all mankind."[33] This "twofold commandment of love" is for Wesley, as for few other Christian theologians, the initial basis for and the cardinal point of ethics, and indeed for the whole Christian life: "Loving God with all our heart, soul, and strength, as having first loved us, as the fountain of all the good that we have received, and of all we ever hope to enjoy; and loving every soul which God hath made, every man on earth, as our own soul." That is the content of "better religion" and at the same time "the never-failing remedy for all the evils of a disordered world. . . ."[34]

Everyone has a soul that must be saved,[35] a soul for which Christ died.[36] This constitutes the unforgettable value of all people, but especially of the poor—they have very little or nothing of value to call their own, except that they are bought with the blood of Christ.[37] The lower strata of society should better discern the love of God bestowed upon them because God's love is concerned with even the slightest and the least. This love now forms a new basis for the Methodists' aid to the poor.[38] It also heralds, alongside justification by faith alone, the concept of sanctification, which in its essence is nothing other than love made complete.[39]

Alongside deriving love of neighbor from the doctrines of God, creation, and redemption, still another argument occasionally plays a role in the love of neighbor commanded by God. This commandment is subordinated to love's sole basis in reconciliation and the consequent effectual demonstration in the life of the renewed person.[40] For the person living in communion with God, "this commandment is written in his heart, 'that he who loveth God, love his brother also.'"[41] Wesley points out that the "Master teaches me to love all men."[42] Jesus has become the example for us,[43] for this attitude springs from the mind of Christ.[44] Early Christianity likewise acted accordingly.[45] Thus to the inner necessity arising from the love of God communicated in faith, Wesley added the outward necessity of the divine commandment, fulfilled by Jesus and the first Christians in exemplary fashion.

3. THE METHODIST SOCIETIES AS FIELDS OF SOCIAL PROBATION

Preaching God's love for all mankind and demanding unrestricted love for one's neighbor awakened a sense of responsibility to one's contemporaries in distress. It led not only to much direct aid, but also to giving the Methodist communities a structure of social connections in which society's despised acquired new worth as human beings. The rules for dealing with others, whether recipients of aid within or outside the community, simple members, class leaders, or preachers, were based consistently upon the fundamentally equal worth of all persons. This could be justified in negative terms by human nature's total depravity[46] or in positive terms by God's universal love for his children.[47]

Sympathy and courtesy are owed even to the most utterly corrupt and depraved, the poor and the outcast, who should be loved for the sake of their Creator and redeemer. Their body and soul, their temporal and eternal happiness, are valued equally with others.[48] The point was not just to do good, to help the poor, and to be active in charitable works; this was no more than what the "religion of the world" was already doing.[49] What was involved, rather, was allowing one's fellow human beings to share the high regard and esteem rightfully belonging to them in the same measure, on the basis of God's love, and this could not be denied without incurring guilt before God. The steward's rules, therefore, contain this among other things:

> If you cannot relieve, do not grieve the poor. Give them soft words if nothing else; abstain from either sour looks or harsh words. Let them be glad to come, even though they should go empty away. Put yourself in the place of every poor man, and deal with him just as you would God would deal with you.[50]

From this attitude and from the frequent contact with each other there developed what Wesley called "Christian fellowship," the readiness to share each other's burdens, the solidarity with all who joined the community or needed its support.[51] Poverty was no hindrance to becoming a community member or leader; furthermore, women were not excluded from leadership tasks. The membership card assured traveling workers of acceptance and support in all Methodist communities.[52] Correspondingly, when in London, Wesley and the other preachers shared in the meals at the poorhouse.[53] This reciprocal participation, a newly justified and formed ministry to the socially disadvantaged, arose out of the charitable practices of the past. It also created the preconditions that caused the relationship between the church and the working class in England to develop differently than in the European states.[54] Methodism as a "fellowship movement" (Gemeinschaftsbewegung) communicated to its followers a previously unknown sense of self-worth. It gave a new orientation to their existence and thus laid the groundwork for an otherwise inconceivable social ascent.

CHAPTER III

JOHN WESLEY'S CONTRIBUTION TO ECONOMIC ETHICS

Of primary importance to understanding John Wesley's contribution to economic ethics are his ethical evaluations and demands for the individual and collective economy. Set forth in sermons and treatises, Wesley's evaluations and demands affected not only the Methodists' private handling of goods, but also England's economic and political development.

1. THE ECONOMIC RESPONSIBILITY OF THE INDIVIDUAL

Wesley's most famous statement on the problem of handling worldly goods is undoubtedly his formulation of the "three simple rules": "Gain all you can; save all you can; give all you can."[1] In fact, these rules appropriately sum up Wesley's own practices and his congregational teachings concerning handling money and other economic goods. Wesley's three rules, expanded by the question of his view of vocation, will provide a format for the following discussion.

The Striving for Financial Gain

It may seem odd that Wesley quite independently concerned himself with rules for properly using money, since the Methodist communities consisted chiefly of members who did not own much property, and Wesley lacked any suitable examples, especially at home. Wesley cited two reasons: first, most Christians did not know how to rightly deal with money, and no one offered them any instruction; second, the proper or improper use of money, as such a valuable good entrusted to human beings by God, must have far-reaching consequences for both the

Christian and his or her neighbor, contrary to the opinion of many poets, orators, and philosophers.[2] Because it was highly important for all God-fearing Christians to know how to use this valuable commodity, Wesley undertook the task of instructing them. Through precisely observing his rules, Christians could prove themselves faithful stewards of "unrighteous mammon."[3]

The first rule was generally an explicit challenge to earn as much money as possible; this was limited, however, by emphasizing essential honesty in profit making. Superseding New Testament ethical instructions in general, Wesley was not content with simply doing good with money already in hand. Wesley's writings did not challenge his followers to voluntarily surrender all earthly goods, rather to earn as much money as honorably possible.[4]

As Wesley correctly recognized, diligence and thrift established indispensable preconditions for improving the living standard of the populace's poorer strata, all too often victimized by the fatal combination of lethargy and alcoholism. For this reason, he added a second rule: save as much as you can.[5] Wesley then exhorted them to put away earned money in private treasuries or Bank of England savings accounts, and to refrain from all unnecessary expenditures. In Wesley's eyes, waste and luxury were just as reprehensible as accumulation for one's heirs or one's own appetite for power.

Wesley began with the assumption that money as such is neither good nor evil. In the hands of God's children it becomes "nourishment for the hungry, drink for the thirsty, and clothing for the naked."[6] Wesley thus clearly proclaimed that money afforded the possibilities for effective social help without conceding to it a value in and of itself. All that money could achieve, good or evil, depended on how people used it.[7]

Social Obligations of Property

The first two rules for dealing with money, therefore, were only justified through the third rule: give all you can.[8] Without resorting to elaborate logical proofs,[9] Wesley drew a boundary line between necessary possessions and incipient wealth; between what a person needed to keep and needed to give away. Anyone whose income exceeded the necessities of life and personal obligations should give the excess to meet the needs of others.[10] Wesley did not draw this boundary arbitrarily. He determined it through a far-reaching definition of property as superfluous goods given to us by God to manage or

36

administer. Strictly speaking, we are not the owners of what we have earned or inherited. The true owner of all things in heaven and on earth is God. As our Creator and sustainer, God has provided instructions for its proper use and has promised an eternal reward to us as stewards for obedience to them.[11] These instructions state that everyone who has secured enough for the necessities of life for self and family should return the excess to needy folk, first to those of "the household of faith" and then to others, and thus to God.[12] Wesley declared that he had known no one who in his dying hour regretted saving as much as possible in order to give as much as possible, and Wesley strove to use such examples to win others to do the same.[13]

All those who observed the first two rules and not the third, however, are "twofold more the children of hell than ever they were before."[14] The blame for others' needs rested upon those who "impiously, unjustly, and cruelly" withheld from others what God had entrusted to them for giving aid.[15] Anyone spending money for expensive clothes and other luxuries and asserting: "I can afford it," thereby defrauds the Lord. According to Wesley, the purpose of earning and thrift is to make life's necessities available to all and to ameliorate or eliminate the distress of others. Doing so fulfills the commandment to love one's neighbor, and above all demonstrates obedience to the will of God, the owner.[16] All persons must account before their Creator and Judge for what they have done with their money and all other goods entrusted to them and must receive God's reward or punishment.[17]

Wesley nowhere disputes the right of private property; he merely emphasizes that God is the supreme owner who has delegated the power of administration only for a limited time and with clear instructions for using all goods. Thus Wesley relativized the right of private property to a large degree. He explicitly demanded obedience to God's commandment to love in order for anyone to lay claim to private property.[18] This sheds light on the amazing willingness to give sacrificially that accompanied the growing prosperity of Methodist congregations and individuals.[19]

The Perils of Wealth

Giving away money unneeded for a livelihood was to be motivated by the Creator's commandment and others' needs, but also by the danger that money poses for the "rich." While in Methodism's beginning years Wesley still heavily emphasized diligence and thrift, initiating in many followers an attitude that would lead to increasing prosperity, in his later years he stressed more and more the perils of riches.[20] Contrary to Wesley's intention, the Methodists who adopted his attitudes became well-to-do, and some of them became wealthy, even by today's standards. Wesley attributed this to their observing the first two rules while suppressing or forgetting the third one.[21] Once religiously motivated diligence (i.e., renouncing "foolish, unneeded extravagance" and committing all one's energies to "useful" activities)[22] and religiously justified thriftiness (i.e., renouncing unnecessary expenditures)[23] led many to enjoy ever greater incomes, until finally their conduct became detached from its original motivation. The real aim, namely, the acquisition of means to give assistance to others, lost its significance. In the final analysis, earning money served only the aim of private enrichment. Although Wesley warned against "hoarding" money and amassing wealth,[24] many Methodists became more and more detached from the most important injunction: "Give all you can." Wesley bitterly lamented this attitude, which brought shame not just on them personally, but also on the community and the entire Christian church.[25]

At this point in his socioethical theory, Wesley once again closely connects the individual and social aspects of behavior. Individual and community injury result from heaping up earthly possessions without passing along the excess to the needy as God, the Creator and Owner, wills it. Personal striving for increasing wealth and social injustice are two sides of the same coin.

Of course, Wesley did not require the rich people within his circle of influence to totally renounce their possessions (even the eschatological proviso of the New Testament, the relativizing of what is earthly by the coming kingdom of God,[26] is lacking). Money may be used for commercial and industrial investments as well as for providing the necessities of life.[27] The rich are addressed by a special call from God to help others, to visit the sick and contribute to the spiritual and physical welfare of others.[28]

But it would be better not to possess wealth, which always exposes people to the danger of a temptation that can hardly be overcome, a temptation that is far greater than that which results from poverty.[29] Those who desire to be rich are, as a rule, more likely than those who already have riches to fall victim to irrational cravings for wealth that damage body and soul, destroy faith, hope, and love toward God and neighbor, and blight every good word and work. Their temptation is a trap which they are not able to escape by their own strength,[30] because they all too readily set their hearts on wealth, making possessions their chief joy and God.[31] Toward the end of his life, Wesley summarized his experience with the prosperous Methodists who had risen from lower- to middle-class status:

> The Methodists grow more and more self-indulgent, because they grow rich. Although many of them are still deplorably poor . . . yet many others, in the space of twenty, thirty, or forty years, are twenty, thirty, or yea a hundred times richer than they were when they first entered the society. And it is an observation which admits of few exceptions, that nine in ten of these decreased in grace in the same proportion as they increased in wealth. Indeed, according to the natural tendency of riches, we cannot expect it to be otherwise.[32]

Those who love money cannot love God or their neighbors.[33] The story of Ananias and Sapphira shows that the love of money is the first pestilence to infect the Christian church.[34] Indeed, as wealth has increased in the history of the church, the mind of Christ has diminished in the same measure.[35] By God's grace the rich can be preserved from temptation,[36] but *striving* after wealth always leads to corruption. Only observance of the third rule, which sets forth the social obligations of possessions, can convert an increasing income into a blessing.[37] Therefore, those whose pure intent is to give as much as they can are serving God, their neighbors, and their own salvation.[38]

Work and Vocation

Wesley did not promote earning and saving for their own sake or for the sake of any other economic goals. His attitude toward the methods of earning money, vocation, and the individual's social position is similar. These should not be directed by satisfaction of one's own wishes, but for the glory of God and the use of those dependent upon others' assistance and care. This chapter will conclude by investigating how much this view of early Methodism strengthened the "spirit of capitalism."

Wesley's primary criterion for selecting an occupation was not the consideration of one's abilities and inclinations, but the possibilities of service that is pleasing to God. Money and professional activity in the Christian calling should not be ends in themselves, but rather means leading to a higher goal: fulfillment of the divine will, consisting specifically in the commandment to love.

Therefore, according to Wesley's exposition,[39] love limits the number of permissible occupations. The Christian must exclude all ways of earning money that would injure a neighbor's possessions, body, or soul. Furthermore, the Christian's occupation should not cause injury to his own body or soul, for life is more than food and the body more than clothing (here Wesley cites the Sermon on the Mount, Matthew 6:25).[40] Anyone who injures his neighbor for the sake of personal gain deserves the punishment of hell.[41]

Wesley saw still another sense in which one's occupation is a testing ground for Christian ethics—the possibility to significantly shape one's society, in itself a blessing entrusted to us by God. An independently wealthy person should not "uselessly waste" time but use it for the benefit of others.[42] In any case, available leisure time should be filled with "useful" activities. In addition to charitable work, these include serious dialogue, reading good books (including historical, philosophical, and literary works), making music, or gardening.[43] Love for one's neighbor and useful activity provide both impetus and limitation in choosing professional activity and managing leisure time.

Wesley did not establish any scale of values among permissible occupations; neither socially higher positions nor religious offices are any more pleasing to God than simple manual labor.[44] Everyone should live seriously and work in accord with his calling and responsibility toward God, who will judge not according to wealth and honor but "according to the standard of faith and love" that God has given.[45] The worthy goal of work is not attaining riches, but acting from love for God and one's neighbor.[46]

One further related point emerges in Wesley's thought. Although Methodist attitudes emphasized contentedness and adaptation to existing situations, Wesley unmistakably emphasized the importance of continued occupational development and firmly criticized false self-satisfaction with previous achievements. Methodists should devote understanding and effort to constant learning; they should evaluate experience, and they should acquire new knowledge through reading and reflection, so that everyone might do work better today than was previously possible.[47]

Undoubtedly Wesley's professional ethics exhibit essential similarities to those of the Reformers, especially Luther. A distinction not found in the Lutheran tradition is the challenge to earn as much as possible and to save by doing without things beyond the necessities. Similarities appear, however, in emphases on fulfillment of obligations, fitting one's work ethically into the Christian life, and interpreting work theologically as service to God and one's neighbor without suggesting that as a good work it contributes to one's justification.[48]

2. METHODISM AND THE CAPITALIST SPIRIT

Diligence, thriftiness, and contentedness, which Wesley regarded and taught as an important element of Christian praxis, are also economic virtues that ordinarily benefit their practitioners with economic success. This is immediately evident and has been emphasized frequently enough.[49] It is generally acknowledged that in propagating a religiously motivated inner-worldly asceticism, Wesley was influenced by biblical, and especially by Puritan tradition. It is commonplace that the developmental history of early Methodism registered an upward social and economic migration that largely followed a secularization of the three "simple rules," that is, the detachment of the first two from the all-important third rule. Therefore, how genuine Wesleyan Method-ism[50] relates to the "capitalistic spirit" fostered by the beginning industrial revolution is a highly important question.

As early as the 1760s, Wesley affirmed the necessary connection between diligence and thriftiness, on the one hand, and the economic achievements that almost automatically grow from these qualities, on the other hand. At this time Methodism was only twenty-five years old.[51] Wesley often lamented and censured this development, because it brought to light how people had completely lost sight of the true aim of diligent earning and thriftiness: to devote to the well-being of others everything that God has entrusted to us beyond the necessities of life.[52] Thus it was a fundamental falsification of Methodist ethics to dissociate striving for economic success from ethical obligation. The influence of Methodism undoubtedly contributed to strengthening the "spirit of capitalism" (M. Weber); however, this capitalistic "Methodism" in its essence and nature could no longer properly be called Methodism.[53]

At the same time it must be observed that some fundamental expressions of Wesley's economic ethics thoroughly contradict the "spirit of capitalism" and, historically considered, worked against that spirit. Alongside the radical social obligation connected with property ownership, these elements specifically included demands that the state intervene in the economic process (to be discussed in the next section), and rejection of coupling economic success to favorable standing with God. Indeed, Wesley gave no sign of proving the certainty of faith by good works or earthly prosperity, in the sense of a practical syllogism.[54]

The Christian should strive for neither poverty nor wealth in itself; Wesley neither praised nor commended poverty, and he explicitly and frequently warned against wealth. Both states presented people with a special temptation whose danger must not be underestimated.[55] M. Vester has unjustly made the accusation that Methodism "instead of praising improvement, blessed poverty and postponed happiness till the hereafter."[56] Since everything one legitimately earned is regarded as a good entrusted by God, Wesley perceived economic success as God's gift. Wesley's ethic, however, accents the people's obligation to rightfully administrate all they possess, since God, the sole true owner, has committed possessions to their hands. This applies to every condition in life: no one lives utterly without gifts from God, such as body, soul, abilities, and talents. However, responsibility and the danger of misuse increase with the scope and quality of the gifts.[57] Therefore, the rich and the poor especially, rather than those who are neither one nor the other, fall into temptation in this world.[58]

There were many poor people among the Methodists who had not been able to attain prosperity. We might expect Wesley to respond to them under the presupposition that visible economic success indicates "a state of moral health,"[59] that is, utterances or admonitions aiming to change the *inward* circumstance of the congregation's poor in order to effect a change in their *outward* condition, the increase of their possessions.[60] Such utterances, however, are lacking in Wesley's writings, and we can even find quite different views. Wesley saw the frequently undeserved poverty within and beyond his congregations as a challenge, for the rich to relieve this wretchedness through their gifts, and for the poor to exercise diligence and care. As noted above, Wesley did not set forth any causal connection between poverty and lack of diligence.[61]

The only "contribution" genuine Methodism, along with other Protestant communions, has made toward advancing "capitalism" lies in its high praise of diligence and contentedness and in its emphasis on the significance of the Christian ethic for all realms of life. This contribution, however, cannot be counted as especially favoring capitalism as an economic system. On the other hand, the chasm between the "spirit of capitalism" and Wesley's ethic is immense and, as long as Methodism remains faithful to its origin, indeed unbridgeable: unrestrained striving for profit versus warning against wealth, accumulation of capital versus renunciation of hoarding possessions, exploitation of foreign laborers versus ultimate motivation by love for one's neighbor. To this extent, in spite of many parallels, Wesley's ethic represents an exception among the Protestant ethics of his time.[62]

3. THE ECONOMIC RESPONSIBILITY OF SOCIETY

The shock to society of the social and economic upheavals announcing the forthcoming Industrial Revolution formed one essential precondition for the Methodists' evangelistic preaching and social activity among society's lower strata, who were threatened or already affected by economic distress and social uprooting. Wesley first came to grips with economic problems through his practical assistance to the poor. To the extent that his and his colleagues' limited resources allowed, Wesley was also involved in discussions with various social and governmental groups to achieve effective help. It is true that on occasion he expressed little confidence in responsible agencies' perceptions and readiness to act and that he depended on divine intervention for a thoroughgoing improvement.[63] Nevertheless, Wesley became involved repeatedly with this complex problem, which was then hardly the object of scientific analysis.[64]

Wesley's Protest Against Economic Injustice

Having dealt with the situation of the lower strata of society and with Wesley's efforts to provide help in the first two chapters, we now consider his engaging in public discussion regarding economic matters. The central focus will be to investigate the ethical implications and consequences of Wesley's writings rather than his specific statements on economic issues.[65]

Without statistical documentation, Wesley was obligated to base his assessment of the country's economic situation on his own observations. Due to his extended travels there was hardly anyone in a comparable position to make such assessments.[66] Wesley regarded poverty as an evil to be eliminated through every allowable means, not as a necessary consequence of culpable failure on the part of the poor or as the unavoidable fate of those excluded from God's election.[67] Therefore, he constantly investigated the causes of poverty, denounced the guilty, encouraged and expected diligent labor, and strove to awaken in the rich and influential a sense of responsibility for eliminating social evils.

One of his most important writings on this subject, "Thoughts on the Present Scarcity of Provisions,"[68] was both a flaming protest and an attempt to propose suitable measures for achieving change.[69] Wesley cites inescapably manifest economic evils, their causes as he perceives them, and improvements that he considers attainable. Through moving illustrations, he portrays the wretchedness that has driven thousands into death from starvation.[70] He listed the causes step by step: unemployment, scarcity and high prices of foodstuffs, squandering grain for use in the breweries and for the horses of the wealthy, the monopolizing of goods and the simultaneous elimination of small-holder farms, rising rents and the very high taxes that were a result of the public debt. He then summarized his analysis: "Thousands of people throughout the country are dying for lack of nourishment. This is due to several causes, but especially because of the breweries, taxes, and luxury."[71] As the pronouncements of a lay economist, his study, its conclusions, and its corrective proposals, are in part naive, sketchy, and unrealizable; nevertheless, they are stimulating and interesting from an economic and political point of view. This has already been noted by others[72] and need not occupy us further in the context of a theological-ethical study.

Two things are to be noted, however, as important and typical of Wesley's attitude toward social issues. One is the absence of pseudo-Christian fatalism, and the other is a disregard for the boundaries between the individual's social responsibility to the poor and a general claim by the poor to receive government and parliamentary measures, as well as aid from economically influential groups. Wesley not only urged his followers to be diligent and thrifty, he also contributed to heightening the public consciousness, without which, changes in the social situation probably would not have taken place. In that process his argument appealed less to a religious authority than to analysis of the economic situation (even though often fraught with inadequate methods), comparisons with historical parallels, and the consistency of economic laws.[73] Influenced by Josiah Tucker's publications on economics, Wesley had even adopted a theory that "was much more analytical, much more secular, and in the long run much more fruitful than the one that he had held earlier."[74]

The Responsibility of Social Groups[75]

Wesley's travels and his study of economic theory[76] had made him aware that during the previous two decades the economic development of the country had improved, that trade had increased, and unemployment had declined, in spite of population growth. According to Wesley's estimates, unemployment still stood at 5 percent of the work force,[77] and it led to significant disturbances during regional economic recessions.[78] The "entire civil and religious liberty that all England now enjoys," so he wrote in May, 1776, made possible the amazing increase in trade.[79] Freedom, however, could also be misused. Wesley especially regarded as abuses of freedom the many rich people who lived in the lap of luxury, the smugglers whose business flourished at all times, and the brewers and sellers of spirits. He strove to counter these abuses by direct appeals to the groups involved and by demands for governmental intervention.

The luxury of the rich, who with their great possessions controlled a major part of the national economy, in addition to leading to their own spiritual injury,[80] contributed indirectly to the higher cost of foodstuffs and to unemployment.[81] With their unnecessary expenditures for costly clothing, gluttonous banquets, horse races, balls, expensive furniture, and extravagant diversions, they were robbing God and the poor.[82] Again and again in his sermons, letters, and other publications, Wesley censured luxury as one source of widespread poverty and glaring social discrimination. The meaning and aim of renouncing luxury is guarding the rich against satisfying reprehensible desires such as pride, ambition, and idleness; and in improving the poor's economic situation, directly through material assistance and indirectly by lowering the cost of life's basic necessities. Indeed the wealth of the upper strata could only be acquired and increased in a situation where there existed a sufficiently large potential of underpaid poor people who were merely vegetating, lacking the daily supply of the necessities of life.[83]

Wesley directed his urgent appeals for change not only to the rich people living in luxury, but also to the smugglers. He undertook severe measures to prevent any support in his congregations for this widespread violation of the law, which was frequently regarded as a gentleman's misdemeanor or as a welcome means of reducing the cost of merchandise.[84] In his "A Word to a Smuggler"[85] Wesley defined smuggling as the importing, sale, or purchase of goods on which import duties had not been paid, and he labeled this as theft committed against the king and all honest English people, for it indirectly contributed to tax increases by which the king must compensate the resultant loss in customs charges.[86] The smugglers not only violated God's commandment,[87] but also defrauded their fellow citizens. Here obedience to God's authority and human social obligation served as grounds for a strict and general rejection of any behavior of fellow citizens who through fraud misused their special position in commerce. It appears that through the growing influence of Methodism, Wesley actually was successful in reducing smuggling.[88]

The production of beverages with a high alcoholic content, however, had done graver injury to the people than had luxury or smuggling. Undoubtedly, religious and moral aspects of the matter were foremost in Wesley's battle against alcoholism, but he viewed the production of spirits as a devastating evil from an economic standpoint as well. Besides, as historians have confirmed, the consumption of alcohol was then a widespread abuse, the extent of which is hardly imaginable even in our own time.[89] Wesley warned that alcohol abuse would gradually destroy the body and soul. Furthermore, the amount of wheat and barley used for manufacturing spirits with high alcoholic content contributed to the scarcity of these grains, thereby driving the prices higher and causing many people to suffer hunger.[90]

Once again religious motives were combined with social motives that were strengthened by Wesley's analysis of the economic connections. This time, however, he expected help not from the distillers whom he had addressed directly, but from governmental agencies that should put an end to this evil through legislative measures and more effective controls. Wesley expected the same from the economic power groups of entrepreneurs and large landholders, and the trade and financial enterprises. Wesley did not approach them with specific appeals; he would have preferred to see their conduct corrected by governmental intervention.

The Responsibility of Governmental Agencies

As a high-church Anglican, Wesley favored the political leanings of the Tories. Hence, he viewed the king, his ministers, and Parliament as supreme institutions of governmental power.[91] God gives them the power and therefore also the responsibility of governing the nation and doing whatever will benefit it. Officials whom Wesley publicly defended against unjust accusations did not owe a public explanation, for they, along with their actions, were continually being examined by God during their term of office.[92]

Wesley viewed the most important rights with which God had entrusted the king as police power and taxation.[93] For Wesley, the king's task was therefore to use his power of taxation to more equitably distribute goods and to eliminate grave distresses, to provide food and employment for the people. Lowering food prices would increase demand for other goods; sales would improve and the number of jobs would increase.[94] He regarded a number of governmental interventions as essential to achieving lower prices, and he perceived the national government and Parliament as the appropriate agencies.[95] Above all, legal measures must also restrict luxury and drastically reduce the number of pensions.[96] Wesley indirectly called for limiting agricultural monopolies and easing the indirect taxes that particularly burdened the poorer people's income.[97]

Despite Wesley's slight technical knowledge of economics, he recognized the English people's freedom as a precondition of the favorable economic growth that occurred after 1750,[98] and also the dangers that this freedom posed for providing the populace with life's necessities and also maintaining the nation's internal peace. There had already been initial disturbances due to lack of foodstuffs. In spite of Wesley's unconditional loyalty to king and Parliament, and the many bad experiences with groups of rowdies undergone by the early Methodists, Wesley evoked a great deal of understanding for the hungry people who often violently seized what had been withheld from them for the sake of greater profits.[99] The disturbances were not always peaceful; inflammatory pamphlets undermined love and respect for the king. There gradually emerged a situation which Wesley perceived, as early as 1775, to contain the glowing sparks of a revolution, sparks that only needed fanning to ignite the fire of open rebellion.[100] Wesley informed the prime minister by letter of his estimate of the situation, pointing out his responsibility on behalf of the people to make clear the urgency of new economic decisions by the government. Wesley refrained from detailed proposals, but he expressed a recurrent fear that this evil had been sent by God himself because of general godlessness and the luxury of the wealthy. Rebellion could be averted only by prayer and fasting.[101]

Wesley's achievement lay in the great vigor with which he pointed out wretched conditions and seeking suggestions to resolve the issues rather than in results from pursuing specific plans for change. Wesley's estimate of the entrepreneurs' power was certainly too low, and he overestimated Parliament, which was prejudicially affected in its decisions by various economic interests. In Wesley's day employees' dependence on the profit motive of industry had not been recognized by anyone else, although Edmund Burke[102] and Josiah Tucker, based on a thorough study of the economic situation, had been able to go deeper in their analysis than Wesley. In later years Wesley expected less from public appeals, although it is difficult to determine whether this was due to the improved economic situation or to resignation on his part.

Driven by love for God, Creator and Lord of all, and by love for his fellow human beings, especially the poorest and weakest among them, Wesley nevertheless continued throughout his life to be concerned that a humanitarian spirit prevailed in all areas of life. His limitations are evident: an overestimation, though not entirely uncritical, of governmental authority; a mistrust of all democratic strivings; and his inadequate insight into the laws of economics and commerce. Wesley occasionally undertook to go beyond them or to enlarge them. His success in this respect was imperfect. In his time, however, he remained unsurpassed as a fearless admonisher and unwearying helper who strove directly and indirectly to mold lives of individuals and society preeminently to obedience to God's commandments and love for persons. Wesley always considered participation in this task worth the strenuous effort of the most capable. He saw the first precondition as people turning toward God, and he considered his work to that end to be his most important task. Surely that task did not exclude concern for humanity's earthly well-being, for their happiness in this world, for peace and justice. Instead, it included all these as integral and necessary components of the whole.

CHAPTER IV

THE EDUCATIONAL AND TRAINING WORK OF WESLEY AND HIS COLLEAGUES

One prominent part of Wesley's life work, subordinate to evangelization and social service, was his role as founder, promoter, and theoretician for various diverse educational projects, especially with two groups: the poor, who were excluded from the existing means of education; and the recently-converted Methodist Society members, for whom Wesley felt highly responsible. Previously published literature on this subject[1] is limited, as a rule, to pure description or the discussion of pedagogical principles. The principal emphasis here, however, is the inner connection between Wesley's theological ethic and his underlying view of humanity.

1. ENGLISH SCHOOLS IN THE EIGHTEENTH CENTURY

Strictly speaking, there is only one common mark of all the schools existing in England at this time: an almost unimaginable diversity of sponsorship, equipment, constitution, subject matter, quality of instruction, teaching staff, and pedagogical intentions. Alongside the state church as the oldest and largest sponsor of educational institutions, schools were also established by free churches, associations, congregations, property owners, factory owners, and individuals.

The Latin schools, rich in tradition and often supported by foundations, were frequently in deplorable condition; it was not uncommon for the administration to embezzle foundation funds. Only a few of these Latin schools developed into recognized, qualified educational institutions.[2] The most famous schools of that time, the so-called public schools, were in fact distinguished private schools with humanistic curricula, open only to children of well-to-do families.[3] Less highly regarded than the public schools, but to a large extent superior to them in quality of instruction, were the dissenting academies, secondary schools founded by Independents, Quakers, Presbyterians, Baptists, and other non-Anglican communions for their children, who were excluded from the Anglican-administered schools and universities. Contrary to the public school curriculum, the natural sciences and modern languages were emphasized in the dissenting academies, so that some of them offered the best possible education of the day.[4] Alongside these three types of schools there were also several private establishments in rural areas, in which single women and other teachers who were not formally educated taught children reading, writing, and simple arithmetic for a modest fee.[5] While the nobility could maintain private teachers in their courts and castles, the masses of the children of ordinary people, unable to pay the cost of schooling, remained largely without any regular formal instruction.

As a remedy, church societies, particularly the Society for Promoting Christian Knowledge, assumed the task of providing elementary instruction without cost in charity schools for the children of poor families.[6] Considerable progress was made in this area in the first quarter of the eighteenth century.[7] Yet, measured against the total population, this was far from a solution to the school problem. About mid-century the education issue lessened for these societies sponsoring the charity schools, because their interest turned more strongly to foreign missions.[8] As a result, the quality of the teachers and instruction in many schools declined.[9] Nevertheless, thousands of children from the lowest social strata received their only education in charity schools. For the first time in English history, there was a successful effort to address a large part of the children who previously had no access to schools, to give them at least minimal instruction in the most important subjects, to secure good clothing for them, and to find apprenticeships for them after they left school.[10]

Apparently the chief hindrance to providing a basic education for all children regardless of their families' social status was that at this time only a few persons perceived the necessity of such an education. The existing educational system by no means questioned class distinctions, and even frequently confirmed them in the children's self-awareness.[11] The commonly held opinion among both rich and poor was that a poor child's most important task was to earn money as early as possible and not to "waste" time in school.[12] Fundamental reforms of the educational system could not be expected until it was possible to change such an outlook decisively. Until that time, social discrimination only allowed measures designed to treat symptoms rather than the illness itself, in spite of well-meant attempts at improvement.

2. METHODIST SCHOOLS AND SUNDAY SCHOOLS

The influences of German Pietism (Herrnhut, Halle) and the example of the English Society for Promoting Christian Knowledge—as well as Wesley's own observation of the neglected, deficient, or utterly lacking education of many children—strengthened Wesley's devotion to their care and education. His lifelong interest in pedagogical problems and tasks stemmed from his own childhood. Wesley's mother, who taught her children, exerted a far stronger influence than did their father, the pastor of Epworth. Wesley's experiences in the famous Charterhouse School in London and at Oxford University also shaped his educational endeavors.[13] Even though the schools sponsored by Wesley, his colleagues, and his successors did not succeed in covering the quantitative and, to a large extent, qualitative deficiency in the English educational system,[14] they still made a noteworthy contribution to reducing that deficiency, and they facilitated the process that finally in 1870 led to a law guaranteeing universal elementary education.[15]

Methodist School Projects

When viewed from the outside, the Methodist schools that arose essentially from John Wesley's direct or indirect initiatives operated entirely within a traditional framework.[16] Nevertheless, Wesley succeeded in significantly advancing the English school system toward providing an adequate elementary education for all the country's children. The explanation for this success springs primarily from Wesley's view, shaped by basic ethical convictions, that all persons are of equal worth. Wesley could not passively accept the imposition of widespread disadvantages, especially in such an important area as education.

From the very first, instruction for children from poor families was a project of Methodist social work. During his time in Georgia, Wesley attended to the education of the children in his congregation.[17] Soon after his return he undertook building the first school for the Kingswood miners near Bristol (1739), for which his friend George

Whitefield laid the cornerstone.[18] Soon after, other schools for the poor arose in Bristol, London, Newcastle upon Tyne, and other places. Such schools met in residences, institutions, chapels, and other locations, and often in buildings erected for this specific purpose. Teachers, pastors, and preachers, as well as capable laypersons, provided instruction in reading, writing, arithmetic, and the Christian faith. This schooling was offered without charge when the parents were not able to make a financial contribution.[19] In addition, needy children were given clothing and meals.[20] The resources that made these measures possible were supplied exclusively by gifts, which were overseen by special administrators in the larger schools.

Wesley's chief motive for establishing such schools and developing them within his sphere of influence was primarily a religious and humanitarian one. In his 1748 report on the Methodist movement intended for publication, he wrote:

> Another thing which had given me frequent concern was the case of abundance of children. Some their parents could not afford to put to school; so they remained like "a wild ass's colt." Others were sent to school, and learned at least to read and write; but they learned all kind of vice at the same time: so that it had been better for them to have been without their knowledge than to have bought it at so dear a price. . . . At length I determined to have them taught in my own house, that they might have an opportunity of learning to read, write, and cast accounts (if no more), without being under almost a necessity of learning heathenism at the same time.[21]

This description applies *cum grano salis* to all the Methodist schools. They were intended to provide elementary knowledge precisely for those who otherwise would have foregone it; they were designed to protect the children against a nonChristian way of life, dangerous influences, or influences that were perceived dangerous; and, above all else, they were meant to guide the children into basic Christian truths and lead them to a life in harmony with the will of God.[22] This intention formed the indispensable presupposition that governed everything else for Methodist instruction, not only within the family, but also in the schools.[23]

The historically most influential aspect of the Methodist schools, however, appears not to have been in the imparted secular and religious content, but rather in the breadth and depth of the sense of duty that

Wesley instilled in his congregation members for the children's education and training. It is fair to say that hardly any other Christian communion has given so large a place in its preaching and pastoral care to the education of children as did Methodism in its formative period. This significant development among Methodists occurred precisely at a time in which other groups' interest in the education of children was diminishing or already extinguished.[24]

Wesley was not satisfied with lamentations about deplorable conditions or accusations against the responsible agencies; instead, he committed himself to remedying the deficiency through the strenuous efforts of the Methodist communities. To that end he employed repeated sermons and conversations on the education and training of children,[25] regularly checked the schools he had founded,[26] conducted conversations with the children,[27] gave hours of instruction himself,[28] wrote his own school books,[29] outlined instructional plans,[30] counseled parents on questions of child-rearing,[31] enlisted teachers,[32] and regularly assisted with various emerging difficulties.[33] From the very first he shifted the leadership of the schools to other shoulders, but he did so without surrendering the overseeing of "his" schools.[34] The preachers were required to include questions of child rearing in their catalog of sermon topics regularly[35] and to report to the congregations, especially on the second Kingswood School—the only advanced Methodist school of this time and Wesley's pet project—as well as to take up collections for it and other schools, something Wesley himself continued to do even into his old age.[36]

Thus there arose in all of Britain's Methodist Societies a relatively high degree of knowledge in this area. There was an increasing awareness of the necessity, arising out of individual responsibility before God, for creating places of education and carefully teaching children. Hence, it is not surprising that a considerable number of smaller elementary schools appeared at the local level; these often provided the only educational opportunity for the children of the poorer families.[37] These may only partially be compared with the already existing charity schools, since in most cases the local schools were supported by the commitment of women and men who had been won to a new life, people from the lower social strata who had taken upon themselves the responsibility for educating poor children rather than depending on the charitable gifts of well-to-do donors.

The Sunday School Movement

The emergence of the Sunday school movement without doubt belongs to the realm of Methodism's impact, even though the chief credit belongs to an Anglican newspaper publisher for its dissemination throughout the country.[38] In 1780, with the help of the clergyman Thomas Stocks, Robert Raikes, owner and publisher of the *Gloucester Journal*, founded in his city a Sunday school for children of poor families, and saw to it that this undertaking was quickly publicized. Consequently, by the year 1785 the "London Society for the Establishment of Sunday Schools" was founded, and twenty thousand English children could receive regular instruction in Sunday schools in 1786.[39]

The first Methodist Sunday school, however, had already been established in 1769 by a woman, Hannah Ball, in High Wycombe,[40] apparently without Wesley's direct influence. Nevertheless, the prevailing sense of responsibility in Wesley's congregations for the education of children probably provided the soil for this initiative, which effectively supplemented the other measures for education. While attendance at the regular day school presupposed that the children did not need to go to work, the Sunday school was open to all children, regardless of their attendance during work days. Here children learned the basics of reading, writing, and the most important portions of the catechism; in some Sunday schools they also learned arithmetic. The school book that was readily obtainable, least expensive, and most suitable for the religious educational needs of the Sunday school was the Bible.[41]

In this connection church historians have occasionally pointed to the forms of Sunday instruction that existed in earlier centuries, to Christian teaching, prayer, and catechetical instruction that were conducted not only in Protestant churches, but also in Catholic and nonconformist communities. In some cases these forms were also supplemented with instruction in reading and writing.[42] These references are appropriate in that they identify an actual parallel between earlier established patterns and the Sunday schools of the late eighteenth century, but do not suggest any direct causal connection.

Wesley advanced the establishment of Sunday schools with a readiness, astounding for his age, to recognize these new undertakings and to see them as still another possibility of helping the needy.[43] To assist in their further expansion, in 1775 Wesley published in his periodical, the *Arminian Magazine*, a report from Robert Raikes about the "Sunday Charity Schools." In view of later official Methodist criticism,[44] it should be noted that even on Sunday, secular and religious knowledge were simultaneously imparted without any legalistic narrowness. Also, in spite of attacks from within and without the churches,[45] more and more helpers made themselves available (at least in this inadequate fashion, though under the existing social circumstances hardly any better was possible) to provide without cost a general basic knowledge for the children of the lower social strata.[46] But what concerned Wesley more than imparting knowledge was the Sunday school children's developing into Christians who might lead an inner renewal of the entire nation.[47]

3. ADULT EDUCATION IN METHODISM

From the outset this educational work was not limited to children. Adults, too, were the object of Wesley's efforts to impart substantive knowledge. Wesley also wished to develop them into knowledgeable Christians, who not only felt the assurance of God's love, but also grasped for themselves rationally the consequences of faith for their lives. This occurred in three ways: by special school courses for adults, by availability of inexpensive and suitable literature, and by sermons and conversations in the classes and societies.

Instruction for Adults

After the first school in Kingswood was founded (1739), John Wesley wrote concerning its aim:

> It is proposed, in the usual hours of the day, to teach chiefly the poorer children. . . . The older people, being not so proper to be mixed with children (for we expect scholars of all ages, some of them grey-headed) will be taught . . . either early in the morning, or late at night, so that their work may not be hindered.[48]

Here Wesley obviously had in mind adults of the same social level as the children,[49] particularly the illiterate miners and simple people who had been denied the opportunity of attending school in their childhood. Wesley was not content to simply preach the gospel to those who already found themselves largely outside the sharply drawn boundaries of the established society and church. Instead, he strove to help them, within the narrow range of possibilities open to him, to attain an existence worthy of human beings, a new self-awareness and greater self-esteem.

In some of the Sunday schools that arose later, special courses were developed to provide adult instruction in basic school subjects.[50] Seen as a whole, however, these projects were of little consequence, because they apparently remained quite limited in number, scope, and longevity. Nevertheless, they significantly indicate Wesley's attitude toward the distresses of his time, which he felt obliged to recognize and to ameliorate.

Special attention should also be given to the intention, arising out of both a pedagogical perspective and a bad experience, to establish in Kingswood a high-caliber academic institution. For a long time Wesley had recommended to his pupils—partly in accordance with their own desires—that they complete their studies at Oxford or Cambridge, which he held to be the best of all the English and continental universities.[51] In view of the many defects and deficiencies that he had to reprove in these institutions,[52] his positive attitude developed in large measure, as he himself concedes,[53] out of his bias in favor of the two tradition-rich universities, especially Oxford. Only after six Methodist students were expelled from Oxford and another had been refused admission[54] did he make a virtue of necessity and follow his conviction that it "was highly expedient for every youth to begin and finish his education in the same place." Thus he established at Kingswood, where there already existed an elementary and a secondary school, an academy as well, for diligent students who would learn more in three years than most of their Oxford contemporaries would learn in seven.[55]

In spite of objections, difficulties, and disadvantages, he carried through with this intention. The Kingswood curriculum embraced not only theological subjects and ancient languages, but also ancient authors, history, philosophy, mathematics, physics, geography, and contemporary and classical literature, so that upon its successful completion, the student had attained the highest academic standard.[56] In principle, the class barriers were in this way dismantled for a small number of young men, barriers that had made elementary schooling, to say nothing of higher education, inaccessible for the majority of poor children.

Education Through Literature

Education of the poor in the eighteenth century was left entirely to voluntary organizations, and the establishment of a sufficient number of schools far exceeded the capabilities of these organizations. Thus, a special significance accrued to another kind of communication of knowledge: the provision of good and inexpensive literature for the existing schools, and especially for reading by individuals and groups. Wesley devoted the full force of his energy to carrying out this task, whose urgency had quite early been impressed upon him. Wesley was convinced that printed materials, especially publications of his own writings, were a suitable means for advancing the preaching of the gospel beyond the circle of his immediate hearers, of confirming and deepening the faith of Christians, and of conducting theological discussions with his opponents. In addition, however, the imparting of specialized knowledge, as well as guidance in the use of one's own reason, which complemented his largely argumentative style, played an important role. Wesley's famous saying that he wanted to be a "man of one book" (*homo unius libri*, that is, the Bible)[57] was first understood (or rather misunderstood) by others in the sense of a depreciation of all other literature. A later admirer even thought that it would be a good thing to destroy Wesley's copy of Shakespeare that contained his handwritten marginal comments.

The late seventeenth and early eighteenth centuries brought some revolutionary innovations in printing and publishing: the first newspapers and inexpensive brochures were printed, making possible the development of a broad public opinion and the distribution of numerous writings even in the middle and lower strata of society; and in 1702 the first daily newspaper appeared in England.[58] Wesley very quickly made use of these technological advances for a comprehensive and well-organized publishing program in order to supply "his" poor people with books. The majority of the publications were on religious and ethical problems, but along with these there was a broad spectrum of other materials: practical issues of life and the times, biographies, travelogues, poetry, philosophy, and school books.[59] Some brochures treated in simple language a long list of diverse topics once accessible for discussion only to a small circle of well-informed people, but now made familiar to a large circle of readers. The books were to be given to anyone who was not able to pay for them despite the low price.[60] Wesley supplied Methodist schools, especially those in Kingswood, with textbooks that he himself had written or had revised on almost all subjects.[61] His book *Primitive Physic* was to be available (along with Thomas à Kempis' *Imitation of Christ*) to practically every family,[62] and in

57

spite of its many peculiarities it rendered a valuable service to those who could not afford a physician.[63]

Between 1749 and 1755,[64] there emerged what is probably the most important of Wesley's editorial achievements, the fifty-volume *Christian Library*, which was supposed to contain "all that is most valuable in the English tongue, . . . in order to provide a complete library for those who fear God."[65] Wesley himself took the trouble to select all the works intended for inclusion in this edition, work through them, abridge them, and supply introductions for them.[66] In that process he was fair enough to preserve opinions that did not fully agree with his own, if they appeared reconcilable with Holy Scripture.[67] He was concerned, above all else, that the texts be practical and understandable, and that they present "the height and depth" of the Christian faith.[68] From these concerns it naturally follows that these fifty small volumes contained only religious literature. Moreover, controversial discussions were excluded in order to avoid over-extending and confusing the simple reader, instead equipping him for every good work and deed.[69] Along with Wesley's expositions of the Old and New Testaments, his sermons and treatises, the *Christian Library* was meant to serve the theological education of his preachers and congregations. Understanding the faith was not meant to replace practicing it; rather it was to provide a basis for that practice, to correct it, and to strengthen it. Therefore, the preachers themselves were to read diligently, and to engage in reading publicly to others[70] and in selling or giving away the books.

A monthly periodical, the *Arminian Magazine*, which the founder of Methodism published in London beginning in 1778, presented Wesley's doctrine of God's universal love and defended it against the Calvinist theory of election. It also disseminated Christian poetry and testimonies of the experiences of "God-fearing people." Controversial theological discussions, too, found a place here if they had not already appeared as separate publications because of their length. The content of the first years' issues, which appeared during Wesley's lifetime, made it clear that his chief concern was the clarification and confirmation of perceptions of the faith as well as spiritual edification. The authors' denominational affiliations—be they Lutheran, Anglican, Calvinist, or Arminian—were not to pose any barrier to publication, as long as they were "holy men." According to Wesley's view, this meant people whose lives and teachings were in harmony with his understanding of the will of God.[71]

The fact that he spared neither cost nor labor in introducing the books into his congregations shows how seriously Wesley desired the dissemination of the works that he wrote, edited, or recommended. As early as 1740, a bookshop was established in London as a central distribution point; preachers and members of the societies served as agents, and stewards chosen specifically for the purpose operated the business.[72]

The Methodist Societies as Centers of Education

In stating that the Methodist Societies provided for such a wide distribution and so intensive a use of good literature, it is important to note *who* was led to hear, to read, to join in thinking, and to share in discussions. This audience was predominantly people who had not attended school or had enjoyed only a brief span of instruction; many of them had first learned to read as adults. Most of them were financially unable to buy books and were hardly interested in doing so because of their background and lack of education. Thanks to Wesley, the Methodist Societies became educational agencies with a systematic pursuit of reading. Reading Christians were knowledgeable Christians; and the uneducated people, of all people, were not to be excluded from this opportunity. It was precisely for them that Wesley published his comprehensive list of books.[73] Inexpensive editions comparable to our pocket-sized books afforded opportunity to all who wanted to gain a better education and become intentional Christians.

Because of extensive psychological and social barriers, many would not have made use of the opportunity if a crucial precondition for the effectiveness of his publication program had not been developed within the small groups that Wesley had created. A systematic program of reading prompted them to think about the issues of life and their faith, and to talk with each other about them.[74] Here no one was considered more important than any other, not only because most of them had the same social status, but also because the message of the sinner's justification had leveled all human distinctions of rank.[75] Everyone had the sense of belonging as a full-fledged member of the group; that shared sense of solidarity gave them self-confidence and courage for self-expression. They were no longer lost in the mass of the proletariat, despised by society, but were accepted as fully valuable individuals.[76] Due to the expansion of their religious, moral, political, and cultural horizons, a number of impulses and stimuli arose that had an impact upon the entire English educational system.[77]

Seen from the perspective of general education for the public, the content of the books that Wesley wrote, published, or recommended appears one-sidedly religious. Nevertheless, Wesley's recommendations for reading were by no means limited to this basic theme. To a preacher who strictly refrained from any reading except the Bible, Wesley made clear the folly of that attitude and rejected it as enthusiasm.[78] He also recommended a regular and persistent reading of "the most useful books."[79] By this he meant textbooks in arithmetic, geography, logic, ethics, and philosophy (natural philosophy, Locke's *Essay on Human Understanding*, metaphysics), poetry (Spenser, Shakespeare, Milton, and others), and newspapers.[80] His criterion for selection was usefulness to the reader. This functioned as an over-arching characteristic for secular and religious literature: whatever advanced faith, character, and knowledge was good, and whatever was injurious—whether because of false, incomprehensible, or erroneous statements—was bad.[81] In his social work and in instruction and education, Wesley envisioned the well-being of the whole person and not merely the immortal soul. This enlightens the significance of the doctrine of creation within his theological ethic, which will be worked out clearly in the following section.

4. EDUCATION AND TRAINING IN THE CONTEXT OF WESLEY'S THEOLOGICAL ETHIC

Wesley's work in education and training is important for a study of social ethics and discloses an important part of his anthropology. Wesley regarded humanitarian tasks as an essential part of Christian life. This emphasis gave him the theoretical foundation and the frame of reference to set goals for his manifold educational work.

The Basic Theological/Anthropological Affirmations

Wesley has no place in the history of modern pedagogy; his methods of education resemble those in medieval families and schools rather than those prevalent in modern times. Pestalozzi (d. 1746) and Fröbel (d. 1782) were unknown to him. He had read Rousseau's *Emile* and analyzed it on an extremely superficial level, since his own firmly fixed principles made him neither willing nor able to evaluate and to understand a position that so strongly differed from his own.[82] Without doubt, it was Wesley's mother who exerted the greatest influence upon his views, and even in his later years he still placed great value upon her counsel.[83] German pietists (Francke, J. E. Stolte, the Herrnhut people) also made a great impression upon him and helped to shape his style.[84] Finally, specific statements by Comenius, Milton, and Locke are also included among the pedagogical rules that he appropriated.[85]

But what can be said on specific points about his theological/anthropological conceptions? Wesley's narrow and often harsh rules for education in the family and school did not result from any deprecation of children, a widespread attitude in the eighteenth century.[86] Instead, he assigned them a place in family, church, and society that was clearly distinct from the prevalent one.[87] In his personal relationships with children he was less severe than one might expect; such attachments correct the picture of the harsh zealot for the faith who deprived children of all joy.[88] Even his strictness was grounded in his love for the children,[89] a love that was, however, led astray by a defective knowledge of the child's psyche. Wesley's perception of the soul of a child is clearest in a brief treatment of 1783:

> The bias of nature is set the wrong way; Education is designed to set right. This, by the grace of God, is to turn the bias from self-will, pride, anger, revenge, and love of the world, to resignation, lowliness, meekness and the love of God. And from the moment we perceive any of those evil roots springing up, it is our business immediately to check their growth, if we cannot yet root them out. Insofar as this can be done by mildness, softness, and gentleness, certainly it should be done. But sometimes these methods will not avail, and then we must correct with kind severity.[90]

Thus the anthropological starting point for all educational measures (as also for the preaching of the gospel) that must be countered is the corruption of human nature from birth onward.[91] Therefore, the child's will, as a will that is basically of the devil, must be broken and obedience imposed upon it.[92] From this perspective, it appears consistent and suited to the children's welfare that all available means be used to bring them to an unresisting submission to an authority commissioned by God to keep them as much as possible under constant supervision. It is not surprising that the educational measures included, if necessary, severe punishment.[93] What is surprising is that Wesley showed such optimism about these measures' effectiveness, namely, that they could at least partially make good the "loss of original perfection."[94] This optimism, nurtured of course by confidence in the efficacy of divine grace, pervaded the whole of Wesley's ethic.[95] Through God's grace, the maladies of human nature must and can be healed little by little.[96] This optimism also renders understandable his great efforts, as well as his profound disappointment, in the case of failures.[97]

The same roots nurtured Wesley's sharp opposition to Rousseau and his principles. Putting aside all subjective and polemical comments, and laying bare the kernel of Wesley's accusations, it is clear that Wesley viewed Rousseau as an atheist: that is, not taking the sinfulness of the childish nature as the point of departure, and developing a humanity independent of Christian revelation and redemption. Against this view Wesley set the assertion that there is only *one* happiness, which in the same way as the only true religion has God as its center, and that the cause of human misery is human sin. On this point Scripture, reason, and experience agree.[98] Thus Wesley would first change human nature: that is, by the grace of God and through educational methods, form nature as it was originally (before the fall) and as it should be according to God's will. Rousseau, on the other hand, would begin with the existing disposition of the child, respect its individuality, and claim validity for its original natural quality (not yet corrupted by any civilization).[99] The fact that Wesley succeeded in having many children brought up to be diligent, well-educated, responsible citizens is not to be disputed. However, it is equally incontestable that his narrow principles and rules share the blame for emotional harm to many people, and not only in England or during his lifetime.

Wesley's impact on the field of education was thus ambivalent: on the one hand, a stimulus to the entire English educational system and the education of an increasing number of children and adults from the underprivileged classes; on the other hand, an introduction or maintenance of harsh and narrow principles in education. This ambivalence can ultimately be traced to the religious basis to which Wesley felt unconditionally obligated. This basis included both love for the disadvantaged and needy, and also the pessimistic anthropology that saw the only road to individual and social happiness in the absolute submission to God's authority that is manifested in the canon of biblical commandments, and in parents, teachers, pastors, and other officeholders. Because this constellation of motives has such foundational significance for Wesley's social ethic, it will be more particularly examined and explained in the following section.

The Religious Definition of the Theory of Education

During a critical phase of his schools in Kingswood, Wesley wrote in his journal: "I will kill or cure: I will have one or the other—a Christian school, or none at all."[100] The basic Christian character of all education and training was for Wesley simply indispensable. Why?

According to Wesley's conviction, children are to be regarded as creatures of God who are destined for blessedness, but who must fall short of this destiny unless they are granted renewal through forgiveness of their sins and the transformation of their nature.[101] Although forgiveness of sins is accomplished by the merits of Christ, as Wesley taught in harmony with his church,[102] in baptism, and indeed as far as original sin is concerned, even already at birth,[103] the evil inclination still persists, and can only be changed into a good inclination by the continuing influence of the grace of God. It must be recognized that for Wesley the love of humankind, a means to make provision for the working of God's grace in children and adults, was the driving thrust for all his activity. However questionable his methods for doing justice to this commission may appear to us today, there can hardly be any doubt that love for God and people was his essential motive. Only love can awaken love in people; even when punishment is necessary, love must motivate and soften the reproof.[104] The Spartan life-style in Wesley's schools[105] had the aim, above all, of guarding the children against a mistaken love for the world that would only hinder their happiness.[106]

Since Wesley saw a vital connection with God as the only way to attain this goal, he was obliged to direct all his efforts to bring children and adults to the point where this connection could develop, namely, to an encounter with the gospel. Preaching and pastoral care therefore had a fixed place in his overall educational and social work.[107] His deep-seated aversion to all merely "outward piety" and the conviction of the necessity of an inner, vital faith meant that he was not satisfied with the usual communication of knowledge via catechism. Instead, he sought to bring home to the children at the earliest possible age in completely understandable terms the greatness of God and his love.[108] To the objection that such statements went beyond the children's capacity to understand, Wesley responded with the blunt observation that the same was true also for adults if God himself did not open their understanding.[109] With great delight he told of children whose wisdom, faith, and earnestness of life confirmed the correctness of his view.[110] Nevertheless, the dominant impression that one gains from the children under Wesley's care is that they were treated like small adults,[111] who, because of a misguided zeal concerning their souls, had been robbed of the joys of childhood.

Thus there is a tension, readily understandable from the perspective of Wesley's educational aims and principles, between an affection for children and a helpful, sacrificial commitment to them, on the one hand, and a great severity, sharp discipline, and Spartan regulation of life on the other. In addition to this tension, there is another intrinsically contradictory attitude whose effects likewise extend to other aspects of Wesley's ethic. Alongside a rational analysis of the psychical and social data and the willingness to draw practical consequences from it, there stands an attitude of expectancy that saw God's grace at work in a supernatural and direct, often magical, fashion.

It is not my intention here to discuss the belief in the real existence of spirits, witches, and other supraterrestrial beings that Wesley shared with other famous and educated contemporaries.[112] However, during Wesley's sermons there were outbreaks of hysteria, exhibitionism, and other psychic-based disturbances in which he saw effects of supraterrestrial powers, signs of a battle between God's Spirit and evil spirits that occasionally appeared even among children.[113] Some Methodist teachers attempted to elicit convulsive conversions without being reproved by Wesley.[114]

Against oft-repeated assertions,[115] we must maintain that Wesley did not deliberately strive to evoke such phenomena, nor did he attempt to further them. Although others diagnosed the hysteria differently, Wesley interpreted them to be a direct working of the Holy Spirit upon the souls of his hearers that produced a greater understanding of religious utterances, a greater seriousness in the conduct of life, and a sense of joy, happiness, inner peace, faith, and readiness for total obedience to the will of God.[116] He believed that conversions of children at the tender age of three to eight years could be demonstrated[117] and that the Holy Spirit imparted the insights necessary for such conversions, even if the powers of understanding were not yet present.[118]

It is noteworthy that Wesley was not satisfied with the declaration that God's Spirit works solely in a supernatural, direct fashion that is inexplicable to us. This would necessarily have led, in the final analysis, to a renunciation of any further reflection and action. He also considered it insufficient merely to cling to some biblical or traditional, churchly instructions, although he by no means devalued tradition and Holy Scripture as possessing the highest authority. He intensively concerned himself with the presuppositions and conditions of understanding, with information about the development of the human mind as well as methods and means of instruction.

Among modern philosophers Wesley concerned himself especially with John Locke (1632–1704) and his *Essay on Human Understanding* (1690).[119] Along with Locke's reverence for God and his Word, Wesley emphasized Locke's rejection of innate ideas (Lord Herbert of Cherbury, Descartes), because for the sake of revelation it was important to emphasize yearning for knowledge as a universal human principle, as well as the limited scope of this knowledge.[120]

Wesley's theory of education attempted to harmonize revelation and reason by taking into account the human yearning for the most widely varied and comprehensive knowledge and at the same time emphasizing the abiding importance of the illumination of the understanding by the Holy Spirit. The religious content of our knowledge (God, creation, providence, grace) can only be derived from revelation,[121] while experience and reflection represent the sources of our knowledge of finite things.[122]

These principles of knowledge are highly significant for Wesley's ethic because they guard against pride and arrogance and at the same time identify an unquenchable desire for learning and knowledge as willed by God and therefore legitimate.[123] For this reason Wesley can, without thereby falling into a contradiction, exert every effort to investigate the learning abilities of children and youth, accordingly criticize and correct textbooks and teaching methods, and at the same time accept the possibility of special knowledge acquired at an early age. The content of this special knowledge is not the result of sense experience or reflection, although it never conflicts with the declarations of Scripture. It results from an infusion of the Holy Spirit.[124]

Therefore, Wesley was strongly in favor of modern school subjects, the natural sciences and the living languages.[125] Thus in spite of his stern opposition to deism, which in his view was atheistic, Wesley adopted significant impulses from the early Enlightenment in his theory and practice of education, thereby contributing to the establishment of a positive relationship between modern science and ecclesiastical tradition.[126] In defining the relationship between religion and education, Wesley even went so far as to assert that the latter is rarely found without the former.[127] Consistent with that perspective, he was concerned not only with developing his converts into intelligent Christians, but also with setting forth and awakening a lively piety as a precondition of genuine education. The schools that were founded for the glory of God were intended also to produce responsible members of society.[128]

Culture and piety, education and faith, secular knowledge and the mind of Christ—all should be reconciled with each other and imparted as such to children and adults alike,[129] but especially to those for whose self-esteem and social ascent Wesley did more than any of his contemporaries.

CHAPTER V

JOHN WESLEY'S BATTLE AGAINST SLAVERY

I n terms of its injustice and inhumanity, slavery was the gravest and probably the most difficult to resolve social problem of the eighteenth century, despite the burgeoning distresses resulting from rapidly growing industrialization. The misery caused by slavery grew with every shipload of Africans brutally robbed of their freedom. The proportion of blacks among the laborers increased along with a growing demand for plantation laborers. Thus this important branch of the economy became more dependent on importing even more slaves. Economic calculations of politicians, slave merchants, and slave owners, as well as the general public's almost total oblivion to the injustice of enslavement, worked hand in hand to multiply this evil.

A brief survey of the rise of black slavery in modern times will set the stage for examining the attitude of the churches and of Wesley toward it, and finally for analyzing the theoretical foundation for Wesley's late but stout advocacy of the abolition of the slave trade and of slavery itself.

1. SLAVERY AND THE SLAVE TRADE IN EIGHTEENTH-CENTURY ENGLAND AND ITS COLONIES

As early as 1500 the Portuguese began buying blacks on the west coast of Africa and soon began transporting them to America. England began participating in the black slave trade in the mid-sixteenth century, as it became an ever stronger sea power and contested the Iberian supremacy in the high seas. Soon England was transporting more than half the total number of slaves appearing on the American market. Furthermore, from about 1620 the colonies were compelled to accept them.[1]

National interest in the slave trade had been heightened by royal privileges, parliamentary laws, international agreements, and above all, the *Asiento* clause of 1714, a part of the Utrecht peace accord guaranteeing England and Spain a monopoly on the slave trade. Consequently, a large part of the British population was receiving a profit from slave trading. Its security and development was the political goal of a strong lobby in the House of Commons.[2] Between 1680 and 1688 the English Africa Company and unlicensed interlopers transported more than two hundred thousand black slaves to America; between 1783 and 1793 the ships departing from Liverpool alone carried some three hundred thousand.[3] According to one source, "The profit from a single round-trip, including the goods that were bartered in Africa and the general cargo that was brought from the West Indies, often returned far more than one hundred percent of the originally invested capital."[4] Because of these vested interests, and the fact that thousands of black slaves had also been brought to England, it is not surprising that proposed legislation to abolish the slave trade, initiated by Wilberforce in 1791, failed to pass the House of Commons.[5] Only in 1807 did the English Parliament prohibit the slave trade; only in 1833 did it order slavery abolished in the entire empire.[6]

It is inexcusable that king, cabinet, and Parliament did not oppose on behalf of foreigners the violation of fundamental rights guaranteed to their own citizens in the British constitution. England was rightly regarded as one of the states with the most extensive individual rights. However, the slavery situation must be understood altogether in terms of prevailing economic and political factors.

2. THE CHURCHES' ATTITUDE TOWARD SLAVERY

What was the attitude of churches and Christians toward slavery and the slave trade?[7] The Anglican state church tolerated slavery and the slave trade without objection. Individual protests from pastors or from Bishop Warburton[8] echoed ineffectively or encountered outright resistance from the church. Thus in 1727, Edmund Gibson, the bishop of London, who was also responsible for the colonies, wrote against the demand that Christianized slaves should be freed by their Christian owners: "The Freedom which Christianity gives is a Freedom from the Bondage of Sin and Satan . . . but as to their outward Condition, whatever that was before . . . their being baptized, and becoming Christians, makes no manner of Change in it."[9]

In this statement the bishop uses Paul's theological rationale to deliberately refrain from fundamentally altering the contemporary social structure. However, as is typical of the churches' line of thinking, the argument is detached from its original apocalyptic context and employed to generally justify the status quo.

Recent theological research no longer seriously denies that Paul's ethical directives must be understood in the context of his deep conviction that the end of the world was imminent, instead of elevating them to the rank of timelessly valid rules binding upon all Christians.[10] For Paul, in an eschatological sense baptism into Christ radically relativized all social and racial distinctions (Galatians 3:28) without consequentially affecting societal structures. Slaves who became Christians should explicitly renounce any possibility of emancipation and instead serve their masters all the more submissively for the sake of the Lord Christ (I Corinthians 7; Colossians 3). The Christian's very slavery was the place to prove himself or herself a Christian, a place from which he or she should not seek to be released (I Corinthians 7:25).

Neither the Old Testament nor any of the Gospels contains any fundamental protest against slavery; in fact, many passages assume its existence as a given. The church has repeatedly appealed to such passages to justify its renunciation of social change. Religious and secular freedom, religious and secular justice, have always been regarded as independent and nonmediated entities (aside from fanaticism in Corinth and at the time of the Reformation).

The Pauline refusal to derive slavery from the will of God[11] has played no role in church history down to modern times. It did not prevent the perception in the Church of England or in early Catholicism that slavery is a component of the divine order of the world.[12] It is true that some Anglican Christians freed their converted slaves, but as a consequence they endured a reprimand from their bishop,[13] who appealed to the New Testament as many before him had done. Leaders within the Anglican state church down to the mid-eighteenth century posed no opposition to slavery. Bishop Warburton and a few pastors who opposed cruelty and advocated the emancipation of Christian slaves were the exception. The official view held by the overwhelming majority of the church's members remained unaffected, however, by these few exceptions.[14]

3. THE BEGINNING OF THE BATTLE AGAINST SLAVERY

The Quakers were undisputedly the first to raise their voice against this inhuman form of controlling humanity, a voice that expressed profound sympathy with the burdensome lot of the black slaves. As early as 1671 George Fox spoke out for the emancipation of slaves; in 1727, the Society of Friends in a formal declaration condemned slavery in the face of the churches' and the general public's indifference. In 1761 the Society of Friends decided to withdraw fellowship from any of its members who were connected with the slave trade.[15] Aside from these English Quakers and the North American Mennonites, only isolated individual Christians or denominations decisively opposed this deeply entrenched evil at the beginning of the nineteenth century.[16]

These limited, religiously motivated protests were effectively furthered by a new philosophical and literary current originating in the French Enlightenment, particularly in Diderot, the Encyclopedists, and Rousseau: the idealizing of the natural. Idealization of the "noble savage" was strengthened by writers of fiction (Defoe), travel narratives (J. Thomson and G. Addison), and individual tractates and public statements of position (S. Johnson, F. Hutcheson, and J. Beattie). The numerous exaggerations in such writings combatted the prejudice that black people were inferior, precisely because the majority of readers could not test these depictions.[17] Romantic enthusiasm for natural man along with newly arising demand for universal, naturally bestowed human rights gradually created in broad segments of society an awareness that constituted a favorable climate for the emerging anti-slavery movement.

Nevertheless, without the religious motivation that shaped the leading representatives of this movement, its final success would have hardly been possible. The content and strength of this motivation was exemplified in John Wesley's attitude toward slavery and his commitment to its abolition.

4. JOHN WESLEY'S ATTITUDE TOWARD SLAVERY

The Early Phase (to about 1770)

Wesley's consciousness of slavery, in terms of his desire to first humanize and later abolish it, emerged relatively later than his concerns for other contemporary social problems such as widespread poverty and lack of education. Nevertheless, the roots of Wesley's support of the anti-slavery movement and the abolition of slavery were already evident in the early years of his ministry as an Anglican pastor in the North American colony of Georgia.

When Wesley began work in the colony in 1736 there were no black slaves there, since General Oglethorpe and his board of trustees did not allow them to be brought in.[18] Wesley—in contrast to Whitefield—supported this policy unreservedly, since on visits to South Carolina and through reading the *Negro's Advocate* he had gained insight into the cruelty of slavery.[19] Indeed, he even evoked the wrath of a number of the settlers for daring to attack forms of white slavery.[20] Nevertheless, there is no evidence of any general ethical condemnation of slavery on Wesley's part. In this respect, he coincided with the Anglican position and the attitude of the Society for the Propagation of the Gospel, under whose sponsorship his ministry in Georgia took place.[21] Even his close associations with leading representatives of the Moravians did not change his attitude since these people likewise did not attack what formally accorded with the law.[22]

This early phase of Wesley's activity to improve the situation of black slaves was characterized by a mild protest against certain wretched conditions, approval of the colony administration's refusal to admit slaves, and a pastoral concern for individual blacks. As for the latter, Wesley conversed individually with the black slaves, whom he met in South Carolina, about God and the soul as he did with whites; planned a preaching service especially for them; and instructed them in foundations of the Christian faith.[23] By collecting funds for a school, securing literature, and establishing contact with other pastors active among the black slaves, Wesley saw to it that educational work could be conducted among them.[24] Wesley continued this pastoral and pedagogical care, as time and opportunity allowed, even after his return from America (1738).[25] In evangelistic and pastoral praxis Wesley did not distinguish between white and black, free and slaves; people from both groups were won to the Christian faith by his preaching. Slaves were baptized and admitted to the Lord's Supper together with white persons.[26] Similarly, in America Methodist preachers and slave owners gathered slaves into "classes" and accepted them into their congregations.[27]

With astounding freedom from prejudice, people of another race, to whom most of the English populace denied equal worth and equal

71

rights, thus were received as sisters and brothers in the faith, persons to whom the gospel of God's love applied without restriction. Here a certain parallelism to the Pauline communities is unmistakable.

In spite of Wesley's negative experiences with the Native Americans during his missionary activity in Georgia, he insisted upon publicly emphasizing the special qualities that he perceived among his black hearers.[28] Based on his own experience, his feelings of esteem for all human beings made it easier to deal with the black slaves as persons with immortal souls to be rescued because God created them for that end.[29]

Nevertheless, in this first period Wesley did not arrive at a public protest against slavery.[30] In spite of all the reforms he initiated, perhaps he was still too much a captive of political conservatism, the ecclesiastical tradition, and an uncritical attitude toward the law, for he protected these throughout his life. Yet such a conclusion cannot be drawn with certainty. More importantly, however, Wesley's emancipation of the blacks in the religious and ecclesiastical realm, motivated by his doctrine of creation and soteriology rather than by eschatology, laid the foundation for his later opposition to and rejection of slavery.

The Later Phase (After 1770)

Even before the Quakers presented the initial proposal for abolishing slavery to the English Parliament in 1783,[31] the first Methodist conference in the United States in 1780 proclaimed its opposition to slavery as "contrary to the laws of God, of man, and of nature, and injurious to the society," adding "that it contradicts the instructions of conscience and of pure religion and does that which we would not wish others to do to us or to our folk."[32] After the decision of the Conference of 1784, all Methodists were required to abandon all connection with the slave trade and to free all slaves in their possession, as some had already done.[33] The significance of these decisions is aptly indicated by Siegfried Schulz:

> For the first time in the history of humanity and Christianity, not only is there a protest against the institution of slavery—the Greek Sophists did this in the fifth century B.C., not only is there once again an attempt to humanize the institution—as had the pagan Stoa, early catholic Christianity, and the Roman Catholic Church, not only is slavery radically eliminated in a religious community's own circle—as the late Jewish Essenes had done, but the anti-slavery movement is introduced in church and society. . . . What is disclosed is nothing less than a world-transforming praxis of faith, and the ideologically generated dominion of the slaveholder was broken.[34]

These courageous decisions could not be carried out fully and universally because of civil laws, some of which forbade emancipation of slaves. Certainly, Methodists, Quakers, Mennonites, and Baptists, due to their negative attitude toward slavery, suffered attack and experienced divisions among their own ranks.[35] Nevertheless, they sent an effective signal that restored freedom to hundreds of slaves and introduced a movement that ultimately led to the prohibition of slavery in England (1833) and in the United States (1865).[36]

The theological manifesto underlying these decisions was Wesley's small, frequently issued, and widely distributed 1774 publication, *Thoughts upon Slavery*.[37] Wesley's impetus to write it came from a Quaker, Anthony Benezet, whose writings he received and carefully studied in the early 1770s.[38] Wesley was also influenced by accounts of travels in Africa and practices of American slave owners and traders, as well as his own observations, experiences, and independent theological reflections. The position Wesley set forth in 1774 on this problem of slavery was clear and, to many of his contemporaries, convincing.

What, then, was the shape of Wesley's argument? After briefly defining and concisely surveying the rise of slavery, he began by refuting widespread prejudices concerning the blacks' lands of origin, manner of life, and character. Wesley assembled facts from travel narratives relating to the geographical, economic, social, and political conditions in the various countries of the west coast of Africa. Some omissions and exaggerations caused Wesley's picture to appear more attractive than was actually the case. This should not be attributed to a tendency to idealize nature, which Wesley had explicitly contended against when dealing with Rousseau. Rather, it should be attributed to Wesley's uncritical appropriation of literary portrayals and to his intention to correct the perception of blacks that was distorted by prejudice.[39] Besides this, the widely held view that blacks were not authentic human beings deeply contradicted Wesley's fundamental conviction that the value of a person resides first and foremost in the individual soul, created by God for eternal life. According to Wesley's own experience with the "work of God among the blacks,"[40] blacks as well as whites possess such a soul.[41] In this light Wesley's positive prejudgment is understandable.

The second and larger part of Wesley's *Thoughts upon Slavery* concerns the cruelties of capturing, transporting, and selling slaves, as well as inhumane treatment by their owners that reduced them to a status hardly preferable to beasts of burden. This section concludes by questioning whether the creator intended that the noblest creations in the visible world should lead such a life.[42] Not only the slaveholders, but also those responsible for unjust legislation must expect God's punishment for their misdeeds.[43]

The third major section[44] forms the center of Wesley's total argument. It explicitly refrains from using the Bible as a basis for discussion, and examines instead the possibility of reconciling slavery, on the one hand, with justice and mercy, on the other.[45] The concept of justice employed here derives from natural law.

This perception of natural law, which appears in Anglo-Saxon Protestantism from its Calvinist traditions, gained an importance in underlying the emergence of modern democracy in the early eighteenth-century Enlightenment.[46] Surpassing all positive law in rank and validity;[47] natural law was endowed to every person, of whatever race, religion, or nationality. Slaveholding could not be brought into harmony with this law in any way. The only argument, then, with which slavery's defenders could avoid moral condemnation and justify their actions was the argument of economic necessity. Wesley denied that this necessity existed on the grounds of experience, pointing out that white people could also work in the climate of the West Indies and the southern states, but that there had been no major effort to encourage this. Wesley's dispute of the economical argument was by no means erroneous, as was later demonstrated by Adam Smith and others with their demand that slavery be abolished for economic reasons.[48]

Wesley's most important argument, however, was to demonstrate the injury to fundamental human rights that was bound up with slavery: "Better no trade, than trade procured by villainy. It is far better to have no wealth than to gain wealth at the expense of virtue. Better is honest poverty, than all the riches bought by the tears, and sweat, and blood, of our fellow-creatures."[49] Wesley argued that this disregard for the rights of blacks had reduced them to a low moral and social position, for which the slaveholders bore the full responsibility. Thus an argument from psychology was added to the argument from natural law.[50]

Wesley's presentation up to this point was convincing precisely because he refrained from a method based upon biblical ethics and a proof-text approach. However, his position's weakness appears in his addressing his suggestions for eliminating slavery to those who were chiefly responsible: the slave ship captains, the slave traders, and the slaveholders. Wesley regarded general appeals to the public and the English nation as ineffective as an address to Parliament. Until the appearance of Wesley's *Thoughts upon Slavery*, certainly both Parliament and the public were lamentably silent. Wesley's hope, however, of changing those vitally interested in the continued existence of slavery can only be understood in light of an optimism that greatly overestimated the power of a humane appeal and its effect upon these men, their social consciousness, and their readiness to accept responsibility before the bar of morality.

Except for a few consciously Christian slave owners who obeyed the demand for emancipation, those whom Wesley addressed did not respond. Moreover, antipathy toward Methodists and abolitionists was growing. These realities soon convinced Wesley that it was necessary to seek other ways to accomplish his purposes. No longer content with public statements of position[51] and sermons,[52] calling for prayer and fasting for the emancipation of slaves,[53] Wesley became more and more involved in supporting the anti-slavery leaders, particularly Granville Sharp, Thomas Clarkson, and William Wilberforce. These men also believed that political measures were necessary and undertook to win their struggle in Parliament.[54] Wesley warned them of increasing resistance by their powerful opponents, though not without encouraging them to rely on God's help.[55] Methodist conferences in America and England submitted petitions to Parliament calling for the prohibition of slavery,[56] a measure that Wesley approved as a "truly Christian plan."[57]

Thus what began as a work of love among the blacks became through Wesley's influence a broad movement that worked toward fundamentally changing the great social injustice of slavery, using every available means of agitation as well as partial emancipation and education. This movement began with two powerful forces: a denunciation of slavery as a sin against God's commandment and an injury to the natural rights of all people, and a demonstration of love for those in distress. Above all, this love provided the necessary impetus for carrying through with this self-appointed task. John Wesley's method of sensitizing people to existing injustice in order to inspire them to abolish it ultimately made the decisive contribution to the success of the anti-slavery movement.[58]

CHAPTER VI

CONCERN FOR PRISONERS AND PRISON REFORM

W esley's intense interest and multifaceted involvement with the black slaves occurred relatively later than his concern for inmates in British prisons. Wesley and his friends had expressed concern for the latter even during the period of the Oxford student groups.[1] This task never relinquished its hold upon him; he took it up again with renewed intensity after his return from Georgia and his evangelical conversion in 1738. Presumably General Oglethorpe, who was concerned with improving the situation of deported prisoners, gave additional impetus to Wesley's interest.[2]

1. THE ENGLISH PENAL SYSTEM IN THE EIGHTEENTH CENTURY

The plight of criminals or debtors was especially unfortunate for three reasons: the extremely harsh penal law, the inscrutable arrangement and procedure of trials, and the disastrous conditions prevalent in the penal institutions.

Penal Law

After the Glorious Revolution of 1689, judges were given immunity from attempts to remove them from office, and thus they acquired greater independence. Added to this, the growing strength of the legislative body over the power of the king and his ministers undoubtedly led to the English citizen's increased security before the law, which contemporaries in other European states did not enjoy. In many people's minds, the events preceding the revolution established the conviction that the law's validity transcends royal privileges and powers.[3] However, the harshness of penal law took on proportions that minimized the citizens' security before the law and undermined their respect for the law and for the executive bodies charged with its enforcement. Thus, for example, in the course of the eighteenth century Parliament lengthened the list of crimes punishable by death to more than two hundred offenses,[4] a significant number of these being major and minor crimes against property: "A person could be hanged for shooting a rabbit, damaging a bridge, cutting a young tree, or stealing five shillings."[5]

Thus many people from the poorer strata of society were affected by penal laws governing offenses that today would largely be seen as misdemeanors or in a good many cases not regarded as punishable.[6] These people were driven by need and hunger to deeds of self-preservation for which they could expect the death penalty if they were identified and arrested. Frequent public executions[7] were heavily attended popular festivals attracting spectators from near and far.[8]

The severity of justice also dealt harshly with the imprisoned debtor who became even less capable than before of meeting financial obligations.[9] Against all reason, the law concerning debts and debtors also provided that citizens without a large income had to appear before the judge to be committed to prison.

The law's harshness was compounded by its various inadequacies. Penal law was steadily becoming more extensive; police power and control were so ineffective that in most cases soldiers had to be called upon; justice was becoming so increasingly corrupt that "of any six thieves who were brought before the court, . . . five could escape in one way or another, while the one who was unlucky was hanged,"[10] to say nothing of those who were not even arrested. This situation expressed contempt for any human sense of justice. It was not significantly improved by the practice, adopted by a number of the courts, of deporting persons instead of sentencing them to death because deportation often enough heralded a painful death.[11] The legislators in Parliament and the majority of people who by major or minor offenses became criminals belonged to two separate strata of society. Instead of a needed humanizing and simplifying of the penal law, this social division led to an effect incomprehensible in itself: "penalty after penalty was added" to "the bloody law book" and justice, to a large extent, turned into a farce.[12]

Trials

The majority of those responsible for passing judgment belonged to the ruling class; they were neither able nor willing to ignore its interests (or those of the state church, the Methodists often found) when performing their judicial duties.[13] This rendered objective proceedings against lawbreakers difficult:

> In spite of William Pitt's proud assertion that the laws of the land guaranteed to the high and the lowly, the rich and the poor, the same security and the same protection, a boy ten years old could be condemned to death, and poor hungry wretches, who were almost compelled to steal in order to live, could be forever banned from their homeland.[14]

Many prisoners had to wait for months or even years for their trials.[15] On the other hand, anyone who had enough money to secure a skilled lawyer could usually find a loophole in the rules of proceedings to circumvent punishment—if the matter came to an indictment and the beginning of a trial at all.[16] Far from helping do away with such injustice and furthering equality before the law, the Anglican episcopate perceived itself obligated to urge judges and other judicial authorities to more effectively enforce the laws. In reality, this necessarily led to a still more frequent penalizing of trivial offenses, especially those regarding public order.[17] Despite the recent separation of powers, the administration of justice was still largely influenced by the executive branch; the jury had only to determine the question of law;[18] and civil authority remained closely connected to ecclesiastical hierarchy. These facts suggest the fateful unanimity of the demand aimed not at improving but reinforcing more strongly the already existing legal situation.

The Methodists of this earlier period frequently discovered to what extent the judicial authorities would manipulate existing citizen protection laws in the purported interest of civil order. Annoyances, disruptions, and even violence committed against Methodists by other groups were neither hindered nor punished, but at times were even approved and encouraged.[19] The harshness of the authorities, even to the point of brutality that incited riots, was considered acceptable procedure against perpetrators of crimes involving property and public order, until reforms improved the legal situation toward the end of the eighteenth century and in the following decades.

Undoubtedly the legal standing of English citizens improved after

1689. Consciousness of law steadily grew stronger in the eighteenth century and ultimately forced the introduction of far-reaching reforms. Yet deficiencies of the penal laws and of the administrative and enforcement agencies repeatedly provided for measures that would have to be labeled as illegal even in the most charitable assessment, and that often led to unwarranted decisions against citizens' rights.

Punishment

The worst cruelties, however, arose because of the desolate condition of many prisons. With a few exceptions, jailers did not receive a fixed salary and thus were compelled to secure their income in other ways. Because the responsible authorities "wanted to save the trouble and cost of having the prisons administered by regularly paid officials,"[20] the ambitious contractors in charge of the prisons practiced extortion on the prisoners. Their aim was to secure money, and in exchange for money, to allow certain privileges (for example, the removal of fetters for a specified time). They sold alcohol and drugs, allowed prostitution (as a rule, men, women, and children were not housed separately), and permitted notorious prisoners to be viewed by the public for a fee. Inmates who could not pay their "fees" were tortured to death by some prison contractors; others were not allowed to leave the prison even after being acquitted or serving their sentences because they still owed money to the prison contractor.[21] It is understandable, if macabre, that many brutalized, defenseless prisoners placed their hopes in the irregular official opening of the prison doors to relieve overcrowding.[22]

In addition to the jailers' cruelty, the grievous situation of the prisoners resulted from their accommodations, and particularly from the catastrophic hygienic conditions that often led to serious illness and death. Those incarcerated while under indictment and those already sentenced, debtors and criminals alike, were housed in old towers or forts, in space beneath town halls, or in dark cellars of inns. Sanitary facilities were rare or even nonexistent; filth and stench prevailed everywhere. Chains, irons, and straitjackets made up for lack of external security. It hardly needs to be said that such places, which were often overcrowded, provided ideal breeding grounds for infectious diseases.[23] The later prison reformer John Howard tried in vain "to cause the judges in Bedfordshire and the neighboring counties to pay the jailers regular wages, [in order to discourage their] extorting money from the prisoners."[24] Not even the simplest and most fundamental provisions for improving prison conditions were made, nor indeed were they even acknowledged. Few persons in the general public knew what actually went on inside the penal institutions.

2. WESLEY'S AID TO PRISONERS

After his Aldersgate experience, John Wesley was involved in some noteworthy activities to assist prisoners. The aims of Methodism, which first manifested itself as an evangelistic movement, were also consistently applied among prisoners: Methodism was concerned with the salvation of the soul as well as with care for personal well-being. Wesley scrutinized and exposed the causes of these scandalous prison conditions.

Preaching and Pastoral Care

Especially in the London and Bristol prisons, Wesley conducted services from the spring of 1739 onward, preaching the gospel and pastoring the prisoners. He held innumerable conversations with individual prisoners, particularly those sentenced to death, praying with them and helping them not only to bear their grievous fate but to view it as an occasion for God's leading them to repentance and eternal salvation. Wesley's sermons, offering the grace of God available to all without exception or desert, did not fail to find a response. Many prisoners were moved by these sermons and found their way to a Christian faith with the power to relieve them of the fear of death and to accompany them to the scaffold with inner peace.[25] As a result of Wesley's activity, prisoners repeatedly sought his conversation and asked him to preach in their prison.[26]

Wesley obviously understood that his commission primarily to the poor did not exclude the poor in prison. Just as he had found that one after another church pulpit closed against him, he encountered early in his prison work the resistance of authorities and pastors. Accusing Wesley of leading the people astray, the sheriffs responsible for Newgate in Bristol forbade his daily worship services and limited his activity to one sermon per week.[27] The alderman of the same district refused him permission to converse with some who had been condemned to death, even though the prisoners had requested this privilege.[28] The pastor responsible for the prison also prevented another such proposed visit with some condemned prisoners.[29]

Obviously, Wesley was not content with the customary pastoral care of the clergy assigned to the prisons. Instead, he took a personal interest in the prisoners, and in some cases even pled for clemency.[30] Because Wesley incurred the disfavor of ecclesiastical authorities in other activities, too, civil and ecclesiastical officials collaborated to curtail or disrupt his work in the prisons.

The content of Wesley's preaching, according to information in his journal, consistently focused on texts proclaiming God's limitless love for all humanity.[31] Wesley's sermons demonstrate his capacity to think through and apply in currently relevant preaching a theological precept: the justification of the sinner by grace alone. Wesley declared that this grace extended precisely to those who were alienated from church and society. He did not gain a hearing from all prisoners, because their bitterness often was too intense. Many prisoners, however, responded to Wesley's concern with personal affection and accepted his offer as a gift of God.

Other Methodists very quickly perceived Wesley's activity as exemplary and therefore imitated it. As early as 1743, visiting prisoners was incorporated into the rules of the societies that directed members' religious and social activities.[32] This led to the second area of Methodist activity on behalf of the prisoners, humanitarian aid, which took the foreground for Wesley's non-theological colleagues.

Humanitarian Aid

As he did to assist the poor and in his educational efforts, Wesley secured a growing number of co-laborers to care for prisoners. Their visitation of the sick and imprisoned was an almost self-evident activity of their faith. Some of them exhibited an unprecedented selfless involvement that exposed them, not only to ridicule, but also to physical and psychological abuse, danger to their health, and even damage to their limited financial assets. They visited the prisoners to read the Bible and pray with them. They submitted petitions for them, provided ties to their kinfolk and the outside world, comforted and encouraged them, and accompanied condemned prisoners to the scaffold amid the hooting of crowds eager for a spectacle.[33]

The Methodists did not confine their concern to their own incarcerated countrymen; they extended it also to foreign prisoners.

French, Dutch, and American prisoners who had fallen into English hands as soldiers often had to suffer even worse living conditions than those previously described. The Methodists' preaching, pastoral care, and humanitarian aid were offered to them also.[34] Money was collected in the Methodists' worship services to buy them clothing, food, and mattresses. To incite others to follow his example, Wesley publicly pointed to these distressing situations and the steps that could be taken to relieve them. He had significant success in this effort.[35]

Abel Dagge, the jailer at Newgate in Bristol, exemplified the effectiveness of the Methodists' preaching and social work in improving the prisoners' situation despite the restrictive legal framework. (Samuel Johnson erected a literary monument to Dagge in his *Life of Savage*.)[36] Wesley bore witness to the results that a single sermon brought to the Bristol penal institution: the entire building was cleaned, drunkenness and prostitution were eliminated, disputes were settled on the basis of testimony from those involved rather than through brawls, and the observance of Sunday and regular services of worship became a part of the routine order. Above all, though, the inmates were provided opportunities for work. They received materials on credit, which they could then repay with the profits from their labor.[37] Instead of being victimized by idleness and waiting, which resulted in much injurious behavior, prisoners now had meaningful tasks, an income of their own, and thereby the possibility of wiping out their debts and preparing themselves for the time after their release from confinement.

From the very beginning, ministry to prisoners was part of the established repertoire of Methodist activity. In 1778 it was confirmed by a Conference decision and made obligatory for all preachers.[38] Although this did not set in motion a comprehensive prison reform, a considerable number of people became aware of the prisoners' lot. Accepting this as a challenge to their Christian commitment to "love thy neighbor," they committed their energies and money to alleviating the situation of the prisoners. Because of their altered awareness and their own experience from working in the prisons, they proved themselves willing and able in later years to support the many efforts of prison reformers like John Howard and others.

Wesley's Publications on Prisons and Aid to Prisons

Wesley has been accused of not creating any new methods of aid to prisoners.[39] Moreover, the silence of much literature on the history of prison reform suggests that Wesley has not been seen as having any significance worthy of mention.[40] Nevertheless, if the impartial historian considers the preceding account and looks more closely at Wesley's public declarations on this subject, Wesley's significant influence upon improvement of the prison situation will become evident. That influence affected not only acute distresses but also fundamental grievances grounded in the legal structure, trials, and punishment. In addition, the limits of Wesley's reform activity can be viewed as drawn for him in advance by his theological and political stances.

Wesley did not confine his activity to providing pastoral and charitable help for prisoners. Publicly and with praiseworthy clarity, he protested against shocking abuses. Before John Howard published his disturbing report, *The State of Prisons in England and Wales* in 1777, Wesley had visited many prisons on his travels and inspected them thoroughly, in order to gain a perspective on prevailing conditions. In fact, Wesley had provided the impetus for Howard's reforming work. Wesley's complaints, reported in several newspapers and in his own publications, were primarily directed against the following:

(1) The condition of most of the prisons, for which there was nothing comparable "this side of hell."[41] Darkness, filth, disease, and the absence of any amenities made the prison a valley of death where people, separated from all friends and acquaintances, were delivered into the hands of "such masters and such companions."[42]

(2) The effect of a stay in prison upon moral behavior. The released prisoners usually "go from this school" having been prepared for all kinds of crimes, brutalized, and fully equipped for all sorts of wicked words and deeds.[43] Thus punishment did not serve to improve the punished but rather set them on the road to still other criminal acts.

(3) The long judicial proceedings. Wesley referred especially to civil proceedings. While capital offenses often were handled and decided within a single day, others frequently had to wait months or years for trial, while the court was untroubled about difficulties resulting from the delay.[44] The complexity of the laws and the differing judgments that resulted, even in similar cases, led to still further insecurity before the law.

(4) The unequal legal treatment of poor and rich. Wesley protested, "If the one is rich and the other poor, doth not justice stand afar off? And is not the poor under the utmost improbability (if not impossibility) of obtaining it?"[45] The lawyers were said to be seldom honest and

reportedly took a great deal of money from their clients. Those who could not pay a lawyer to initiate proper proceedings sought in vain for their rights. The oppressors who had taken everything from the victims were so secure from the victims that they might as well be dead. Even a judgment against the rich, which was very unlikely, would not help the poor, since the rich individual would appeal the decision, and the entire process would begin all over again.[46]

(5) The inhumane treatment of prisoners of war. French, Dutch, and American as well as British prisoners were among the groups visited by Wesley. He did not allow himself to be guided by feelings of revenge, a common occurrence against prisoners of war. Instead, he included them in his concern just like any other people in dire straits. In order to persuade others to share in providing help, he published accounts of their distress and of the measures taken to help them.[47] In a widely noticed sermon to his countrymen, Wesley addressed the need to bring about a changed attitude toward prisoners of war. His text was: "Also thou shalt not oppress a stranger; for ye know the heart of a stranger, seeing ye were strangers in the land of Egypt."[48] Wesley's public laments proved effective on individuals, churches, and authorities who were moved to action.[49]

Here, as in Wesley's appeal for the abolition of slavery, it is striking that he did not polemicize on the basis of biblical and theological arguments alone for carrying out a measure he deemed right and good. It was necessary to help the French prisoners not only "for the credibility of our religion and for the glory of God," but also "for the glory of their city and their land."[50] After he had received an anonymous gift of twenty pounds, he expressed the conviction that the gift would provide "a much more noble satisfaction" for the donor than if he had given it for other things, even if there were no hereafter. And Wesley added, "Men of reason, judge!"[51]

Here, too, Wesley attempted to go beyond the circle of those motivated solely by religious arguments and to stir to action all those from whom he could expect some help. However, Wesley's expressions do not contain any direct attack upon the parliamentary legislation or the executives of the king and his ministers, who ultimately were responsible for introducing and worsening the unbearable prison conditions. Wesley's respect for the institutions of monarchy and Parliament and his political conservatism were too pronounced for him to have been willing to engage in any direct attacks. Against this background, however, his stance appears courageous and unconventional, realistic regarding measures that might be achieved speedily, and primarily oriented to socially sensitizing and mobilizing individuals, groups, and those responsible for regional decisions. Wesley's contribution to the reforms that began near the end of the century and to the preparation of a considerable reservoir of people who furthered and helped in these reforms[52] has never been appropriately described. Although modern society may be more humane, Wesley's implied wish that there might be no prisons at all[53] has not yet been achieved.

THE PRINCIPLES OF WESLEY'S SOCIAL ETHICS

CHAPTER VII

PRESUPPOSITIONS OF WESLEY'S SOCIAL ETHICS

E xamining the most important arenas of Wesley's social activity provides a basis for interpreting and evaluating his social ethics within the overall context of his theological stance. The preceding section could also have been extended to still other problem areas, such as marriage, the family, and the state. However, these are distinguished by Wesley's more limited personal attentions and reduced intellectual and practical energy. These distinctions legitimize the previous approach to restricted topics.

The remaining discussion concerns the inner connection among the principles of Wesley's social ethics within the total context of his theology,[1] resulting in a well-founded assessment of his social ethics. Treatment of such comprehensive theological topics as the doctrine of grace, law, sanctification, and others, will be strictly limited to their significance for social ethics.[2] The preceding investigation of Wesley's social praxis will provide a criterion for judging the usefulness of Wesley's theories. Wesley's theological pronouncements reflect the implicit theological foundation underlying his practical work.

This chapter is less concerned with social relationships[3] than with presuppositions about the human race that relate to the necessity and meaning of ethical conduct. Wesley inquired whether such presuppositions first appeared in the believer on the way to holiness, or whether they already existed in the unconverted "natural man." He also tried to distinguish these two states in terms of the ethical quality of individual decisions and deeds.

1. PREVENIENT GRACE

The Inability of "Natural Man" to Do Good

Wesley shared the view of the Reformers that all the works of the natural, or sinful and unjustified, humans were "unholy and sinful themselves" and that "only corrupt fruit grows on a corrupt tree."[4] Deeds derived their quality from the nature of the one performing the act. It was not that an individual was evil because of evil deeds; it was that the deeds were evil because the individual was evil: "The heart of man is desperately wicked."[5] Individual sins were only the leaves and fruit growing on the evil tree.[6] Through the fall human moral likeness to God was completely lost.[7] "Thou canst do nothing but sin, til thou art reconciled to God."[8]

The "natural man's" inability to do good had two causes: on the one hand, inability to love, or the corruption of the will and affections; and on the other hand, ignorance of God, or utter lack of knowledge of the divine will. Wesley preferred to describe the corruption of human nature with the metaphor of an illness that has fallen on the entire person after rebellion against God.[9] This illness had numerous manifestations: godlessness, willfulness, love for the world rather than for the Creator, thirst for revenge, egoism, and the like.[10] The actual cause, however, lay in the depravity of the human will and of its passions.[11] For this reason Wesley could not be satisfied with a righteousness understood purely in terms of imputation. Instead, he placed an unmistakable emphasis on the curative effect of grace.[12]

The corruption of human nature, initiated by the first creatures' rebellion against their Creator, was irreparable apart from God's gracious intervention.[13] People could not change their nature through any personal striving, or any religious or moral effort.[14] The "free will" of the "natural man" was free only to sin in everything.[15] Wesley's schooling in the natural sciences and the English philosophy of the Enlightenment[16] made it impossible for him to deny the existence of morally good deeds.[17] However, before God, who was ultimately the court to weigh every deed, "all morality, all righteousness, mercy, and truth that possibly exist outside the Christian faith, . . . are worth nothing at all."[18] Wesley was convinced "that all works done before justification have in them the nature of sin; and that, consequently, till he is justified, a man has no power to do any work which is pleasing and acceptable to God."[19] The corrupt nature was the seed of all evil.[20]

Thus sinful deeds, at the very core consisting of lovelessness, were the consequence and visible image of the sinful person: "But none of our works can be done in this love, while the love of the Father . . . is not in us; and this love cannot be in us until we receive the 'Spirit of Adoption, crying in our hearts, Abba, Father.'" [21] In good Augustinian fashion, Wesley also described the essence of the "spiritual sicknesses" from

90

which all people suffer since Adam's Fall[22] as *hubris* and love of the world, which have usurped the place of obedience to and love of the Creator.

It is striking that in Wesley's doctrine of sin metaphysical speculations about the devil are almost totally absent, and occasionally are even explicitly rejected—apart from the theological interpretation of the Fall[23] where they play a subordinate role.[24] Wesley emphasized human responsibility more clearly than does Reformed theology, but he underscored that human corruption could only be healed by divine grace. This can hardly be overemphasized when studying Wesley's ethic, particularly since it appears to have never received substantive treatment.

The same held true for the other consequence of the Fall that continued to affect all subsequent generations: the utter darkening of human knowledge of God and his will. Consciously borrowing New Testament conceptions without citing individual biblical passages,[25] Wesley described the condition of the "natural man" as asleep: "His spiritual senses are not awake: they discern neither spiritual good nor evil."[26] Just as natural knowledge was impossible without functioning sense organs,[27] any knowledge of divine things was impossible for the spiritually "sleeping" man. The "natural man"

> is utterly ignorant of God. . . . He is totally a stranger to the law of God, as to its true, inward, spiritual meaning. He has no conception of that evangelical holiness, without which no man shall see the Lord; nor of the happiness which they only find whose "life is hid with Christ in God."[28]

The consequence of such blindness was total ignorance of the divine will and lack of awareness that one was a sinner. Instead, the individual lived in a tragic security, not perceiving his position on the edge of an eternal abyss.[29] Stated more directly, since the essential significance of God's will was hidden, the individual could not perceive the discrepancy between God's claim upon his creature and the individual's ethical behavior, nor was the creature aware of being subject to God's judgment. This deceitful security was often further strengthened by quietistic misinterpretations of New Testament utterances about God's grace and atonement through Christ, thus making any change in ethical stance appear unnecessary.[30] In this way Wesley disclosed the crucial background of "dead Christianity," of the merely "outward piety" of his time and other times, a condition that has cultivated and further developed conventions of the Christianized West without comprehending and making effectual the ethical impetus of the gospel.[31]

Beginning from this position, which characterized the "natural man" as incapable of doing good and ignorant of the divine will, appeared to eliminate from the outset any basis for a universally applicable ethic. How could personal responsibility be asserted and validated where moral insight and strength was lacking? Wesley undertook to offer the solution to this underlying ethical problem in his doctrine of prevenient grace.

The Effect of Prevenient Grace

Wesley's numerous statements about the "natural man," have provided a basis for perceiving his understanding of the necessity of God's grace working upon man. Next to be investigated and explained on points fundamentally significant for his social ethics is Wesley's doctrine of prevenient grace.

Consistent with his exclusive doctrine of sin, Wesley necessarily regarded all acts of the unjustified person as worthless in God's sight, since the sinful creature has no capacity for good. This problem is treated as early as the 1745 Conference in connection with the Cornelius pericope (Acts 10) and resolved as follows: the works of Cornelius before he was justified were not "splendid sins," nor were they achieved without the grace of Christ. Restated in general terms, "The works of him who has heard the gospel, and does not believe, are not done as God hath 'willed and commanded them to be done.' And yet we know not how to say that they are an abomination to the Lord in him who feareth God, and, from that principle, does the best he can."[32]

The crucial comment that guards this interpretation against potential Pelagianism is the reference to the grace of God even in the person who is not yet justified.[33] This reference is not found in all of Wesley's statements on this subject; it is particularly absent from statements connected with the doctrine of creation. Thus Wesley wrote in one sermon that all persons were created as rational creatures, or creatures who are "capable of God."[34] Not only was this what distinguished humans from all other creatures, but also it was the vestige of humanity's creation in the image of God, otherwise lost in the fall of Adam. This remnant of the *imago Dei* can be stated more specifically in three respects:

1. Every person, whether Christian or nonChristian, had a "spiritual

nature," to which belonged his "understanding, and affections, and a degree of liberty; of a self-moving, yea, self-governing power."[35] Otherwise he would be a machine, a stick, or a stone.[36]

2. Every person had a "natural conscience," which aided him to a certain extent in distinguishing between the morally good and the morally evil.[37]

3. Every person had "some desire to please God." This held true even for those who did not know God, and although the level of this desire varied from one individual to another.[38]

Since the Fall did not entirely destroy the desire for good and turning away from evil, even the heathen had a moral law. Its content consisted, though, in condemning morally reprehensible conduct toward their fellow human beings.[39] Thus no one in Christendom had the right to anticipate God's judgment upon "Heathens and Mohammedans."[40] Instead, all Christians should take care to be renewed by the power of God's grace so that they themselves would not fall under God's judgment.[41]

On the one hand, Wesley's statements about a vestige of the *imago Dei* perhaps present in all persons contradicted his doctrine of the total corruption of those not yet born again. On the other hand, Wesley in other passages attributed those abilities to the effect of prevenient grace. Since he could argue that no person was devoid of prevenient grace,[42] Wesley's position might be described more precisely this way: even the desire to please God, awareness of the moral value of human deeds, and the limited freedom of the human will in the realm of ethical decisions, ultimately should be traced to the effect of prevenient grace. Eicken has rightly observed that this emphasis takes on more and more significance in the course of Wesley's theological reflection. Wesley's application of these concepts suggests that his own observations influenced his affirmation of ethical action, while his theory of prevenient grace interpreted these phenomena and reconciled them with the doctrines of original sin and saving grace.[43] The following points provide evidence for such an analysis.

The desire to please God is usually present, wrote Wesley in a letter of November 1762 to Bishop Warburton.[44] Even a certain measure of Christian virtue could be discerned before justification, but this should be traced back to the effect of God's prevenient grace.[45]

Similarly, this held true for the human conscience. In one of his late sermons Wesley did leave open the question whether conscience was naturally given or added by God's grace,[46] because at this point he apparently did not wish to engage in any fundamental discussion. It was his personal conviction, however, that no one lived in a purely natural state, i.e., utterly without God's grace.[47] People were capable of ethical, dutiful conduct because of grace, not by nature. In addition to revealing salvation in the Holy Scripture, God gives every creature a "light of nature" that issues from prevenient grace.[48] Knowledge imparted this way was the knowledge of conscience:[49] it was not connected with the improvement of natural perception or insight but with knowing God's will and each person's own transgressions of this will.[50] This "internal witness" in the human breast enabled one to distinguish between right and wrong in a limited way.[51] It rendered the creature susceptible to moral appeals: "Ought we not to do what we believe is morally good, and to abstain from what we judge is evil?"[52] The internal perception of this conscience related to matters past and present, and inner attitudes and outward manners of conduct; it not only weighed but also excused or accused, approved or disapproved, acquitted or condemned.[53] Employing Paul (especially Romans 1), Wesley defined the conscience as "a faculty or power, implanted by God in every soul that comes into the world, of perceiving what is right or wrong in his own heart or life, in his tempers, thoughts, words and actions."[54]

The common ground for the ideas of the vestige of the *imago Dei* and prevenient grace appears in this passage, which renders unimportant, if not utterly unnecessary, any fundamental differentiation. Both of these ideas clearly indicate that the ability to distinguish good from evil and to decide in favor of the good was in every instance the gift of God.[55]

Not only was the conscience given the ability of moral discernment and evaluation of attitudes and deeds, but also it was the instrument with which God stirred one to specific behavior, giving satisfaction when a person was obedient to the voice of his conscience and discomfort when one acted contrary to it.[56] This "inner check" was also an effect of the Spirit by the grace of God.[57] Without it the conscience could not fulfill its function.[58] Continual disobedience, nevertheless, could also blind conscience and ultimately kill it, while obedience sharpened its vision and heightened its sensitivity.[59]

The chief problem of human ethical responsibility, however, was not yet resolved. Wesley had posed this problem sharply with his doctrine of the total depravity of the human will and its inability to choose the good: insight, although absolutely necessary, was insufficient. In order to avoid diminishing the value of insight and to underscore personal responsibility even prior to justification, Wesley took the theological path characterized by prevenient grace. Following Article X of the Church of England's Thirty-Nine Articles,[60] he taught that doing, like knowing, the good, was impossible without grace; which was the only thing capable of liberating the will to a certain degree[61] and enabling it to do what was good.[62] These good works, however, were good only in a diluted sense, for they did not arise out of faith and love toward God,[63] nor did they have any meritorious character.[64] Nevertheless, they were necessary: "First, God works; therefore you can work: Secondly, God works, therefore you must work."[65] Individual actions must harmonize with God's preceding gracious activity if one did not wish to lose prevenient grace, which could be refused in case of omission or neglect. Grace then was considered personal, not substantial, and cooperation was necessary, although any idea of merit remained excluded.[66] At the same time, it was dangerous to stop short with these "works of repentance," as Wesley occasionally called them,[67] since by stopping short everyone would be excluded from justification and thus from salvation: "It is by no means advisable to rest here; it is at the peril of our souls if we do."[68] Only justification by faith and sanctification in love enabled one, in the proper sense of the term, to perform good works and to act as God wills.[69]

In a general sense the entire intention of the doctrine of grace was aimed at this fundamental transformation. Still, the doctrine of prevenient grace, especially as developed by Augustine and Abelard, had a twofold function for the ethics of the unbeliever: it placed even him in a position of responsibility for his actions, and it rendered him susceptible to ethical appeals that would have remained meaningless without the effects of prevenient grace.[70]

2. RENEWING GRACE

The fate imposed upon mankind by Adam's fall was the fundamental corruption of nature and an utter inability to do good. Prevenient grace had cancelled that fate, though only in a provisional measure limited both in content and time. Moreover, the creature could not climb unaided from this "prevenient" level of ethical awareness and ability to a higher level. Therefore, a further work of grace was necessary,—a work that would bestow a different quality in one before God and in the world.

Such a change touching the very core of one's being, could be accomplished only by the saving, renewing grace of God, which awakened faith and enabled one to love. This central doctrinal element in Wesleyan theology has been described often.[71] It is relevant to this study in that it contains nonnegotiable presuppositions for Wesley's ethic, which are crucial for identifying and appropriately evaluating his social ethics. Two aspects of this doctrine are particularly relevant: a real, effective renewing by grace received in faith and the necessity of good works after one's justification.

The Renewal of Humanity

For works to be considered good in the sight of God prior to justification is impossible. Wesley was in fundamental agreement with the Reformers' doctrine of justification, which had been his abiding foundation for theology and preaching ever since his encounter with the Herrnhuters. Very early on, however, he had taken his stand against narrowing the doctrine of justification to a mere imputation of righteousness. The special formulation of the doctrine of justification was based on the two components essential for ethics: the effectiveness of grace, which leads to a genuine change in man; and the necessity of good works after justification.

God's grace acting through the Holy Spirit was not limited solely to prevenient grace, which in a certain sense prepared the way for justification. Grace initiated a process of complete renewal:[72] the restoration of the image of God.[73] As distinguished from justification, this renewal did not occur in a single moment, but in a lifelong process of sanctification.[74] While one occasionally gains the impression that Wesley regarded the attainment of perfect sanctification in this life as a possibility,[75] it may be objected that he never claimed this status for himself and did not identify it in others. Wesley did, however, allow it as a possibility, and in most of his statements referring to this matter he stressed the process-oriented character of sanctification, which will reach perfection in the resurrection of the dead.[76] Albert Outler fittingly sums up Wesley's expressions: "Grace is the real activity of God in the human heart; it is the actual influence of God's love in human existence. In its several dimensions it suffuses and affects all of life. . . . Grace is God's love in action: in Christ, to reconcile us to himself; in the Spirit, to sanctify us wholly."[77]

Both the beginning of this genuine transformation by grace and its abiding significance were rooted in Christ's reconciliation for all, and thus it must be accepted by faith.[78] F. Loofs, with good reason, defended Wesley against the charge that he mixes justification and sanctification, affirming that "John Wesley's own teaching about the relationship of justification and sanctification is entirely correct. . . ."[79] Like faith, rebirth as the beginning of renewal was a gift of God. Only the Creator could accomplish the new creation.[80]

This characterization of sanctification could thus be described as gift-like. The question must then be posed as to the direction of this change wrought in people and the content of the renewal that the Spirit of God produced. God's work addressed the soul and its capacities of understanding, will, and affections, by which God drew one away from evil and inspired one to do good. Thus the individual's whole way of thinking and acting was changed.[81] The creature was awakened from spiritual death to spiritual life,[82] freed from the compulsion to sin,[83] and released to Christian liberty.[84] The power of sin was broken,[85] and the heart filled with love for God and for all humanity.[86] Sanctification was not merely a holiness imputed for Christ's sake, contrary to the Herrnhuters' belief, but a transforming renewal that instilled the mind of Christ.[87] Wesley repeatedly identifies love for God and all people with the mind of Christ, naming these as the components of this spiritual renewal. They enabled the justified individual to "walk before Him in righteousness, mercy, and truth, doing the things that are pleasing in His sight."[88] The knowledge of God's love in Jesus Christ liberated from the guilt and power of sin and from the fear of God's wrath. It poured God's love into the heart, so that the new creature did evil to no one but diligently strove to do good.[89] This constituted real freedom, evangelical freedom, experienced by every believer. It was not freedom from God's law or God's works, but from the law of sin and the works of the devil.[90] Thus, through the work of Christ, God had not only wrought a redemption *for* us but also a renewal *in* us, which set us free and empowered us for a life in the spirit of Jesus.[91]

Wesley did not believe it necessary to carefully nuance the language used to describe this activity of God.[92] Clearly, however, he understood faith as a trust in God's grace that provides the strength to overcome sin. He also ascribed to faith a level of knowledge that facilitated the renewal of humanity through grace and thus was of great importance for Christian action. Faith was "a divine evidence or conviction wrought in the heart that God is reconciled to me through His son."[93] It illuminated the mind, clarifying a person's calling—namely, to glorify God—and

97

revealing Christ to the heart through "a divine evidence or conviction of his love, his free, unmerited love to me a sinner."[94] This knowledge was hidden from the "natural man."[95] It was only faith that enabled a person to have a clear and certain knowledge of self and the invisible world of God.[96] Imperfect knowledge of the divine, like weakness and temptation, remained as a sign of the earthly limitations.[97]

Good Works

This knowledge of self and of God bestowed upon the believer, along with the renewal by grace that liberated from the power of sin and restored to the likeness of God, now also empowered the believer to do good works. There was thus a causal connection between justification or regeneration and the practical performance of the divine will in the Christian's daily life. For Wesley, two things were inescapable: the irreversible sequence of faith and good works, and the necessity of good works for faith. "First believe," he says in a sermon, "and then thou shalt do all things well."[98] "Good works follow this [true, justifying] faith; they cannot precede it."[99] Sanctification may therefore be described as "a continued course of good works."[100] With this unequivocal affirmation Wesley detached himself from his pre-1738 dogma and with conviction adopted the Reformers' position, never to abandon it as long as he lived.[101] Wesley's emphasis on human rebirth through God's action further confirmed and established the irreversibility of the sequence of faith and works.[102]

Wesley no less clearly pointed to the necessity of good works. He used a twofold line of argument: good works belonged in essence to justifying faith, and the believer needed them for growth in holiness. Just as a diseased tree could produce nothing but bad fruit, so also good fruit must grow on a healthy tree. What Wesley meant here was obviously not an external compulsion imposed upon the believer, but an inward necessity grounded in faith itself. The fruits of faith issued from it directly.[103] Faith without works was not faith; it was dead faith, devils' faith.[104] The good works that one performed after being justified were essentially God's deeds.[105] God through Jesus Christ had recreated His children for good works,[106] placed His Spirit in their hearts, and affected the "genuine fruits of the Spirit of God in their lives."[107] In the believer's life,[108] these fruits served a central deictic function; in the life of the unbeliever, who was prone to question the authenticity of faith,[109] their role was less important. The unbeliever's works, at least as far as "outward" good works were concerned, were not fruits of the Spirit or essential elements of faith that came about without human will. One might deliberately omit these[110] and by neglect forfeit faith, the "free gift of God."[111] To avoid forfeiting one's faith, then, the believer should be careful not to ignore opportunities to do good, but to strengthen faith by employing it in good works.[112] It was not the power of faith that produced good works, but the Spirit of God who worked through the believer. The more the believer submitted to being used as an instrument of the Spirit, the more personal faith, the believer's connection with God, was strengthened. Good works were both the consequence of renewal through grace and a means for advancing and perfecting the sanctification of the justified person.[113]

In this way Wesley not only more firmly anchored faith in personal experience, but also guarded against misunderstanding faith as a rational scheme, which to a large extent it had become in Protestant orthodoxy. (By doing so Wesley admittedly paid the price of increased danger of assault on the soul precisely through experience.)[114] Wesley also defended faith against two other tendencies of Christian theology that seemed to falsify the proper understanding of the relationship between faith and works: quietism or antinomianism, which he perceived in the Herrnhuters and the mystics, and works-righteousness, which he perceived in Catholicism and in his own Anglican church.

By his own statements, Wesley owed the knowledge that man is justified by faith alone to his encounter with Lutheran theology through the Herrnhuters. Wesley was also conscious of an abiding obligation to them in other ways. Wesley's relatively early separation from the Herrnhuters occurred for one fundamental reason: their different placement of good works in the doctrine and praxis of believers. Wesley accused his German pietist friends of representing a "solafideism" or quietism. That is, they denied the essential necessary connection of faith and works, as did the mystics, to whom he had given so much attention and esteem in his early years.[115]

Something, however brief, must be said about Wesley's attitude toward the Herrnhut teaching on good works, because it brightly illuminated Wesley's own doctrine. Wesley was thinking of Moravian teaching and representatives of Roman Catholic mysticism especially when he asserted that it is under the devil's counsel that faith and works were so often set in conflict with each other. He then continued: "Some have magnified faith to the utter exclusion of good works, not only from being the cause of our justification (for we know that a man is justified freely by the redemption which is in Jesus), but . . . from having any place in the religion of Jesus Christ."[116] For Wesley the activity of faith and responsibility for the world were indispensable elements of the Christian life that were missing in the dogmatics of the Moravians, and indeed rejected by them as injurious to faith. Wesley, on the other hand, claimed that "If good works do not follow our faith, . . . it is plain our faith is nothing worth [sic]; we are yet in our sins."[117]

Anyone who agrees with Wesley's understanding of justifying faith as a work of God's grace renewing the whole man must label any mere imputation of righteousness as too abridged, wholly inadequate, and therefore wrong. Wesley not only was defending his own theology on this point but, ironically in the history of theology, was also defending Luther against a Lutheranism that had become one-sided. In the context of Wesley's battle against "solafideism," he read and strongly criticized Luther's Galatians commentary[118] without distinguishing Luther from scholastic Lutheranism. Yet—like Wesley later—it was Luther who wrote polemically against fideism as "human folly and dream":

> O, when it comes to faith, what a living, creative, active, powerful thing it is. It cannot do other than good at all times. It never waits to ask whether there is some good work to do; rather, before the question is raised, it has done the deed, and keeps on doing it. A man not active in this way is a man without faith. He is groping about for faith and searching for good works, but knows neither what faith is nor what good works are.[119]

For Luther, too, a new obedience was the distinguishing mark of real faith.[120] The inner necessity of works following faith linked Wesley's theology with Luther's.[121] The ethical impetus in the teaching, preaching, and social activity of the founder of Methodism grew precisely from this starting point, strengthened by the manifestation of God's love for us and by our resultant love for God and neighbor (see below, chapter VIII).

It is evident that Wesley's struggle to demonstrate the necessity of good works for a life lived out of faith, even if not for justification by faith, prevented grace from being misunderstood as a cloak for wickedness.[122] Yet by this very thing Wesley made himself vulnerable to the accusation that he taught justification by works. During a brief period of his life, in fact, Wesley actually crossed over the boundary that he himself had drawn between faith-righteousness and works-righteousness. In the heat of battle he forgot that he had once described justification by faith as the "cornerstone of the whole Christian building"[123] and had often defended it as such.[124] At the conference of 1770 "there arose . . . the impression that the whole movement had gone back to the merit-character of works."[125] This contention over works of repentance might lead to the conclusion that the person who feared God and did righteous deeds was accepted by God, although on the basis of "works as a condition," not on the meritoriousness of the works themselves. Wesley answered this previous dispute by saying it constituted an argument, "Over words, I fear."[126] The debate with antinomian Calvinism had brought Wesley to this exaggerated formulation, which was bound to be misunderstood. At the very next conference, however, the matter was once again clarified and the doctrine of justification by works was unequivocally rejected.[127]

Nevertheless, Wesley's simultaneous emphasis on justification by faith alone and the necessity of good works looked like a case of constant tightrope walking, and his effort to avoid slipping off the tightrope towards a mild synergism was not always successful.[128] As J. Weissbach has correctly observed, this is due partly to the fact that for Wesley, "the *sola gratia* in repentance as well as already in prevenient grace is not insured by the *sola fide* but by the Holy Spirit."[129] This potential misunderstanding was also due to Wesley's understanding of grace, which renewed human beings in such a way that faith was not only their gift, but also their obligation:[130] because God worked in them, they themselves could and must work if God were not to cease working.[131] Using biblical passages[132] and Augustine's words,[133] Wesley solidified his view that ethical passivity and justifying grace are mutually exclusive. This theological dialectic, which appropriately placed Paul and James side by side,[134] made it possible for Wesley to emphasize equally the doctrines of justification by faith alone (against Anglican legalism, which accused him of fanaticism) and the necessity of good works (against any mystical or pietistic quietism). It is through this synthesis that Wesley laid the foundation for his social ethics.

CHAPTER VIII

STANDARDS FOR SOCIAL ETHICS

It has been established that based on Wesley's understanding of God's grace, he attributed to everyone the possibility of responsible action. But what was the content of the ethical action commanded, and what motives and standards provide points of reference and direction for that action? The Christian has been given biblical commandments to guide moral behavior. However, because of historical conditions, which Wesley recognized, the commandments vary in their applicability. It is necessary to inquire anew in each case to determine what is obligatory, and, in light of the ethical demands of a new situation, to seek standards that can provide a basis for ethical action in different social settings.

1. LOVE OF GOD AND NEIGHBOR[1]

Along with Paul and Augustine,[2] Wesley regarded love as the indispensable condition for all deeds that might in the strictest sense be called good. It is true that a person could do good and avoid evil before the love of God was poured out in the heart, but the value of such action remained provisional and relative. It is true that prevenient grace rendered one capable of outward piety, of works of penitence and good deeds; however, with a clear reference to I Corinthians 13, Wesley asked, "What does it profit us to have done everything good and nothing wicked, to have given all our goods to feed the poor, if we do not have love?"[3]

Wesley distinguished between the outward performance of good, which was not without value but nevertheless only provisional, and the performance of good that followed the inner renewal by God's grace, prompted and shaped by love. Only this latter activity should in the proper sense be characterized as good. Only a person who acted out of love was really doing good.

Love as the content of true piety was a legacy that Wesley owed first of all to William Law's influence.[4] After his (1738) conversion this concept remained determinative for his ethic, though not without undergoing profound revision. Law's contention for human striving toward love for God had driven Wesley deeply into a legalistic piety.[5] But he recognized, in connection with his discovery of justification by faith alone, that it was faith alone that opened the way by which love for God and neighbor filled the heart and became the motivating force for one's actions.[6] After this discovery, loving God and one's neighbor was no longer a means of self-justification before God—as had been the case with the members of the Holy Club—but the response of a joyous assurance of having experienced God's love. Anxiety about one's own salvation had given way to gratitude for the justification bestowed by God's free love.

In faith, Wesley discovered "that love of God, and of all mankind, which we had elsewhere sought in vain."[7] Faith mediated "the revelation of Christ in our hearts; a divine knowledge or conviction of his love, his free, unmerited love for me as a sinner. . . ."[8] Faith was the straight road to the religion of love, the sense organ for the love of God.[9] Faith and love were not described according to the "form-and-matter principle" of Scholasticism. Instead, using a concept prominently employed in the doctrine of justification, faith and love were described as the renewing of persons after God's likeness, caused by love of God and its consequence, which was the renewed creature's love for God and neighbor.[10]

Only the believer perceived the unlimited love of God poured into the heart, enabling him or her to act out of love. Faith and love now belonged inseparably together. Neither was a substitute for the other, nor could the sequence of faith and love be reversed: "It is in consequence of our knowing that God loves us, that we love him, and love our neighbor as ourselves."[11] The love of God poured out in the heart produced love for God and neighbor.[12] Our gratitude toward our Creator and benefactor,[13] the redeemer from sin and guilt who first loved us,[14] set us free from self-concern; freed us from anxiety about others as well. From this gratitude there "arises true, unselfish goodness toward all men."[15] Wesley's putting first God's love received in faith guarded him against falling into a works-righteousness by which one's love became the means of justification. Wesley's emphasis upon love following from faith guarded him against a self-satisfied quietism concerned first and foremost about its own blessedness.

God's Love for All

Beginning with this priority of God's love that preceded all human love and applied to all people, Wesley rejected two other views: atheistic humanism and the Calvinistic doctrine of predestination. Although these indeed differ in content, the one thing they have in common is devaluing the love of God.

Wesley encountered the doctrine of predestination, philosophically expanded in the sense of a *gemina praedestinatio* (a "double-edged predestination"), particularly in the Puritan tradition. It appeared to him to be a perversion of the gospel because it rendered preaching futile, for those who were elect did not need such proclamation, and it provided no help to those who were reprobate.[16] It destroyed the comfort of faith as well as the zeal for good works, but most of all, it destroyed an individual's love for the greater part of humanity.[17] Certainly Wesley differentiated too little among the predestinarian positions and did not recognize their value for the assurance of those who believed themselves to be among the elect.[18]

To Wesley, that assurance appeared too much like a slap in the face of God's love for all humanity, making the loving Father into an all-powerful tyrant.[19] Such a view would be incompatible with love for Christ and the work of grace.[20] The doctrine of the universal love of God was such a cardinal point of Wesley's dogmatics and ethic that he even neglected to unequivocally support it exegetically,[21] arguing his case more systematically instead[22] by laying claim to non-exegetical arguments for his position.[23] Although Wesley was tolerant enough not to deny Christian faith to those who held a predestinarian view,[24] he firmly insisted on the indivisibility of the love of God, who was the Father of all humanity[25] and had mercy on all without respect of persons. For Wesley the doctrine of predestination not only perverted the love of God, but also destroyed Christian happiness imparted through the experience of God's love.[26] Out of this conviction Wesley could cry out, "Behold the amazing love of God to the outcasts of men! His tender condescension to their folly!"[27], and could follow it with corresponding deeds. The whole of Wesley's social activities appears inconceivable without this "theology of love."[28]

Because God's love alone was the power enabling human love, Wesley

105

also rejected atheistic humanism. Anyone who denied or deleted the cause—the love of God—had no way of accounting for the consequence—love for all people. Hence Wesley especially took a stand against the humanism of the *Aufklärung* (Enlightenment) as he had come to know it in the works of Rousseau, Voltaire, Hume, and others:

> . . . call it humanity, virtue, morality, or what you please, it is neither better nor worse than atheism. Men hereby willfully and designedly put asunder what God has joined—the duties of the first and second table. It is separating the love of our neighbor from the love of God.[29]

Thus a deficiency in love for God would be an offense with respect to an obligation toward God, a disobedience of God's commandments. But Wesley was not content to stop here; he continued with clearly antideistic sharpness, saying that God not only created the world but also watched over it and governed it without spatial or temporal limitation: "We know that as all nature, so all religion, and all happiness, depend on him; and we know that whoever teach to seek happiness without him are monsters, and the pests of society."[30] Hence it was not only commanded but also reasonable for people to love God, the "Father of all good,"[31] who constantly loved them and gave them everything to enjoy.

Wesley attempted to refute the atheistic humanism of the Enlightenment by its own methods, without being conscious that his premises, especially his belief in God as Creator and Sustainer of the world, constituted an assertion. It is true Wesley could gather evidence from the psychological and empirical realms to support his thesis that love of neighbor resulted from love of God. Wesley was unable, however, to verify his assertion that the love of God was the exclusive source for the love of neighbor. Ultimately he retreated to a position based on a consensus of believers and formulated it as an assertion that this love came only from faith and that faith and love were wrought by the Holy Spirit:

> You, to whom I now speak, believe this love of humankind cannot spring but from the love of God. You think there can be no instance of one whose tender affection embraces every child of man (though not endeared to him either by ties of blood, or by any natural or civil relation), unless that affection flow from a grateful, filial love to the common Father of all.[32]

Even though Wesley's philosophical argumentation was not completely convincing, his definition of faith linked with love, oriented to a combination of Pauline and Johannine theology,[33] provided a basis for his ethic that merits the highest recognition in its practical application. Indeed, it could have led to even more far-reaching results if Wesley had held to it consistently, and if after his death official Methodism had not extensively and all too quickly reverted into a legalistic orthodoxy.[34]

Love of Neighbor as Effect of God's Love

Wesley viewed the love of God as reciprocal and personal, and believed it to be necessary for the emergence and implementation of unselfish love. Equally necessary as a result of the love of God known and experienced in faith was active love of one's neighbor. Anyone renewed by God's love and given the gift of faith could not resist sharing the love he had received. Faith, the beginning point of sanctification, and love, its essential content, both remained the gift of the Creator and Redeemer.[35] As there could be no love without faith that received that love from God, so there could also be no faith that did not actively share that love with others. Those renewed by God "'love him, because he first loved us,' and withheld not from us his Son, his only Son. And this love constrains them to love all mankind, all the children of the Father of heaven and earth. . . ."[36] For that reason, love for God and love for one's neighbor belonged together so indissolubly that one did not exist apart from the other.[37]

But love for one's neighbor was characterized not only by its selflessness, but also by its absolute refusal to judge the person to whom it is given. Out of the relationship with God defined by love grew unlimited love for all humanity, even in the face of a neighbor harboring hatred.[38] In the context of Wesley's theological ethics, it is an untenable idea that national or racial differences, social position (as outsiders), or religious or philosophical differences make a person unworthy of love. Every person deserved love because he or she was loved by God.[39] Again and again Wesley emphasized that one's neighbor was "every child of man, every son of Adam,"[40] "everyone who breathes the breath of life."[41] Because the love of God was indivisible and addressed to all, so was love of neighbor. To make it applicable only to certain persons was to pervert its character as universal love. Therefore, in a sermon on Romans 15:2, Wesley proclaimed:

107

> Let love not visit you as a transient guest, but be the constant temper of
> your soul. See that your heart be filled at all times, and on all occasions,
> with real, undissembled benevolence; not to those only that love you, but
> to every soul of man. . . . Be not straightened or limited in your affection,
> but let it embrace every child of man. Every one that is born of a woman
> has a claim to your good-will.[42]

Because God was the Father of all, who were therefore brothers and
sisters as children of the same Father,[43] it is not only commanded, but
reasonable, to do good to all people when opportunity permitted. With
this word Wesley sought not only to address those who had perceived
and gratefully accepted God's love in faith, but also to confront
representatives of the Enlightenment way of thinking on the level of
their own argument and convince them of the rightness of his ethical
perspective.[44] Yet here the subject was only a secondary aspect that his
debate with philosophical adversaries prompted him to accept into his
ethic. This love capable of prompting corresponding reactions in other
persons[45] was free from any consideration of advantage or gain;[46] it was
capable of helping people attain that happiness for which they were
created. "It is in consequence of our knowing God loves us, that we love
him and love our neighbors as ourselves. . . . This is religion, and this is
happiness, the happiness for which we were created. . . ."[47] Seen from
the human perspective, holiness means the deepest fulfillment,
blessedness.[48]

In the tradition of Pauline theology, Wesley attributed this infilling
with love to an influence of the Spirit of God in the heart as the center of
personhood. Here Christology did recede into the background, though
it still occupied an important place: awareness of God's love arose
primarily not through gratitude to the Creator, but through "the
revelation of Christ in our hearts"[49] that led believers to the confession,
"the life that I now live I live by faith in the Son of God who loved me and
gave himself for me."[50] Only faith opened the way to a life lived out of
love, which was constituted by the work of Christ. This work was not
significant merely in initiating love through justification; this connection with Christ was a constant necessity for the Christian to maintain in
him the mind of Christ and enable him "to walk as Christ walked."[51]

This direction by love was constantly under threat throughout one's
earthly life: wealth,[52] disturbance of the mind and emotions,[53]
weakness,[54] temptations,[55] and even sin in the believers[56] could affect or
disturb the mind of Christ in them. Only God's grace that brought about

108

repentance and renewal could restore it.[57] Perfection in love, which is the sole content of sanctification[58] and found in the angels and in Adam before the fall,[59] cannot be attained by the Christian in this life.[60] Even entire sanctification should be understood only as a work of God and acceptable to Him only on account of Christ.[61]

More important in Wesley's ethic than speculation over what "degree of perfection" can possibly be attained (a notion that is basically a contradiction in itself) was his view of the possibility and necessity of growth in love. Although Wesley could not muster any understanding of the total aspect of Luther's *simul iustus et peccator*, its partial aspect was all the more significant for him:[62] "Yea, and when ye have attained a measure of perfect love! . . . think not of resting there! That is impossible. You cannot stand still; you must either rise or fall. . . ."[63] Because human nature was not basically good and perfect,[64] people must let themselves ever anew be filled with love in a relationship with God marked by faith. They must activate this relationship in service to others and thereby strengthen the mind of Christ within them. Growth in love therefore was just as much a gift of God as a human obligation,[65] so that love became the dominant motive and measure of all human actions. Only faith working through love was true faith, a "lively, saving principle";[66] its aim was to actualize love among all people.[67] Recognizing it as the highest thing among human beings, Wesley could cry out, "What is all beside loving faith!"[68] With this proclamation, Wesley laid the foundation for his social ethics and his numerous social activities.

Having clarified that for Wesley the basic motivation for sanctification and its essential content was love, which represented the basis for social ethics as compassionate action within acknowledged responsibility for others, in what fashion was love to be expressed? In other words, how was the person filled with God's love to behave in the concrete situations of life? What actions shall he or she decide upon to obey the universal commandment of love? Such questions might be superfluous in many cases since the person was molded and shaped by love; in other cases, however, more precise standards of measurement might be needed for ethical action.

Wesley offered three possible ways to recognize the will of God, which was to love all people, in concrete individual and social situations: divine commandments, the example of Jesus and other persons, and personal insights based on rational reflection.

2. THE DIVINE COMMANDMENTS

The law of God, or the sum of God's commandments written down in the Bible, had no significance for human justification, because justification was received solely on the basis of atonement wrought by Christ through faith. In contrast to the opinion held by many of his Christian contemporaries, however, Wesley explicitly refuses to draw from that the conclusion that the law is without any validity for the believer.[69]

Wesley attempted to speak of God's commandments without falling into either antinomian views or the doctrine of justification by works,[70] of which he was unjustly accused because he acknowledged the significance of the law. Since it is neither requisite nor possible to treat this subject comprehensively here, we shall inquire only into the law's significance for ethics,[71] particularly for one's actions following justification.

The Content of the Law

God's will was originally written in the hearts of angels and human beings. Once human rebellion against God obliterated it, God, unwilling to abandon His creatures, gave them a written law, the moral law, which is "holy, just, and good" (Romans 7:12).[72] This law was communicated by Moses, the prophets, and finally by Christ and the apostles,[73] but also, in the sense of the human capacity to distinguish good and evil, it was written in the heart of the sinful creature.[74] The law contained the goodwill of God as "unalterable rectitude."[75] It included the Decalogue and its exposition by the prophets[76] and by Christ,[77] but not the Old Testament ceremonial law, from whose validity humans had been freed by Christ.[78] The law was summarized in the commandment to love God and one's neighbor;[79] therefore, love was the law's fulfillment.[80]

Christ had abolished the ceremonial law as an unbearable yoke that indeed was given by God but not forever and always.[81] Christ did not, however, abolish the moral law, which as God's will remained unalterable.[82] Believers were indeed free from the law's curse and the law's power of sin and death, but not from God's law. Human freedom was a freedom to obey God, not to disobey Him;[83] it was freedom from the ceremonial law, not from the moral law.[84] Even Paul in his Epistle to the Galatians only intended to establish that no one is justified by the works of the law, but rather by faith in Christ.[85] Therefore, the law belonged to Christ's preaching just as the gospel did.[86]

But the law remained valid for all for still another reason: through the Fall, the human will became corrupted, wrongly oriented, and therefore evil. The good could only be done by a person living in harmony with God's good will and denying his or her own will insofar as it conflicted with God's. Only the Creator could show the fallen creature the right way, and this by means of the law that revealed His will.[87]

In addition to explicitly mentioning the Decalogue, the Sermon on the Mount,[88] the commandment of love, and the Golden Rule,[89] Wesley gave concrete specific commandments as examples, expounding their current application.[90] Thus Wesley indicated the Decalogue's inadequacy as an ethical standard of measurement. Instead, it constantly required new applications as well as supplement by other biblical commandments (especially the Sermon on the Mount), by examples, and by personal insights. The Decalogue, however, indicated the obligatory direction for all who would live a life in obedience to the will of God.[91]

The Use of the Law

Although the law, or ethical commandments of the Bible, applied inviolably and constantly as the distillation of God's unchangeable will, Wesley distinguished various functions of the law. By so doing, Wesley took his stand in the tradition of Reformation theology, which can be confirmed especially by the criteria of content. Paradoxically in relation to everything said up to this point, Wesley plainly declared in his comprehensive treatment of Christian perfection that Christ was the end of the Adamic as well as of the Mosaic law since His atoning work took away the validity of both for humankind.[92] Yet in order to avoid misunderstanding and self-contradiction, he added: "I mean, it is not the condition either of present or future salvation."[93] Instead of that law, ". . . Christ hath established . . . the law of faith. Not every one that doeth, but every one that believeth, now receiveth righteousness . . . that is, he is justified, sanctified[!], and glorified."[94]

Thus the law's fulfillment[95] was not and is not a means of justification. It nevertheless retained a significance that was irreplaceable by anything else, not even the gospel, both for unbelievers and for those who were justified. For both groups of people, God's claim as Creator to total obedience exhibited a diverse series of consequences.[96]

The effect of the law upon unbelievers was twofold. First, it was meant to convince them of their sinfulness and guilt.[97] The Holy Spirit produced this conviction in the conscience,[98] which became aware of the wickedness of the heart in contrast to the good law of God, rendered any transgressions "extremely sinful" since they were now committed in awareness of their blameworthiness,[99] and punished these transgressions with inner condemnation.[100] Second, the law was meant to impel them to repentance, to destroy confidence in their own achievements as justification in God's sight, and to drive them into Christ's arms.[101] Faith came from the preaching of the gospel, not from the law,[102] but the law was the "schoolmaster" to bring individuals to Christ.[103] It taught them to call on God for help, thus preparing the way for the act of faith[104] and serving in its very severity as an expression and instrument of God's saving love.[105]

Certainly justified persons no longer stood under the law's condemnation, after God for Christ's sake had freed them from their guilt and their inability to obey.[106] Their faith, however, did not remain inactive, but manifested itself in a new obedience doing out of filial love what they previously were incapable of doing while enslaved to sin.[107] The works of the law were not necessary for their justification; moreover, they could not precede justification, but instead must follow it as fruits of that faith by which they had been justified.[108] Therefore, the law's purpose is to bind the justified to Christ, without whom they cannot do good works.[109]

As an instrument in God's hand, the law led people into an ever closer connection with Christ, an ever more comprehensive participation in the life that comes from God.[110] It did so in three ways. First, it convicted them of remaining sin, so that they would cling to Christ, who could cleanse them of it.[111] Through their conscience it revealed the true nature and disposition of their thoughts, words, and deeds,[112] for even those who had been born again could sin.[113] The *usus elenchticus legis* (admonishing function of the law) thus applied not only to unbelievers, but also to those who were justified insofar as they also remained sinners. Second, the law brought the believers to the point of accepting from "the head of the church" the strength that enabled them to do what God's law commanded,[114] for faith in Christ and life in accordance with God's will must be in harmony among Christians.[115] Such a faith did not render sanctification superfluous but produced it;[116] that faith constantly holds before their eyes the love of Christ, so that from it "they might draw fresh life, vigour, and strength to run the way of His commandments."[117] Third, the law confirms "our hope of whatsoever it commands and we have not yet attained—of receiving grace upon grace, till we are in actual possession of the fulness of His promises."[118]

These last two effects of the law are closely interconnected and clearly set forth an essential component of Wesley's teaching: for those who live in communion with Christ, what God commands can be fulfilled because He bestows both the freedom and the power to do so. Thereby the ethic of the "Holy Club" was turned upside down. Religious and social achievements were not the means for attaining and growing in God's love. Instead, the love of God, which a person received through faith, first enabled him or her to do God's will, which consisted in essence of nothing more than a responsive love for God and all people. God promised and bestowed what He commanded.[119] Christian life was obedient love.[120] Through God's grace, or His freely given love and the power of His spirit, a believer could do what he or she had previously found impossible.[121] Guided in his or her conscience by God's will, a person could fulfill God's commandments—to the extent that he or she remained in communication with Christ.[122] By gladly submitting their own wills to the will of God, followers of Christ could "constantly transmute the love of God into love for our neighbors."[123] For the entire law under which we now are is "fulfilled by love."[124]

Wesley fit the doctrine of the law entirely within the doctrine of grace, so that for the believer the law almost completely lost its compulsory, oppressive, and restrictive character. It became the basis for happiness and the occasion for gratitude and joy.[125] It provided an example, to be followed gladly, of a life lived in accordance with God's good will, which was always being better realized. Christian perfection was not freedom from all conscious or unconscious transgressions, but a growing state of being filled with and determined by God's love,[126] for love was the end of the law, its fulfillment and its aim.[127] That perfection was a realization of the freedom of God's children, because it was a mutual gift and commandment. It is fitting that people help to make the "law" of this love effective and real in their hearts and lives.[128]

3. EXAMPLES

Standards of measurement and guidelines available to help the Christian lead a life in accordance with God's will in love included, in addition to the biblical commandments, examples from past and, more rarely, present times.

Christ as Example

For Wesley, Christ was first of all quite certainly the bearer of God's love, the Redeemer from guilt and the power of sin, the one who filled the justified person with faith and love and made it possible for that person to have a new humanness according to the likeness of God. But Christ was also the great Teacher able to interpret the commandments of God for the believer clearly and authoritatively, as He did particularly in the Sermon on the Mount.[129] Moreover, Christ was the perfect example for the believer, infinitely superior to all others, helping the believer better to recognize and fulfill God's will. Wesley identified the perfect person as the one in whom "the mind of Christ" dwelt, who walked "as Christ walked."[130] These expressions occur repeatedly in Wesley's writings as a description of sanctification and of the proper tenor of the Christian's existence.[131]

Wesley did not view the imitation of Christ[132] as a reduplication of Christ's deeds but above all in being filled with love, as Christ was, and letting love control all one's deeds: "Indeed, his soul is all love . . . and his life agreeth thereto. . . ."[133] Wesley's reasoning exists quite apart from the matter of the possibility of such an attempt. Such a person was friendly, helpful, compassionate, and considerate toward all people without thinking of his or her own advantage.[134] Like Christ, he or she was filled with love for his or her neighbor,[135] as long as he or she lived out of the inner communion with Christ.[136] It need not be explicitly stated that Wesley considered this possibility of imitating Christ to occur only after one was born again if it were to be internal discipleship and not merely external imitation.[137]

Beyond these very general statements, that following Jesus means having His mind, walking as He walked, and doing good, Wesley gives few concrete indications of how this should happen in particular.[138] This state of the texts indicates that Wesley was not concerned with imitations of Jesus' deeds, but with action growing out of Jesus' mind, the particulars of which appeared only in confrontation with a concrete ethical situation. However, one must not underestimate the effects on the compassionate behavior of the hearers when Wesley attempted to hold the figure of Jesus before his congregations' eyes and to emphasize especially Christ's illimitable love even for the poorest and most deeply despised. For those congregations Christ as the Son of God possessed the highest authority, which was manifested not in claims to power, but in ministering love that was for their benefit and should be passed along to others in a life of daily discipleship.

Other Persons as Examples

Among the examples to which Wesley assigned high rank after the authority of Holy Scripture and the example of Jesus, primitive Christianity holds the preeminent place. After Wesley's first conversion to an ascetic-legalistic Christianity (1725), he made a part of his life program the imitation of the first Christians,[139] whose strength of belief and knowledge of Scripture he hoped in this way to maintain.[140] Wesley's voyage to Georgia must also be considered in this perspective.[141] This attitude placed Wesley altogether within the tradition of an important stream in the Anglican church that had been significantly strengthened by the revival of patristic studies and by the rise and spread of the "religious societies."[142] To be sure, in that time Wesley was served also by the attempt to imitate primitive Christian piety, especially in his striving, which was definitive for him at that time, to earn God's favor. Yet even in the years after 1738, the actual beginning of the Methodist proclamation and social work, primitive Christianity did not lose its significance for Wesley as a criterion for Christianity in whatever setting or time.

In doctrine, Wesley emphasized, Methodism fully agreed with the "universal basic principles of Christianity" valid since the primitive era of Christianity. What others set forth as a charge against him, Wesley felt to be instead a confirmation and a mark of distinction.[143] Without idealizing the first Christian communities as worthy of imitation in every respect,[144] Wesley was impressed above all else by "the degree of love which they enjoyed."[145] What served as examples for his congregations were not the prescriptions and customs concerning outward appearance (such as coiffure, clothing, and so on),[146] but deeds and activities arising out of love: visiting the sick, sheltering the destitute, and helping those in distress.[147] In many projects undertaken, their similarity to examples from primitive Christianity was noted only later as opposed to their having served as models or motives from the outset.[148] These parallels then served Wesley especially to justify his decisions, such as including women in the visitation ministry,[149] forming associations, or issuing membership cards as "letters of recommendation" to Methodists who were moving away.[150]

115

The primitive Christian communities as Wesley saw them[151] thus served as a measuring device, either generally, through the exemplary spirit of love, or subsequently, as justification for undertakings already realized, not as an example to be copied directly.

Wesley's conviction that conformity with the "simple, ancient Christianity" was more important than the correctness of dogmatic opinions gave him the inner breadth and ability to be tolerant. His mother and the venerated William Law became his models among the people of his time and of the recent past, as did an entire series of Christian personalities with whose views in part he did not agree. Unity in central matters was more important to Wesley than difference on particular issues. In this respect, too, he learned from the English Enlightenment as well as from German Pietism. The series of authors whose writings Wesley edited in the *Christian Library* eloquently testifies to this fact.[152] A. H. Francke, whose work Wesley had come to know in Halle during a trip through Germany, became a revered example for his social activism.[153] The extent of the actual influence of those Wesley venerated as exemplary Christians in their teaching and living can be surmised at many points but not determined with any scientific exactness. However, Wesley always highly treasured the value of the *exemplum* for children and adults.[154]

4. PERSONAL INSIGHTS

As the first part of this study indicates, commandments and examples as standards for social ethics did not suffice to cover Wesley's numerous social activities. Instead, he required many other observations and considerations in order to perceive the social demands of the time, to develop theories suitable for dealing with them, and to place the corresponding practical measures in operation.

The Significance of Reason

Ernst Troeltsch, in his assessment of Methodism and other movements, writes that it is "a radical opposition to the whole spirit of modern science and civilization."[155] What is to follow reveals that this verdict does not apply to Wesley's theology.

In a letter of 1745 in which he defended Methodism against public attack, Wesley outlined the relationship between his religion and reason: "By this religion [i.e., Methodism], we do not banish reason, but exalt it to its utmost perfection; this being in every point consistent therewith, and in every step guided thereby."[156] Was Wesley correct in this assertion?

Undisputedly Wesley did not reject the remnants of belief in the existence of witches and ghosts still generally held in his time, nor did he denounce the practice of rolling dice and casting lots. Yet such views were so peripheral to his perspective that they played only an extremely small role in his preaching and practice. On the other hand, Wesley most decisively rejected any obscurity, any appeal to dreams and visions, as a source of present religious knowledge.[157] Wesley's use of language,[158] the argumentative style of his sermons, and his readiness to test all his utterances by Scripture and reason and to let himself be convinced by better insights[159] all attest to Wesley's high estimate of reason.

One of the most important objections voiced against mystical, as well as theological or philosophical writings, is that they contradict reason or are incomprehensible.[160] "Our guides are Scripture and reason"[161] is another way of stating the same argument. "Prompted by the great controversy over reason and revelation," Wesley placed "emphasis upon the rational component of biblical Christianity"; he was "no advocate of Christianity's opposition to reason."[162] Still less was he ready to base any obligatory declarations on feeling, in spite of the high value that he assigned to Christian experience.[163] Wesley perceived the relationship of Scripture, reason, and experience thus: the latter two taught people to understand and apply Scripture, but could never contradict it in fundamental declarations.[164] It is evident here though it cannot be traced out further, that Wesley learned and adopted much of importance from the English Enlightenment, especially from John Locke, in spite of Wesley's vigorous opposition to Deism.[165] In addition to a fundamental affirmation of reason's use even in theological questions, these included in particular the assumption that God has equipped His creatures with certain rights without distinction[166] and an affirmative acceptance of the results of experimental physics.[167] There was only one thing that reason could not achieve in the realm of knowledge: it could not replace God's revelation or render it superfluous in any respect.[168] Therefore reason would also never conflict with that revelation because God was the source of both revelation and the knowledge supplied by reason.[169]

117

The Tasks of Reason

Wesley's concise ontological statements about reason were not thought through in all their connections and even their tensions with each other. Instead, they were more vigorously pursued to their effect upon the use of reason and its tasks in the area of ethics as well as in all of theology. Wesley found this exemplified in Jesus and His apostles, especially Paul, who were constantly debating their opponents.[170]

Reason served the understanding and the exposition of Holy Scripture,[171] in which there could not be any contradiction "in any fundamental point of faith or practice."[172] Therefore, no one was obligated to believe any doctrine that was not clear and understandable.[173] Anything in the Bible going beyond this was not an object of faith.[174] The basis for the exposition of Scripture was the literal sense of the text within the total context[175] unless this yielded an absurd result.[176] Even the authority of the church's tradition remained subject to the Scripture expounded in this way.[177]

Examples of Wesley's use of "reason, knowledge, and human education" as "preeminent gifts of God"[178] for understanding the Bible reveal that he always had the courage to apply his hermeneutical principles himself and to draw the implications for rejecting a biblicistic exegesis.[179] This indicates in principle what reason could signify and achieve for ethics: it made relevant to the conduct of life both the commandments and universal love, which could also be rationally grounded,[180] and suggested how to properly apply and actualize them both.[181] The Holy Spirit illumined the understanding to recognize fellow human beings' need for help and, filled with love for them, effectively aid them.[182] In many cases no special commandments were needed to know God's will, only application of the universal rule to be good and to do good.[183] Even what should be avoided often became evident from experience with reason reflecting upon it.[184]

By incorporating reason into the process of religious knowledge and deriving from it principles of ethical obligation, Wesley gained great inner mobility and freedom to meet the social challenges appropriately and insightfully, to win others to similar actions, and to supply the commandment to love with a universal validity for ethics, without inadmissibly restricting the authority of Holy Scripture and of the will of God laid down in it.

CHAPTER IX

AIMS OF WESLEY'S SOCIAL ETHICS

I t is indispensable for understanding and assessing Wesley's social ethics to recognize its point of departure as explained in the previous two chapters. Yet the founder of Methodism went beyond motives and methods to consider and formulate the aims of social action as well.[1] So far this topic has been dealt with only implicitly; now a more comprehensive and basic topical treatment is needed in conclusion.

1. THE RENEWAL OF THE INDIVIDUAL

Wesley's evangelistic preaching, like his pastoral care, related to the individual although it was frequently delivered before large congregations of listeners. Wesley's preaching was meant as direct discourse to the individual person and as a call to conversion. Analogously, Wesley's social work and ethical preaching focused first on the individual, then the entire English nation, other nations, and finally human society, regardless of its structure, culture, or political and economic order. They were social in the sense of eliminating social distresses and referring to life with other persons and in society. Nevertheless, the temporal and substantive priority doubtless lay with individual renewal, which preceded social renewal as its necessary precondition. Admittedly, individual renewal acquired its meaning through more than just the social effects it produced. Nevertheless, according to Wesley's pointedly formulated statement about Christianity as "essentially a social religion,"[2] no real transformation of an individual by God's grace could fail to immediately affect the shared life of all people. The aim of Wesley's preaching was therefore twofold: to lead individuals to renewal through God's grace in justification and sanctification and thus to a meaningful life, and to guide them into activity suited to transform the whole of society from within.

Self-awareness and Moral Conduct

In his high estimate of the individual's creaturely value and immortal soul, Wesley revealed the modern influences of the rediscovery of antiquity and the onset of the Enlightenment, which tended to oppose thinking in corporate terms.[3] Wesley strove to combat the incipient submergence of the individual with all its negative consequences, particularly for members of the industrial proletariat, by declaring every individual's worth to be immeasurably great and independent of social status. Wesley did so by basing that worth in God's universal love that has destined them to be happy.[4]

In the confrontation between this proclamation and the wretchedness of the masses lay the stimulating challenge that seized Wesley and that he sought to answer through his social work, which in this context was nothing other than preaching God's love with other means. Many understood that this promise was meant for them and found their way into a new life. People who had become religiously indifferent, left in the lurch by state and church, and often enough morally depraved,[5] found a faith in God that not uncommonly led to a surprisingly rapid moral transformation in their lives. Evidently feeling the impact of astonishing effects, Wesley describes these changes:

> The drunkard commenced sober and moderate; the whoremonger abstained from adultery and fornication; the unjust from oppression and wrong. He that had been accustomed to curse and swear for many years, now swore no more. The sluggard began to work with his hands, that he might eat his own bread. The miser learned to deal his bread to the hungry and to cover the naked with a garment. Indeed, the whole form of their life was changed: They had "left off doing evil, and learned to do well."[6]

Wesley's basic thesis, that the sick will must first be healed, was confirmed in innumerable cases. The individual's alienation from God and hence from self and neighbor was overcome by the preaching of the gospel in word and in deed. The preaching of the law preceded the preaching of the gospel, making people conscious of their lostness in sin, and it followed the preaching of the gospel as well, providing instruction for a new life.

The ethical power thus awakened and preserved, and firmly founded in connection with Christ, overcame the fatalism of the predestinarians and Deists and enabled many to bring about social change in their vicinity.[7] Ernst Troeltsch has already correctly described the results of Wesley's effectiveness:

> To begin with, Methodism gained its victories in the middle and lower classes, among the miners and in the industrial towns. To the middle and lower classes it brought a new sense of the sacredness of personality; it appealed to the popular imagination, and awakened a devotion which found expression in a most self-sacrificing charity. . . . It had brought the impulse of personality and individuality into the life of the masses, who were being brutalized by the industrial system, and with its charity it helped them in their distress.[8]

The doctrine of sanctification and its possible and necessary growth at the same time filled this new morality with a dynamic that caused its growth and improvement to become an integral element of sanctification itself: the community of the converted became the core of a growing renewal movement that had an effect upon its environment.

Responsibility and Solidarity

Because love for God could not be separated from love for neighbor, the combination and interweaving of the two formed the basic principle of the new ethic. Therefore an essential element in Methodist piety was its commitment to the world. Hence Wesley's social ethic might be described as an ethic of responsibility and solidarity, as far removed from utilitarianism as from the altruism of contemporary English thinkers.[9] This ethic viewed social obligations and involvements primarily from the perspective of individuals, their destiny, and their tasks, although from the very first it struggled against the alternative of "change and transformation of the individual or creation of new social conditions, diaconal compassion, loving activity, and caritas, or engagement for social justice."[10] Instead, it "rests on the dialectic of person and society"[11] and thereby filled an important precondition of any rightly understood social ethic.[12]

Wesley explicitly rejected the religious self-satisfaction of the believer and any restriction to a personal I-God connection; this was one of his essential objections to mysticism.[13]

Central foundational concepts were neighborly love resulting from love of God, and stewardship, or human responsibility not only for all one's possessions but also for one's fellow human beings, independent of relationships of kinship or affinity.[14] In this context Wesley's definition of the ethically good and evil was instructive: "By good I mean, conducive to the good of mankind, tending to advance peace and goodwill among men, promotive of the happiness of our fellow-creatures; and by evil, what is contrary thereto."[15] The physical and spiritual well-being of the other person thus became the yardstick for measuring one's own ethical actions. This commandment to love was more precisely defined in terms of a normative ethic in which the underlying relationship with God prevented one's slipping over into altruism.

Wesley understood such conduct to be "the medicine of life, the never-failing remedy for all the evils of a disordered world, for all the miseries and vices of men."[16] This healing was not to wait for the hereafter;[17] it was to occur here and now, and was to include both body and soul.[18] This holistic understanding of salvation was grounded in Wesley's high regard for the Old Testament and the doctrine of creation. In spite of any inner-worldly asceticism, it allowed him to regard delight in the beautiful as important and good.[19] Gratitude for God's goodness and love, not a compulsion obliging one to deserve them, and liberation of the will by grace bestowed on Wesley's followers the desire to communicate to their contemporaries what they had received and prompted their keenest attention as instruments of God's love to suffering persons.[20]

Distinct from the charity being practiced elsewhere at that time was still another crucial characteristic added to this social sensitivity: solidarity with those who received aid. It arose, in the first place, because many of those who turned to Methodism and undertook social work were once themselves the recipients of such help. In the second place, Wesley imprinted upon his followers his understanding that all persons fundamentally were of equal worth, and he spoke to them as "fellow-creatures" and "fellow-sufferers."[21] Aid should be accompanied by internal and external attitudes of solidarity with the poor, not by condescending charity that helped the poor but at the same time humiliated them.[22] This solidarity implied refraining from any sort of prejudice along with a readiness to forego, for the sake of others, many personal comforts of life.[23]

Measured against the great social tasks of the eighteenth century, the achievement of the Methodists and their communities could hardly be described as a satisfactory solution. Yet Wesley and his co-laborers created an essential precondition for solving all social problems in all times: they communicated to people a social sensitivity and an awareness that solidarity recognized urgent demands and attempted to respond to them as fully as possible.

2. THE RENEWAL OF SOCIETY

As previously noted, Wesley considered the religion of love to be the remedy for all the world's evil, and he was not satisfied with the conversion of some, nor indeed many, individuals. Instead, he added: "This religion we long to see established in the world."[24] As far as his home country was concerned, this actually happened to a relatively high degree, as historians confirm.[25] But how did this happen? Did Wesley consider it sufficient to renew society from below, that is, through the transformation of individuals, or did he include the transformation of social structures and of governmental institutions in the process of renewal that he perceived in comprehensive terms? In other words, did social ethics extend beyond the social environment of individuals and groups and lead to preparatory analysis and instructions including the possibility of transforming foundational social orders? Or did social ethics merely remain an individual ethic extended to include broader social connections that emerged from time to time?

The Source and Task of Civil Power

Without reference to Wesley's statements regarding civil power, one might conclude from his statements about the universality of God's love and the fundamental equality of all human beings that he opposed with inner consistency a civil order still oligarchic despite parliamentary rights, and irrational claims to power by governmental organs. However, such a conclusion would be incorrect. Influenced by parental teaching and his Oxford education, Wesley remained until his death a convinced Tory of the moderate (non-Jacobite) wing,[26] to which most of his Anglican clerical colleagues also subscribed.[27] As he himself confessed, this "deep-rooted prejudice"[28] in favor of the existing constitutional monarchy was explained and justified in three ways.

First, every civil authority is derived from God, the sovereign over all.[29] Irrespective of the particular form of the existing state (dictatorship, oligarchy, aristocracy, democracy), power ultimately originated from God.[30] Certainly Wesley correctly acknowledged that this still says nothing about those dispensing the power derived from

God. In a rather unconvincing attempt, Wesley undertook to carry the idea of popular sovereignty ad absurdum. He did so by trying to demonstrate the impossibility of clearly delineating the sovereign "people" without arbitrary exclusion of individual groups—asking who constituted the people (all men, women, and children?)[31], and with the historical argument that only once in the history of the world had there been a democratically chosen ruler.[32] Thus he argued that democracy should be rejected on rational, historical, and theological grounds, for "the people" could not bestow what they had never possessed: power over life and death,[33] liberty, and property,[34] which was the very essence of civil power.

Lest it appear that with such arguments Wesley advocated a dictatorship, it must be emphasized that at the same time he derived governmental authority from God,[35] he also stressed its limitation: in all decisions its bearer remained accountable to God, who permitted no ruler to rob his subjects of their civil or religious liberty. Legitimacy and responsibility were inseparably derived from God.[36] Therefore Wesley stood against any misuse of power in such forms as religious compulsion, burning of heretics, persecution on grounds of conscience, and other arbitrary acts. He regarded as necessary the sovereign's obligation under the law to protect person and property, as that assurance existed in England; and for this reason, he regarded the constitutional monarchy as the best of all existing forms of the state. In distinction from his threefold reason for rejecting democracy, his favoring of the form of the state that existed in England in his time was given only an empirical justification.[37] In distinction from the Puritanism that was potentially and sometimes actually hostile to the monarchy,[38] and from the dissent that was friendly to the Whig point of view,[39] Wesley regarded the order established in England since 1689 as essentially excellent. Therefore, like all moderate Tories, he worked to support preservation of the status quo.

In Wesley's case this attitude was further strengthened by the biblical commandment to honor the king. The same authority from which all earthly dominion was derived commanded loyalty to the monarch, a loyalty which thus became a religious obligation. This meant that anyone who feared God must treat the king with respect[40] and obey him as long as that obedience did not become disobedience to God.[41]

Alongside this argument that all power derived from God, which has proven insufficient to justify the English form of government, lay Wesley's second argument—his doubt that the people were capable of governing. Here again Wesley refrained from developing his own theory of the state and argued exclusively in terms of apologetics. He thus set out the requirement that governing should be left to those who best understood something about it. These were, as a rule, the king, his ministers, and Parliament (even with a Whig majority!).[42] Ordinary citizens often could not understand the background and rationale for political decisions; false reports could not always be recognized as such; and despite assertions to the contrary, most Englishmen lacked necessary expertise.[43] Wesley did not on this basis prohibit any criticism of the king and his ministers. He even practiced such criticism himself on occasion, especially against the ministers, whom he did not regard, however, as any worse than their predecessors.[44] The king, however—and this was decisive—believed in the Bible, feared God, and loved his wife,[45] which distinguished him from many of his opponents.[46]

Claims to authority by the people, who were inadequately informed, unqualified, and led astray by dangerous agitators and inflamed emotions, led only to acts of violence and other injustices; Wesley cited some examples of this from the most recent history of his nation.[47] Such movements' declared aim of gaining more freedom for the citizens not only was not achieved, but also proved unattainable in this way because of the actual consequences of destruction of previous liberties. Hence it was the Methodist preachers' task in their sermons to refrain from making political statements and passing judgment on governmental measures—with the one exception of publicly refuting any unjustified criticism of the person or decisions of holders of public office.[48] It is true that Wesley himself did not follow this instruction; instead, he publicly, even critically, took a position on a great many political questions. At the same time, however, he insisted on strict political abstinence on the part of his preachers, and in so doing he contributed to the maintenance of the status quo.

The third argument has already been intimated; essentially it was this: in England there was no reason for political dissatisfaction and therefore no occasion for publicly calling for more freedom, which was greatest in a constitutional monarchy and least in a democracy.[49] It cannot be denied that the English citizen, measured against his European contemporaries, possessed the greatest freedom and was most fully protected against governmental arbitrariness.[50] Wesley remained untroubled in his praise of British monarchy and unshaken in his confidence in the king even though experience indicated that the laws that were supposed to protect citizens' freedom did not always function.[51]

125

Wesley's reproaches always referred only to individual grievances, not to basic elements of the civil order,[52] whose essential task consisted in the formal, purely negative function of protecting the individual's civil and religious freedom against all perils and attacks as long as that individual observed existing laws. Since this protection provided a free space for preaching and social activity, Wesley saw no need of posing further demands that would have aligned him with agitators and republicans.[53]

Changes to Be Avoided

We Methodists, said Wesley, attempt, as much as we can, "to make mankind happy (I now speak only with regard to the present world); . . . striving, as we can, to lessen their sorrows, and to teach them, in whatsoever state they are, therewith to be content."[54] As previously demonstrated, this attitude did not limit one's rising in society through further education, thrift, and diligence. However, dissatisfaction should not be the driving force behind such ascent, because it only all too easily became contagious and resulted in public unrest[55] or even open rebellion. Admittedly, calm was not the prime obligation of citizens, but as Wesley perceived it, calm was the necessary precondition of any social progress.

Therefore the introduction of democratic order into the sphere of authority of the church or the state was to be avoided. In Wesley's communities, leadership duties were not bestowed by election but transmitted by Wesley himself or his assistants. Stewards and other officials received their rules, which they acknowledged by signature, from Wesley.[56] "As long as I live the people shall have no share in choosing either stewards or leaders among the Methodists. We have not and never had any such custom."[57] Anyone who wanted to introduce such a practice would do well to separate himself without a stir from the Methodists, who were not nor had any intention of becoming republicans.[58] The reason behind Wesley's strict rejection of any democratic tendency was not to be found primarily in either personal ambition to preserve the leadership of a strong movement, or in the view that all civil and ecclesiastical authority derived from God's sovereignty. Both of these interpretations carried equal weight with those always inclined to view such problems from the Tory standpoint.

In addition, another explanation, based on the irrational and grounded in bad experiences, can hardly be overestimated: the Methodists were suspected of being disturbers of the public peace, secret papists, and traitors—followers of the pretender to the throne, Charles Stuart. Precisely in the formative years of Methodism, all the invectives of widespread prejudice were unleashed on this small and despised movement. Such accusations deeply affected Wesley as a convinced Protestant, a loyal subject, and a Tory faithful to the king; they rendered him super-sensitive to such attacks throughout his life. This, too, was part of the reason behind his vigorous and uncompromising rejection of all attempts at a democratizing of ecclesiastical, civil, and social life.[59]

This also explained why, after Wesley's death, Methodism would produce the most determined opponents of the trade union movement and of liberalizing tendencies in politics, for it elevated Wesley's attitude grounded in specific historical circumstances and personal experiences to a general law of the church. In its working out in society, the egalitarianism immanent in Wesley's social ethics was utterly smothered by an apolitical conservatism of the leading Methodists.[60] For Wesley and his followers in church leadership, democracy, republicanism, and unbelief were various sides of the same thing and therefore must be rejected as possibilities of social change.[61]

Also to be rejected, according to Wesley, was a route taken in his time by the British North American colonies, namely, independence from the English king and Parliament. This example is especially instructive because a sharp change can be observed in Wesley's attitude toward the American struggle for independence, making his attitude toward the ethical problem of war especially evident.

In June 1775, Wesley wrote to the English minister for the colonies and, in almost the same words, to the prime minister, that in spite of his high-church-Tory prejudice he could not help thinking "that an oppressed people asked for nothing more than their legal rights." Leaving aside the problem of rights and injustice, however, Wesley felt obliged to pose the question whether it was reasonable for the English to use force against the Americans.[62]

This understanding for the Americans' struggle, which indeed had not yet led to military action but had already produced some illegal actions (the Boston Tea Party, among others), was astounding in light of Wesley's previous political statements. It reveals that on this matter his reflections started from a different point: the natural rights of human beings.[63]

In his discussion concerning slavery (1774), Wesley had already distinguished between legality and legitimacy. He answered the objection that slavery was legally justified by saying: "Can law, human law, change the nature of things? Can it turn darkness into light, or evil into good? By no means! Notwithstanding ten thousand laws, right is right, and wrong is wrong still. There must still remain an essential difference between justice and injustice, cruelty and mercy."[64] This right derived from God, who had not authorized any person to deprive others of their freedom,[65] and as a natural right it had to legitimize any positive right.[66] Parties responsible for impairing this natural right owed an accounting to God, and must have that wrong called to their attention.[67] Yearning for freedom, the glory of all rational beings, preceded any guidance and education.[68] Freedom was an inalienable God-given right belonging to all persons;[69] it existed in the freedoms of the conscience, religion, and private opinion, and in the right to enjoy one's own life and one's possessions in the way one chose.[70] Any deprivation of this freedom—whether by civil authorities or based on positive laws—was unjust and ought to be so labeled so that it could be eliminated.[71] This was precisely what Wesley did, not only in his struggle against slavery and the unjust penal justice system, but also in his vigorous opposition to war.

Excursus: Wesley's Stance on War

The Quakers once again were the only Christian community pioneering the struggle for the elimination of this terrible evil. In Wesley's time, no other church held war as such to be incompatible with the gospel of Jesus Christ.[72] Despite Wesley's extreme loyalty to the king, and his ignorance of the brutal perfection of modern weapons that were unknown and inconceivable to him, like no other well-known author or theologian of his time he protested against every form of war. He often attempted to lay bare its underlying causes and establish its unavoidable consequences in terms of their inhumanity as sufficient reason for outlawing any and every war. Wesley could not provide any insight based on his own experience for the war-torn eighteenth century.[73] In his earlier years he had offered military advice on the defense of his country;[74] however, the naivete of patriotic enthusiasm had long since given way to sober reflection, from which he sought to communicate with a growing sense of responsibility, for in case of war, no one might claim to be unaffected or even innocent.[75]

Wesley's inclusive evangelistic activity also led to the conversion of soldiers, whom he by no means charged to abandon their military profession, however.[76] Yet as early as 1757 Wesley wrote in his treatise on original sin: "There is a still more horrid reproach to the Christian name, yea, to the name of man, to all reason and humanity: there is war in the world! war between men! war between Christians!"[77] But Wesley did not let the matter rest with a general lament. Instead, he inquired further into the causes of wars in order to single out a few important ones: ambition of rulers and corruption of their ministers, differences of opinion, and the struggle of the powerful for colonial possessions. Thus people were always responsible for war. Lacking were reason and humaneness, which might in time prevent the death of thousands brought about by such causes.[78] In the final analysis, humanity's natural depravity manifested itself, and only reconciliation with God would also bring with it a comprehensive reconciliation in the world.[79]

Nevertheless, Wesley described in his letters and publications the absurdity of war and the inhumanity of the consequences unconnected with its causes and aims. He attempted to portray these so impressively that others, if possible, might be moved to an active commitment to ending the current war and preventing any further armed struggles from beginning.[80] Since war even before its outbreak has a way of stirring up passions and causing prejudices to increase inordinately;[81] Wesley contended all the more for a rational investigation of these controversies, even though he himself was not entirely free from prejudices.[82]

In the case of the disagreement between England and the North American colonies, Wesley warned emphatically against underestimating the expected severity of the struggle, which no longer concerned simply the right of taxation, but the more extensive rights of the defense of possessions and families, and the maintenance and preservation of freedom.[83]

In a country preparing for war, it took a great deal of courage to publicly espouse the opinion that the enemy, "an oppressed people asked for nothing more than their legal rights, and that in the most modest and inoffensive manner which the nature of the thing would allow."[84] Wesley likewise challenged his friends on both sides of the Atlantic, and indeed all reasonable people, to end the strife, not feeding the flames but doing their utmost to extinguish them.[85] Indeed, only with every war ended and no other begun could people once again claim to be rational creatures;[86] but God's help must be sought as an indispensable precondition for reconciliation and renewal; only He will at last create eternal peace.[87]

The fact that Wesley's attitude toward the Americans, at first well disposed, changed into a strict rejection of their position does not impair the credibility of his plea for peace and the elimination of all war. Wesley appropriated for his *A Calm Address to the American Colonies* a considerable part of Samuel Johnson's *Taxation no Tyranny*, an argument opposing the American independence movement (probably with the knowledge of the author, who was his friend).[88] With this argument Wesley retreated to the principle of legality and demanded that the Americans submit to the British government. Once again he surrendered his own independent position, which he still held, in favor of the official legal view.[89] The crucial reason for this change, however, was that the discussions in America had assumed the forms of open and violent resistance. This caused Wesley to take up the side of king and Parliament, for peace and order, against war and bloodshed. He opposed the Americans' comparison of their situation to slavery, and their claim that they were obliged to obey only those laws that their own representatives had helped to legislate in Parliament. Employing a historical survey using almost the same arguments he had used against altering the British constitution, Wesley attempted to make clear that the Americans had no grounds for lamenting a lack of freedom or demanding a greater measure of freedom.[90] The price to be paid in a civil war would be too great. Rational insights must convince them of that fact and make them abandon those seducers whose aim was not the welfare of America but the overthrow of the king.

Thus only after all efforts at settlement had failed did Wesley take sides, partly because he was able to supercede his limitations only to a small extent, but also because he expected from the king the quickest possible end to the unfortunate war between brothers.[91] However debatable Wesley's methods might have been, his efforts ultimately served to establish and secure peace, not to participate in psychological warfare. Wesley's partisanship favoring established laws was a partisanship favoring reason and agreement along peaceful lines, in spite of all the justifiable indignation that it unleashed. Wesley certainly was not a pacifist in principle, but concern for the well-being of men, the maintenance of peace, and the preservation of freedom brought him to the point of appealing to the reason of the combatants and proscribing war as a means of resolving conflict. War was not a means of changing society for the better.

Possible Ways of Renewal

In Wesley's eyes, the most important and most effective means of renewing society was the individual's moral transformation. Human wickedness was the greatest hindrance to society's well-being, while human righteousness was its most effective promoter.[92] Peace and well-being for all would be produced by purification from lies, injustice, lack of compassion, pride, a partisan spirit, wrath, revenge, bitterness, prejudice, hypocrisy, narrow-mindedness, and contentiousness, and by new patterns of behavior wrought by the obedience of faith, such as friendliness, sympathy, forgiveness, and compassion, as well as sobriety, moderation, and diligence.[93] The elimination of sin as the cause of all evil, along with living life out of love for God and all people, would achieve a comprehensive reform of the life of individuals as well as society.[94]

The Methodist congregations and their fields of social work were places for the practice of this conduct and for mutual corrections.[95] Struggle against public abuses was the appropriate means for working beyond the limits of these areas,[96] for restricting widespread corruption,[97] and for eliminating smuggling, luxury, alcoholism, and other vices injurious to society.[98] Wesley publicly attacked even legally protected evils such as slavery and the sale of seats in Parliament. In his demands, however, he never went so far as to call for changing the system.[99] Ministers and members of Parliament were not immune to his attacks;[100] occasionally he even demanded specific measures for eliminating public abuses of these offices.[101] Nevertheless, his general confidence in the governmental system's ability to function remained essentially unshaken.

Wesley's fear of causing or promoting unrest and his inveterate Toryism, along with his fear of overtaxing the capacities and possibilities of individuals or smaller groups, prevented him from actually demanding comprehensive and fundamental reforms that only the state could have carried through: representation in Parliament of *all* Englishmen, regardless of their income and their possessions; and a just apportionment of the electoral districts.[102] Wesley did not call for new ordering of the school system that would assure all children up to age fourteen an education that John Locke (1697) and Adam Smith (1776) had demanded.[103] He did not offer any fundamental objections to the cruelty of the penal laws; he did not see that a reform of the prisons would require other measures than the conversion of their wardens. His

131

unique efforts toward relieving the plight of the poor did not have the reform of the poor laws as their aim. Without doubt Wesley correctly recognized that institutional measures without the personal ethics of the persons responsible for them would bring few positive effects in the long run. He did not see that the social efforts of small groups and individual persons in a system burdened with injustices could not produce any effective changes in the long run because they only addressed specific points and remained utterly dependent on the personal and necessarily narrowly limited initiatives of their agents.

CHAPTER X

CONCLUDING OBSERVATIONS

After surveying the essential elements of Wesley's social ethics, its principles as well as its practices, a final systematic statement must be made with a dual aim: first, to trace individual observations and analyses on the whole back to their foundations; and second, to explicate points of strength and weakness in a theological evaluation.

1. THE WEAKNESSES OF WESLEY'S SOCIAL ETHICS

Partly due to one-sided exaggerations, Wesley's teaching and example lamentably led to some faulty developments, which can easily be recognized from the vantage point of subsequent history.[1]

The Conservative View of the State

The state and especially the king were elevated above any criticism seeking to attack anything more than the individual, the negative, or the peripheral. This position of Wesley's originated from several causes: his belief that civil power derived from God; his inherited, unquestioned Tory conviction; his own experience with fomenters of unrest; and his understandable need to exhibit the new movement's loyalty convincingly while keeping it clear of any suspicion of enmity to the state. In addition, the representatives of republican movements, who conflicted with the state church because of their political convictions, appeared godless and hostile to Christianity, thus making it even easier for Wesley to take sides in favor of the existing order.

In spite of the courage Wesley exhibited even before highly placed persons, it must be said in relation to the state that he lost a great part of his critical ability and therefore was guilty of applying two different standards of measurement.[2]

Wesley's prohibition against his preachers' addressing political topics allowed only one exception: exculpating and defending the king and his government. In the long run, this stance made the official representatives of Methodism uncritical supporters of a society that largely worked against the movement's dynamic, society-changing force or drove those motivated by it out of the newly emerging church.

Rejection of Structural Changes in Society

A further deficiency resulting from this attitude was Wesley's renunciation of any demand for fundamental changes in societal structures. One certainly cannot blame Wesley for failing to foresee the evil consequences of the Industrial Revolution that the nineteenth century would recognize. Without demanding changes in the laws or even a reform of Parliament, Wesley did, however, denounce the deprivation of many farmers by land enclosures, the catastrophic conditions in the prisons and poor houses, the luxury of the rich, the economic distress of broad strata of the populace, injustice in the penal system and in tax collection, and many other abuses. He challenged individuals and groups on the basis of humanitarianism or responsibility to undertake measures toward eliminating distresses, but he was not concerned about having these measures legally and institutionally established and assured.

The opposite side of Wesley's failure to demand that the state in its supreme responsibility for its citizens bring about necessary changes in society was Wesley's desire to awaken society's social conscience. Without this kind of awakening, any private initiative would have been able to achieve only a small amount, in its onset and even more so in the long run. But this kind of social activism would have aligned Wesley with the political reform movements, from which he so decisively distanced himself, except concerning the anti-slavery movement.

These two weaknesses just described were founded less in the system of Wesley's social ethics than in his time-bound personal attitude. His ethical impulse could have led him further in praxis had these limitations not restricted him. Therefore, what appears as a deficiency from a historical perspective can be regarded as unessential in a systematic perspective, and it can be set aside in working out Wesley's fundamental principles. The same holds true for the third and last deficiency left to be cited.

Defective Knowledge of Causal Connections

Wesley's advice for fulfilling major social tasks frequently makes it apparent that he did not perceive the deeper connections of political or economic developments. Thus in many cases his proposed solutions[3] sound naive and superficial. This lack of knowledge was caused by his political bias and insufficient leisure time to study such problems and acquire necessary information, as well as general unavailability of appropriate research and publications. The careful observer should understand this deficiency and guard against hasty conclusions.

2. THE STRENGTHS OF WESLEY'S SOCIAL ETHICS

These can be summed up essentially in four complementary pairs of concepts in tension with each other.

Faith and Works

This combination forms an essential basic element in Wesley's ethic in spite of the inevitable danger, of which Wesley was fully aware, of slipping into a works-righteousness. Untroubled by the debate with medieval Catholicism that determined Luther's theological struggle and partially shaped his doctrine of justification, Wesley could assign works a higher rank without losing the Reformation character of his soteriology. On the one hand, works were always subordinate to faith or the working of God's grace and could never acquire a meritorious function; on the other hand, they essentially belonged to faith as its necessary consequence, so that there could be no faith without works in the normal case when time and opportunity were present. This combination preserved ethics from becoming a mere appendix to dogmatics, and made it a necessary element of Christian existence. Faith must bring forth good works as its fruits if it was to withstand the test of its genuineness and vitality; indeed, faith's continued existence, its perseverance, was gravely imperiled if it did not thoroughly permeate and determine the Christian's whole life and activity in increasing holiness. Thus the true praxis of faith was attached to true faith as a component of the Christian life.

135

Love and Reason

The biblical moral law certainly holds unaltered obligation for the Christian. Since its chief content is love and since present social challenges can seldom be answered with clear biblical instructions, the specific individual commandments of social ethics result in principle from applying the commandment to love, worked out by rational reflection.

The significance of these two elements for ethics can hardly be overestimated. Love for others, born from experiencing God's unlimited love, creates the preconditions of social involvement: social sensitivity, solidarity in community, and compassion for others. Love awakens the conscience to unlimited responsibility for others, regardless of their religious, moral, or social character. To the universal human rights expounded by the Enlightenment, love gives the practical power to transcend the boundaries of race, nationality, and social stratification, and to recognize all persons as recipients of loving gifts. Love also contains the potentially revolutionary element of egalitarianism, which has led historically to Methodism's connection with the labor union movement and political liberalism.[4]

Rational reflection preserves the foundation of ethics while allowing the freedom to adapt to demands of the current situation and to avoid perpetuating ethical patterns that arose in a specific historical setting into a time when their application no longer makes sense.[5] Beyond this flexibility it gives the mature Christian the ability to recognize and perform what is ethically commanded in the situation that confronts him or her without resorting to a comprehensive catalog of casuistic instructions.[6]

Individual and Society

The individual's renewal in justification and sanctification was undoubtedly the primary concern of Wesley's preaching. First of all, Wesley expected from this transformed person the impulses that would gradually transform the entire society. Wesley never lost sight of this goal, which occasionally took on visionary characteristics.[7]

Converts were not snatched from their social connections into Christian circles to cultivate their piety apparently unendangered by nonChristian influences. Instead, they were sent out into the sphere of worldly life to bear witness to their faith and exercise love with full determination. The Methodist groups had the task not of making an other-worldly existence easy or possible, but of practicing manners of social conduct, developing a sensitivity to the needs of others, and setting in motion effective measures of assistance. Only by incorporating socially uprooted people driven by economic developments from their original environment into new social relationships could these individuals be enabled to shape their lives to new standards and thus prepare themselves for social activities. From the first, though not consistently, the Methodist classes had this twofold aim: to help individuals gain a new identity and consciousness of worth, and to provide a starting point for social activity within and beyond the classes themselves. The democratic ground rules learned in these classes would later make a large number of Methodist laypersons into leading personalities of the labor union movement and political reform movements.[8]

Praxis and Theory

With appropriate scholarly hesitancy, it may be asserted that Wesley was the greatest social reformer of his time because he succeeded in bringing socio-ethical theory and praxis into a close connection that served to advance both. His theory almost always operated independently when he allowed social problems to be posed; and despite its limited potential, his theory became so effective because he knew how to translate it into practical measures.

Wesley's lively gift of observation and the contact with all groups among the English populace that he constantly cultivated on his extensive preaching journeys provided him an insight into the multiplicity and severity of problems that hardly anyone else in his time could have possessed. In this connection Wesley was not satisfied with publicly denouncing abuses in his sermons and writings; instead, he also strove, where possible, to initiate practical solutions directly or indirectly, to continue reflecting upon them, to periodically test their effectiveness, and to correct them where necessary.

Thereby Wesley accomplished a dual end: he prompted others to recognize social problems as early as possible and to investigate them all the way to their underlying causes, while he made it clear that analyses alone do not signify a solution until the necessary practical consequences are drawn from them. As this investigation indicates, Wesley did not always make the right judgment, but what he did still served as an

137

example, and thus set in motion "humanitarian waves" leading to more far-reaching reforms than he himself envisioned.[9]

Overall, Wesley's ethic, which began with the universal love of God that repudiates any religious heightening of social abuses,[10] and with the rational analysis of situations that provided the necessary motivation and concrete suggestions leading to practical consequences, must be seen as influential and helpful beyond Wesley's own time. It also provides stimuli worthy of consideration for ethical reflection today and situates comprehensive social responsibility in the conduct of Christians and nonChristians alike.

ABBREVIATIONS

JOHN WESLEY'S WRITINGS:

AM	*Arminian Magazine.* 1778–1797.
Journal	*The Journal of John Wesley.* N. Curnock, ed. 8 vols. London, 1938.
Letters	*The Letters of John Wesley.* J. Telford, ed. 8 vols. London, 1931.
Notes	*Explanatory Notes upon the New Testament.* London, 1831.
Sermons	*Wesley's Standard Sermons.* E. H. Sugden, ed. 2 vols. London, 1921.
Survey	*A Survey of the Wisdom of God in the Creation: or, A Compendium of Natural Philosophy.* 2 vols. Bristol, 1770.
Works	*The Works of John Wesley.* 3rd ed. T. Jackson, ed. 14 vols. London, 1872. Reprinted Grand Rapids, 1958.

OTHER WORKS:

Creeds	*The Creeds of Christendom, with a History and Critical Notes.* P. Schaff, ed. 3 vols. New York, 1877.
EStL	*Evangelisches Staatslexikon.* H. Kunst and S. Grundmann. 2nd ed. H. Kunst, R. Herzog, and W. Schneemelcher, eds. Stuttgart, 1975.
HMC	*A History of the Methodist Church in Great Britain.* vol. I. R. Davies and G. Rupp, eds. London, 1965.
LQHR	*London Quarterly and Holborn Review.* 1932–1968.
NCMH	*New Cambridge Modern History.* 14 vols. Cambridge, 1964–1974.
RGG	*Die Religion in Geschichte und Gegenwart.* 3rd ed. 6 vols. plus index vol. K. Galling, ed. Tübingen, 1957–1965.
RPTK	*Realencyclopaedie für Protestantische Theologie und Kirche.* J. J. Herzog, ed. 3rd ed. D. Albert Hauck, ed. Leipzig, 1896–1913.
WHS	*Proceedings of the Wesley Historical Society.* 1898—

NOTES

INTRODUCTION

1. A helpful bibliography is that prepared by E. F. Sommer entitled "John Wesley, eine bibliographische Skizze." It was prepared for the two-volume biography of Wesley by Martin Schmidt but was not fully published there. Instead, it was published in the *Mitteilungen der Studiengemeinschaft für Geschichte des Methodismus* 4 (1966/67):4-47. An overview of important secondary literature is provided by V. Schneeberger, *Theologische Wurzeln des sozialen Akzents bei John Wesley* (Zürich, 1974), 18-29, although he does not take into account the dissertation of E. W. Gerdes, "John Wesley's Lehre von der Gottesebenbildlichkeit des Menschen" (Ph.D. diss., Kiel, 1958). For a more recent bibliography, see Henry D. Rack, *Reasonable Enthusiast: John Wesley and the Rise of Methodism* (London, 1989), 555-60.
2. Gerdes; D. Lerch, *Heil und Heiligung bei John Wesley* (Zürich, 1941); H. Lindström, *Wesley and Sanctification: A Study in the Doctrine of Salvation* (Upsala, 1950); W. Thomas, *Heiligung im Neuen Testament und bei Wesley* (Zürich, 1965); J. Weissbach, *Der neue Mensch im theologischen Denken John Wesleys* (Stuttgart, 1970), and others.
3. Cf. Schneeberger, 25-28.
4. Zürich, 1974.
5. Thus in a letter to the author dated December 29, 1973.

PART A
THE MAJOR AREAS OF WESLEY'S SOCIAL PRAXIS

CHAPTER I
THE SOCIAL WORK OF THE EARLY OXFORD METHODISTS

1. The term "social" is used here in two senses: first, in the general sense, having to do with the orders and groups in society; and second, in the particular sense, oriented to specific conduct in critical situations and the consequences

of that behavior. "In this society of ours if we speak of social ethics, this dual meaning will unavoidably acquire validity, and rightly so; for only in a stable, secure, unshakable society could one speak of 'acting socially,' or of 'social behavior,' and the like, without the critical and challenging pathos that (at any rate in Germany since about 1848) arises out of this term." H. D. Wendland, *Einführung in die Sozialethik* (Berlin, 1971), 8.

2. E. P. Thompson, *The Making of the English Working Class* (London, 1963), 194: ". . . the outstanding fact of the period between 1790 and 1830 is the formation of the 'working class.'" Cf. M. Vester, *Die Entstehung des Proletariats als Lernprozess. Die Entstehung antikapitalistischer Theorie und Praxis in England, 1792-1848* (Frankfurt, 1970), 23.

3. J. Kuczynski, *Die Geschichte der Lage der Arbeiter unter dem Kapitalismus*, vol. 22 (Berlin, 1961), 240.

4. Kuczynski, 239; L. A. Clarkson, *The Pre-Industrial Economy in England, 1500-1700* (London, 1971), 210. "Poverty was the pervading condition of pre-industrial England. A small minority of the population was very much wealthier than the great majority and rich, even by the standards of the twentieth century."

5. G. M. Trevelyan, *English Social History: A Survey of Six Centuries, Chaucer to Queen Victoria* (London, 1946), 274ff.

6. Vester, 51-52.

7. In 1764, the invention of the spinning jenny (sixteen to eighteen spindles instead of one); in 1767, the spinning frame, for mechanical operation; in 1779, the combination of the two (the spinning mule); in 1764, the invention of the steam engine; from 1785 onward, the use of steam power for spinning and weaving at first only supplementing manual power, but then, after further improvements, gradually supplanting it.

8. The new poor law was announced in 1834 and amended in 1844.

9. Kuczynski, 109.

10. "The problem of the poor and of unemployment was in its essence national—or at least regional—yet every petty parish dealt with it separately, in a state of hostility to every other. Rural ignorance and parochial jealousy were left to cope with the terrible problem according to their own devices, and the chief anxiety felt was to drive out of the parish anyone who might conceivably become a burden on the poor rate, a policy which checked the fluidity of labour and severely aggravated unemployment" (Trevelyan, 351f.).

11. The Law of Settlement, according to which every English citizen had a claim upon assistance for the poor only in the community in which he was born, prevented many impoverished persons from looking around for better living conditions and taking work where this might be possible, for example in the newly developing centers of industrial expansion. "Nine-tenths of the people of England, all in fact who did not belong to a small class of landowners, were liable to be expelled from any parish save their own, with every circumstance of arrest and ignominy, however good their character

and even if they had secured remunerative work" (Trevelyan, 278). Cf. W.
J. Warner, *The Wesleyan Movement in the Industrial Revolution*, 2nd ed. (New
York, 1967), 9; K. Kluxen, *Geschichte Englands. Von den Anfängen bis zur
Gegenwart* (Stuttgart, 1968), 407.

12. ". . . the impending industrial revolution changed the population statistics
greatly, and during the century, towns like Birmingham and Sheffield
probably increased their population sevenfold and Liverpool tenfold." J. H.
Whiteley, *Wesley's England: A Survey of 18th Century Social and Cultural
Conditions* (London, 1945), 53. More precise figures on the development of
the population and migration are provided by Kuczynski, vol. 23 (Berlin,
1962), 94ff. ". . . the Church of England was hampered by an inflexible
organization in the necessary task of ministering to new concentrations of
industrial workers in areas where formerly people had been more scarce."
NCMH 7:136.

13. "Poverty was a stigma. If men fell out of the race they must be cared for; but
the duty never became a pleasure." M. Edwards, *John Wesley and the
Eighteenth Century: A Study of His Social and Political Influence* (London, 1955),
148. "The typical judgement of the day blamed the unfortunate for their
own condition. . . . The necessity of the poor represented an accepted
economic axiom." Warner, 4-5.

14. Warner, 4-5, 7.

15. ". . . there are whole families in want of every necessity of life, oppressed
with hunger, cold, nakedness and filth and disease. The sufferings indeed
of the poor are less known than their misdeeds; and therefore we are less apt
to pity them." The statement by a Westminster official is quoted by
Whiteley, 28.

16. "The poor were not sufficiently self-conscious to organize for a common
purpose. Indeed, they were even incompetent to recognize or support
existing forces which would promote their own interests" (Warner, 6).

17. R. F. Wearmouth, *Methodism and the Common People of the Eighteenth Century*
(London, 1945), 78, relates: "In the year 1740, foodstuffs being in meagre
supply, cereals being exported, prices rising, discontent raging, the
labouring classes suffered a plague of human misery; with their patience at
breaking point and their behavior surly and angry and passing into passions
of violence, no amelioration came in the shape of cheaper and ampler
supplies of the staff of life; instead, the authorities called up the soldiers,
armed many civilians, arrested most of the ringleaders, sent several to the
gallows." Further accounts in Wearmouth; Trevelyan, 471f.

18. H. Nicolson, *The Age of Reason* (London, 1958), 369f.

19. "In the half century from the Act of Toleration (1689) to the inception of
the Methodist awakening (1739) the Protestant churches of England and
Scotland experienced a total religious and moral slackening. In the social
strata that belonged to the Anglican state-church, churchliness existed only
as purely external custom. Among the nobility, religion generally was held
in little esteem, and among the bourgeois religious indifference prevailed;

the lowest strata, the workers in the industrial districts, were unutterably crude, ignorant, and untouched by any influence of the church. Religious decline was not so deep among the Dissenters as in the state-church; yet even among them one could observe a flagging of religious energy." K. Heussi, *Kompendium der Kirchengeschichte*, 13th ed. (Tübingen, 1971), 423. Cf. *NCMH* 7:4.

20. J. S. Simon gives detailed information about the activities of these societies in *John Wesley and the Religious Societies* (London, 1921). Cf. also M. Schmidt, "England und der deutsche Pietismus," *Evangelische Theologie* 13 (1953):209; Schmidt, *John Wesley: A Theological Biography*, trans. Norman P. Goldhawk, 2 vols. in 3 (New York/Nashville, 1962-1973), 1:35f.; V. H. H. Green, *The Young Mr. Wesley: A Study of John Wesley and Oxford* (London, 1961), 157f.; F. Loofs, "Methodismus," *RPTK* 12:751; R. E. Davies, *Methodism* (London, 1963), 31-33.

21. Davies, 32.

22. Cf. Schmidt, *John Wesley* 1:97ff.; Green, 157f.; K. W. MacArthur, *The Economic Ethics of John Wesley* (New York/Cincinnati/Chicago, 1936), 112; R. M. Cameron, *Methodism and Society in Historical Perspective* (New York, 1961), 35.

23. N. Curnock, *Journal* 1:6 (Introduction).

24. This is followed then by correspondingly practical recommendations as under III: *Letters* 1:128f.; cf. *Journal* 1:96f.

25. *Letters* 1:92.

26. On August 17, 1722, John Wesley wrote to his mother: "What I do is this; when I am entrusted with a person who is first to understand and practise, and then to teach, the law of Christ, I endeavor, by an intermixture of reading and conversation, to show him what that law is—that is, to renounce all insubordinate love of the world, and to love and obey God with all his strength" (*Letters* 1:138).

27. A letter of October 10, 1735 (*Letters* 1:188). To this extent, Loofs (*RPTK* 12:756) in my opinion is entirely correct in saying about the Holy Club, "It was not work for others that they held in view as their aim; their own devout egoism was determinative for them." Schmidt's contradiction of this in *The Young Wesley: Missionary and Theologian of Missions*, trans. L. A. Fletcher (London, 1958), 18f., is not entirely convincing to me, since even more documentation of such an attitude in this period can be adduced. *Letters* 1:168: ". . . when two ways of life are proposed, I should choose to begin with that part of the question, Which of these have I rational ground to believe will conduce most to my own improvement?" To be sure, he does not lose sight of the task of collaborating in the sanctification of others; but it is his own sanctification that constantly appears in first place. Cf. *Letters* 1:180, 190f., and note 31 below. Wesley, on looking back in his "Appeal to Men of Reason and Religion" (*Works* 8:5), confesses that essentially they were basically deficient in love for God and for other persons.

28. *Letters* 1:167; letter of December 10, 1723.

29. "The love which our Lord requires in all his followers, is the love of God and man,—of God, for his own, and of man, for God's sake. Now, what is it to love God, but to delight in him, to rejoice in his will, to desire continually to please him, to seek and find our happiness in him, and to thirst day and night for a fuller enjoyment of him?" Sermon in Savannah of February 20, 1736; *Works* 7:495. In this period John Wesley "always speaks about love for God, never of the love which is God's" (Schmidt, *John Wesley*, 1:123).

30. C. E. Vulliamy, *John Wesley*, 3rd ed. (London, 1954), 51.

31. To this extent Schmidt is incorrect when he declares: "It only requires application on a large scale, and the Methodist movement as a whole can be seen. Even the essential points in Methodism's theological basis are present . . ." (*John Wesley*, 1:101). Cameron (33) concisely and appropriately characterizes the difference in motivation: "Whereas the earnest University Students undertook their regime of self-denial and 'social service' as steps on the way to justifying themselves in God's sight, the later Methodists undertook the same steps out of the joyous assurance that their sins were already forgiven, not of their own desert, but of God's grace. They were not the roots, but the fruits of salvation. They sprang not out of anxiety for self, but out of compassion for others and love for God." Theologically, this distinction is of crucial significance and will be examined more closely in the second part of the present work (see below, chapters VII-IX).

32. A clear delineation in contrast to this possible development is reflected in Wesley's famous later characterization of Christianity as a "social religion" which as such would be destroyed if one were to change it into a "solitary religion" (*Sermons* 1:381f.).

33. "The Oxford Society does not, in a literal sense, represent the 'first rise of Methodism'! The formal High Church practices of the Club, with a definite emphasis upon salvation by works alone, were things entirely foreign to the spirit of later Methodism" (Vulliamy, 51).

34. Schmidt, *John Wesley*, 1:260ff.

CHAPTER II
WESLEY'S AND THE METHODIST SOCIETIES'
AID TO THE POOR

1. *Journal* 4:358 (November 17, 1759).

2. "It is the business of a leader (1) to see each person in his class, once a week at the least, in order to inquire how their souls prosper; to advise, reprove, comfort, or exhort, as occasion may require; to receive what they are willing to give toward the relief of the poor. . . ." (*Letters* 2:297: "A Plain Account of the People Called Methodists," 1748); cf. *Works* 8:248-68.

   Wesley requested the London Society "to give weekly a penny, or what they could afford, for the relief of the poor and sick" (*Journal* 2:454; entry dated May 7, 1741!). Cf. David L. Watson, *The Early Methodist Class Meeting: Its Origins and Significance* (Nashville, 1985).

3. *Letters* 2:305; *Journal* 3:300.
4. One account may be cited as representative of many similar ones. In February 1744 Wesley wrote in his journal: "In the afternoon, many being met together, I exhorted them now, while they had opportunity, to make to themselves 'friends of the mammon of unrighteousness'; to deal their bread to the hungry, to clothe the naked, and not to hide themselves from their own flesh. And God opened their hearts, so that they contributed nearly fifty pounds, which I began laying out the very next hour in linen, woolen, and shoes for them whom I knew to be diligent and yet in want." A second collection yielded about thirty pounds; "but perceiving that the whole money received would not answer one-third of the expense, I determined to go round the classes, and beg for the rest, till I had gone through the whole society" (*Journal* 3:116f., 122). He continued to undertake such begging travels even in old age, without allowing himself to be stopped by difficulties; see *Journal* 6:451 (October 1, 1783); *Journal* 7:42f. (January 4, 1785); and J. W. E. Sommer, *John Wesley und die soziale Frage* (Bremen, 1930), 9.
5. *Works* 7:36.
6. Journal entry of February 24, 1747: "At noon I examined the little society at Tetney. I have not seen another such in England. In the class paper [which gives an account of the contribution for the poor], I observed one gave eight pence, often ten pence, a week; another thirteen, fifteen, or eighteen pence; another sometimes one, sometimes two shillings. I asked Mican Elmoor, the leader . . . 'How is this? Are you the richest society in all England?' He answered 'I suppose not; but all of us who are single persons have agreed together to give both ourselves and all we have to God. And we do it gladly whereby we are able, from time to time, to entertain all the strangers that come to Tetney, who often have no food to eat, nor any friend to give them a lodging'" (*Journal* 3:281).
7. More detailed information on this point is given by A. W. Hill, *John Wesley among the Physicians: A Study of 18th Century Medicine* (London, 1958), and H. R. Flachsmeier, "John Wesley als Sozialhygieniker und Arzt" (M.D. diss., Hamburg, 1957).
8. W. C. Cross, "Wesley and Medicine," *The Magazine for the Wesleyan Methodist Church*, 137 (1914):618. In London the death rate was higher than the birth rate. The growth in London's population at the beginning of the eighteenth century can be traced only to immigration. H. Butterfield, "England in the Eighteenth Century," *HMC*, 7.
9. The city (London) was divided up into twenty-three districts; one district was entrusted to the care of each pair of visitors. Every sick person was to be visited three times each week (*Letters* 2:306; *Journal* 2:454).
10. *Letters* 2:307.
11. *Letters* 2:307.

12. On June 6, 1747, Wesley noted concerning the sick who were treated: "I found there had been about six hundred in about six months. More than three hundred of these came twice or thrice, and we saw no more of them. About twenty of those who had constantly attended did not seem to be either better or worse. Above two hundred were sensibly better, and fifty-one thoroughly cured. The entire expense, from the beginning till this time, was about thirty pounds" (*Journal* 3:301).

13. In 1748: "We continued this ever since, and by the blessing of God with more and more success" (*Letters* 2:308). "Two or three years after, our patients were so numerous that we were obliged to divide them." Wesley had installed a device for giving electric treatments (November 9, 1756; *Journal* 4:190f.) In Ireland, June 14, 1773, "I preached in the evening at Lisburn. All the time I could spare here was taken up by poor patients" (*Journal* 5:513).

14. Cross, 613.

15. J. W. E. Sommer, 10.

16. *Letters* 2:309f. and note.

17. *Journal* 3:246.

18. *Journal* 2:403f., 454. For a time, a kitchen for feeding the poor also was established there. J. S. Simon, *John Wesley, the Master-Builder* (London, 1927), 132.

19. Wearmouth, 139; E. M. North, *Early Methodist Philanthropy* (New York/Cincinnati, 1914), 68; L. Tyerman, *The Life and Times of the Rev. John Wesley, M.A.*, 3rd ed., 3 vols. (London, 1876), 1:357; *Journal* 2:454, note 2.

20. The thesis maintained by the historians W. E. H. Lecky and E. Halévy, that Methodism saved England from a revolution like France's, nevertheless cannot be sustained, even though it continues to be repeated down to the present day. The sharpest rebuttal to it comes from the pen of one of the best-informed Wesleyan scholars: "Now this contention I believe to be wrong. Had Wesley never lived, there would have been no revolution in England similar to that in France." M. Edwards, *This Methodism* (London, 1939), 35.

    A detailed discussion of this speculative assumption seems to me to be neither significant nor necessary. The development of the Parliamentary system and of the trade-union movement, as well as the relatively small number of Methodists in the total population of England allow any expression concerning the influence of Wesley and his congregation only in the limited form indicated in the text. For a discussion of the Lecky thesis see E. Halévy, *The Birth of Methodism in England*, trans. and ed. with an introduction by B. Semmel (Chicago, 1971); Thompson; Edwards, "Did Methodism Prevent a Revolution in England?" in *This Methodism*, 35-50; Edwards, "John Wesley," *HMC*, 59f.

21. *Journal* 7:51.

22. *Journal* 4:422; *Works* 7:118f.

23. Cf. A. Knudson, *The Principles of Christian Ethics* (New York/Nashville, 1943), 268.

24. *Works* 7:219.
25. *Works* 8:168.
26. *Works* 8:9.
27. The text of the sermon was I Peter 1:6, 1760, Outler; see *Sermons* 2:264.
28. *Sermons* 2:270f.
29. *Journal* 4:52.
30. *Journal* 2:453; 5:488.
31. On this writing cf. especially J. W. E. Sommer; MacArthur, 110f.; Wearmouth, 210; and T. W. Madron, "Some Economic Aspects of John Wesley's Thought Revisited," *Methodist History* 4/1 (1965-66), 39f.
32. H. Bett, *The Spirit of Methodism* (London, 1943), 143: "Wesley, at any rate, was always ready to denounce social injustice wherever he saw it."
33. *Works* 8:3 (*An Earnest Appeal*, 1744).
34. Ibid.
35. *Works* 6:298.
36. *Sermons* 2:497.
37. *Letters* 6:208f.
38. Sanctification is no longer placed ahead of justification, nor love ahead of faith, as Wesley thought before 1738, referring to Law; instead, love is the fruit of the faith which God gives and out of which we are justified. Cf. Lindström, 56f., and C. W. Williams, *John Wesley's Theology Today* (Nashville: 1960), 68f. and 79.
39. H. Carter, *The Methodist Heritage*, 176ff.; Lindström, 171ff. Here we can only mention without full discussion the fact that with this conception of love as the fruit of faith and in necessary orientation to one's neighbors, Protestant insights become newly effectual and mystical views that influenced Wesley, especially through William Law, were corrected. For this we refer particularly to the appropriate passages in Lindström (174ff.), Williams (71ff.), Schmidt (*John Wesley* 1:246ff.), and A. Lang, *Puritanismus und Pietismis: Studien zu ihrer Entwicklung von M. Buzer bis zum Methodismis* (Neukirchen, 1941), 281ff., and chapter VIII of the present work.
40. Somewhat more will be said in chapter VIII about the "third use of the law" in Wesley's thought.
41. *Works* 8:343.
42. *Works* 7:145. One can also learn the same from the parable of the Good Samaritan; see *Works* 10:156.
43. *Sermons* 1:97.
44. *Sermons* 1:342f.
45. *Sermons* 1:342f. For more particulars concerning love as the basis and the norm for ethics, see pp. 104-9. of this volume.
46. In the doctrine of original sin Wesley even sees the shibboleth between paganism and Christianity: "Is man by nature filled with all manner of evil? Is he void of all good? Is he wholly fallen? Is his soul totally corrupt? . . . Allow this, and you are so far a Christian. Deny it, and you are but an Heathen still" (*Sermons* 2:223).

47. The arrogance that the members of the upper class saw in this proclamation is expressed with hardly surpassable clarity in a letter from the Duchess of Buckingham to Lady Huntingdon: "I thank Your Ladyship for the information concerning the Methodist preachers. Their doctrines are most repulsive, strongly tinctured with impertinence and disrespect toward their superiors, in perpetually endeavouring to level all ranks, and do away with all distinctions. It is monstrous to be told that you have a heart as *sinful* as the common wretches that crawl on the earth. This is highly offensive and insulting; and I can not but wonder that Your Ladyship should relish any sentiment so much at variance with high rank and good breeding." Quoted from G. Lean, *John Wesley, Anglican* (London, 1964), 84.

48. *Works* 7:144ff.; 8:346; 6:300f. "It matters not, in this respect, whether they are high or low, rich or poor, superior or inferior to you. No, not even whether good or bad, whether they fear God or not" (*Works* 7:145).

49. *Sermons* 1:344. The "religion of the world" is outward, churchly piety without inward renewal of life by God.

50. *Journal* 3:301. Cf. *Letters* 2:305f.; *Works* 7:121. The sick who were in need of help are called "fellow-sufferers" (*Works* 7:123; cf. *Works* 7:124f.).

51. *Letters* 2:297, 304. In this connection, too, Wesley's stressing of Christianity as a "social religion"—that is, as a way of life that essentially is dependent on relationship within the community—is in full force. *Sermons* 1:382. Cf. Schneeberger, 143; J. Walsh, "Methodism at the End of the Eighteenth Century," *HMC*, 312f.

52. *Letters* 2:300. Cf. Thompson, 362f.; Edwards, "John Wesley," *HMC*, 62.

53. *Letters* 2:308.

54. "It was due mainly to Methodism, and to the Evangelical Revival, that English Christianity began once more to recognize in theory and in practice that this world is also part of God's Kingdom, and to reassert, and perhaps to over-emphasize, that element of compassion which led to the Christian fruits of the nineteenth and twentieth centuries." J. Marlowe, *The Puritan Tradition in English Life* (London, 1956), 44. Kluxen (530) calls the "evangelical mentality" the "moral cement of English society" and sees in it a "major reason for the difference between British social history and that of other peoples."

CHAPTER III
JOHN WESLEY'S CONTRIBUTION TO
ECONOMIC ETHICS

1. Sermon on "The Use of Money" (*Sermons* 2:309ff., especially 314ff.), the text of which (Luke 16:9) appeared for the first time in 1748 and then in the following years more frequently in the list of sermon texts. The rules are also mentioned at other places in his sermons, letters, and journal (e.g., *Letters* 5:8; 6:207; *Works* 7:285, and elsewhere).

2. *Sermons* 2:312ff.
3. *Sermons* 2:314.
4. On the question of property in the New Testament, cf. W. Schrage, *Ethik des Neuen Testaments* (Göttingen, 1974), 39ff. On the relationship of the New Testament and John Wesley on this question, Knudson (276, note 20) also offers a brief observation.
5. *Sermons* 2:320ff.
6. The complete quotation reads thus: "In the hands of His children, it is food for the hungry, drink for the thirsty, raiment for the naked: it gives to the traveller and the stranger where to lay his head. By it we may supply the place of an husband to the widow, and of a father to the fatherless. We may be a defence for the oppressed, a means of health to the sick, of ease to them that are in pain; it may be as eyes to the blind, as feet to the lame; yea, a lifter up from the gates of death" (*Sermons* 2:314).
7. So also in *Works* 6:265: money is not "evil of itself," but is "applicable to good as well as bad purposes."
8. *Sermons* 2:323ff.
9. In the enforcement of these rules, he writes in a letter of February 1776, "we must needs be directed from time to time by the unction of the Holy One" (*Letters* 6:207).
10. *Works* 7:9f., 356; *Sermons* 1:480f.
11. *Sermons* 2:324.
12. *Sermons* 2:324f.
13. *Letters* 5:8.
14. *Works* 7:286.
15. *Works* 7:286; cf. 308f.
16. In his personal life Wesley held strictly to the rules that he had set forth. Cf., among others, North, 122.
17. *Works* 7:362; *Journal* 4:103; *Sermons* 2:326, 424, 473ff.; *Letters* 3:122.
18. *Sermons* 2:324ff.
19. *Journal* 3:117, 122; *Sermons* 2:309. Some Methodists, through their cheerfulness in giving, became poorer than they were before becoming members of the community; *Works* 8:124f.
20. Thus especially in the sermon, "The Danger of Riches," *Works* 7:1ff. (1779/80). Hence, Lang's assertion (329) that Wesley in his earlier years had despised money and then later was less otherworldly is incorrect. Lang refers to a passage in Wesley's "Earnest Appeal to Men of Reason and Religion," in which Wesley defends himself against the charge that he had personally enriched himself. There he says, "For as to gold and silver, I count it dung and dross; I trample it under my feet" (*Works* 8:39). Nothing is said there about his estimate of money as a means for doing good, whereby it first acquires its worth.
21. *Works* 7:285f.
22. *Sermons* 2:319. Laziness was regarded as a sin and was no more tolerated in the Methodist communities than was thievery or murder! (*Works* 7:129).

23. In 1746 he offered his congregation in Bristol as an example of frugality who gave up drinking tea (*Journal* 3:245f.; cf. *Letters* 2:164).
24. *Sermons* 1:473ff.; *Works* 7:9ff.: *Sermons* 2:323ff.
25. In 1789 he asked whether of the fifty thousand Methodists even five hundred (i.e., 1 percent) still kept the third rule: *Works* 7:286.
26. See Schrage, 40.
27. *Works* 7:3.
28. *Works* 7:123f.
29. *Letters* 5:80f.; 6:56.
30. *Works* 7:5f.
31. *Works* 7:355, 358f.
32. *Works* 7:289 (1789).
33. *Works* 7:10ff.; 8:176.
34. *Works* 6:256.
35. *Works* 13:260.
36. *Sermons* 1:483.
37. *Works* 13:260.
38. *Sermons* 1:473; 2:324f.
39. "The Use of Money," *Sermons* 2:316ff.
40. In this context Wesley dealt briefly with the relationship of physical constitution and health on the one hand and the dangers caused by unhealthy working conditions on the other hand: *Sermons* 2:315-18.
41. *Sermons* 2:317.
42. *Works* 7:123f.
43. A list is found in M. Edwards, *After Wesley: A Study of the Social and Political Influence of Methodism in the Middle Period (1791-1849)* (London, 1948), 137. Cf. *Works* 7:35.
44. Wesley voiced clear criticism not only against the pride of the wealthy but also against an unjustified pride of office on the part of his clerical colleagues; see e.g., *Works* 8:174ff.; *Sermons* 2:321; 1:484.
45. *Sermons* 1:484.
46. *Works* 7:10, 12, 84f., 216; *Sermons* 1:473.
47. *Sermons* 2:320.
48. On Luther, see, among others, W. Elert, *Morphologie des Luthertums*, vol. 2: *Soziallehren und Sozialwirkungen des Luthertums* (Munich, 1932), 495ff.; M. Weber, *The Protestant Ethic and the Spirit of Capitalism*, trans. Talcott Parsons (New York, 1958), 79ff.; F. Lau, "Christentum und Beruf," *RGG* 1:1076-81. The warning against covetousness, which Elert (495) mentions as occurring with special frequency in Lutheranism, is found in Wesley also: negatively expressed in the warning against any accumulation of possessions, and positively in the application of acquisitions to charitable causes.
49. Cameron, 67; G. C. Cell, *The Rediscovery of John Wesley* (New York, 1935), 373, 377; R. M. Kingdon, "Laissez-faire or Government Control: a Problem for John Wesley," *Church History* 26 (1957):343; Marlowe, 45; Walsh, *HMC*, 310.

50. In the context of our present work we must limit ourselves to this specific topic and thus must bracket out Methodism in England since the beginning of the nineteenth century and all Methodism outside Britain. Unfortunately, Weber, insofar as he concerns himself in his studies with Methodist positions, as a rule refers to later American Methodism, which had already advanced beyond its English origins and had taken different positions, precisely in economic issues.

51. He notes in his journal in September 1763 concerning some "brethren" that they are in great danger that "as they are industrious and frugal, they must needs increase in goods. This appears already. In London, Bristol, and most other trading towns, those who are in business have increased in substance sevenfold, some of them twenty, yea, an hundredfold" (*Journal* 5:30f.).

52. *Works* 7:250, 289f.; 7:176; *Journal* 5:82f.

53. The author is fully aware that concepts such as "capitalism" and "socialism," which first acquired their imprint in the nineteenth century, are to be used here only with caution. Nevertheless, for two reasons it was impossible to refrain from using them: (1) They are contained in Weber's assessment of Methodism, and to this extent they are a given for any discussion with Weber's position; (2) The inward attitude that Weber paraphrases in the term "spirit of capitalism" was already at hand before the above-mentioned concepts came to be defined in more precise form.

54. What E. Fischoff says about ascetic Protestantism does not apply to Wesley: the entrepreneur is said to interpret his success as a "visible sign of God's favor" and the manual laborer is said to derive "from his conscientiousness in meeting the standards for his job, along with his readiness to work, the assurance of his religious state of grace." See Fischoff, "Die protestantische Ethik und der Geist des Kapitalismus: Die Geschichte einer Kontroverse," in M. Weber, *Die protestantische Ethik*, ed. J. Winckelmann, 2nd ed., 2 vols. (Munich/Hamburg, 1969), vol. 2: *Kritiken und Antikritiken*, 356f.

   Documentation is not to be found in Wesley for Weber's assertion (*The Protestant Ethik*, 141-42) that works indeed were not the real ground of the state of grace but only the ground of knowledge of the state—this regardless of how much Wesley stressed the necessity of good works as the fruit of faith. In this connection it should only be mentioned that Weber's interpretation of sanctification (140f.) and the assertion that the sacraments were devalued in favor of an assurance of salvation based on feeling (141) do not apply to Wesley. Cf. *Letters* 4:272: "Lose no opportunity of receiving the sacrament!" and especially the high esteem for the Supper which was widespread among the Methodists ever since the time of the Holy Club in Oxford. Cf. also Lindström, 113ff; and Williams, 158ff.

55. "The dangers of prosperity are great; . . . If poverty contracts and depressed the mind, riches sap its fortitude, destroy its vigour, and nourish its caprices" (*Letters* 5:180; cf. 6:56).

56. Vester, 95. Cf. *Works* 7:324.

57. *Journal* 5:101, 82f.; *Works* 7:250, 324; *Letters* 6:288, *et passim.*
58. *Letters* 6:56.
59. Thus MacArthur, 123.
60. Apart from this, with Wesley's Arminian position on the question of predestination, it is impermissible to characterize lack of success as God's punishment or as a sign of reprobation in the sense of a double predestination. Such a characterization is not to be found in Wesley's writings.
61. *Sermons* 2:319f., 324, 477; *Works* 7:10, 123; 13:260f.
62. Madron, 38, comes to a similar conclusion.
63. *Works* 11:59.
64. Adam Smith's major work *An Inquiry into the Nature and Causes of the Wealth of Nations*, in fact had appeared in 1776, but Wesley apparently had not read it. No traces of any such influence are to be found in Wesley (cf. Kingdon, 347). Concerning the general situation in economic and social science in the eighteenth century, it is stated in *NCMH* (8:92f.) that they were still in the "period of preparation rather than of positive achievement," a phase of gathering data.
65. A more precise investigation of his economic views is offered by MacArthur and Kingdon.
66. Edwards, "John Wesley," *HMC*, 57.
67. Cameron, 41; Marlowe, 54.
68. "Thoughts on the Present Scarcity of Provisions." The first version, a letter, is found in *Letters* 5:349-54; the second version, a pamphlet, is found in *Works* 11:53-59.
69. J. W. E. Sommer (25, note 50) has erred in dating the work: the original version, a letter to the publisher of *Lloyd's Evening Post*, was written on December 9, 1772, and was only slightly revised for publication as a pamphlet. Sommer concludes from a journal entry dated January 8, 1773, that this writing had "literally been prepared with prayer and fasting; it bears the date of January 20, 1773." This date refers only to the new edition.
70. *Letters* 5:350; *Works* 11:53f.
71. *Works* 11:57.
72. Madron, 44; MacArthur, 111; Kingdon, 345.
73. Theoreticians in economics whom Wesley had read were, above all, Josiah Tucker and James Stewart; cf. Kingdon, 348f.
74. Kingdon, 350.
75. Under the label "social groups" we include those groups that, on the basis of a particular economic stance, a great measure of economic power, or a special responsibility for economic events, were in a position to exert some influence and were addressed by Wesley. We leave aside official agencies of government, which are treated in the next section.
76. J. Tucker, C. Smith: *Journal* 6:125f.; *WHS* 4:209; Kingdon, 347ff.; *Journal* 6:104.

77. *Journal* 6:104, 180.
78. *Journal* 7:479.
79. *Journal* 6:104.
80. See what was said earlier, pp. 37-39 about the perils of riches.
81. *Works* 11:55ff.
82. *Works* 7:17ff.; 8:162f.
83. Cameron, 27f.; Kluxen, 406ff.
84. On smuggling cf. Cameron, 55f.; Kluxen, 397ff.
85. "A Word to a Smuggler," 1767; *Works* 11:174-78.
86. *Works* 11:174f.
87. Exod. 20:15; Matt. 22:21; Rom. 13:7.
88. Cameron, 56; Edwards, *HMC,* 65; pronouncements against smuggling are found in Wesley's works as early as the 1750s, when he was hardly concerned with other economic issues, and then on into his old age: *Letters* 2:143; 4:107, 272; 6:59, 249, 254, 265, 378; 7:215; *Journal* 4:220, 325, 530.
89. Cf. Flachsmeier, 3ff.; Trevelyan, 314, 341ff.; E. Mertner, *Englische Literaturgeschichte,* (Heidelberg, 1971), 326.
90. *Works* 11:54f., 58.
91. *Letters* 6:161: "I am an High Churchman, the son of an High Churchman, bred up from my childhood in the highest notions of passive obedience and nonresistance." *Letters* 7:305: a Tory is someone who "believes God, not the people, to be the origin of all civil power." In this sense, his father and his older brother had been Tories, and "so am I."
92. *Letters* 5:371ff.
93. Kingdon, 347. There has not been an absolutist phase in Modern English history.
94. *Works* 11:57f.
95. Among other things Wesley cites the prohibition of distilling gin, taxation on the export of horses (the export trade had stimulated the breeding of horses) and on the horses belonging to the nobility, the encouragement of breeding cattle and sheep, and limitations placed on rents (*Works* 11:58).
96. *Works* 11:58f.; cf. *Letters* 5:354.
97. *Works* 11:56f.
98. Kluxen, 481.
99. *Journal* 4:268 (1758): "The mob had been in motion all the day; but their business was only with the forstallers of the market, who had bought up all the corn far and near to starve the poor, and load a Dutch ship, which lay at the quay; but the mob brought it all out into the market, and sold it for the owners at the Common price. And this they did with all the calmness and composure imaginable, and without striking or hurting anyone."
100. *Journal* 8:327, 334; *Letters* 6:159.
101. *Journal* 8:327f.; *Letters* 6:159.
102. In 1770 Edmund Burke, through his "Thought on the Cause of the Present Discontents," laid bare the underlying cause of the widespread dissatisfaction. Cf. Kluxen, 471, 473.

CHAPTER IV
THE EDUCATIONAL AND TRAINING WORK OF
WESLEY AND HIS COLLEAGUES

1. W. H. G. Armytage, *Four Hundred Years of English Education*, 2nd ed. (Cambridge, 1970); A. H. Body, *John Wesley and Education* (London, 1936); J. W. Bready, *England Before and After Wesley*, 3rd ed. (London, 1939); Cameron; G. D. A. Cole and R. Postate, *The Common People, 1746-1946* (Bristol, 1963); Edwards, *John Wesley*; D. S. Hubery, "Unterweisung und Erziehung," in *Der Methodismis*, ed. C. E. Sommmer (Stuttgart, 1968), 252-61; D. L. Marsh, "Methodism and Early Methodist Theological Education," *Methodist History* 1/1 (1963-64):3-13; North; Trevelyan; J. W. Prince, *Wesley on Religious Education: A Study of John Wesley's Theories and Methods of the Education of Children in Religion* (New York/Cincinnati, 1926); Warner; Whiteley.
2. Trevelyan, 363f.; Whiteley, 278.
3. Trevelyan, 76f., 519ff.; Whiteley, 274.
4. Trevelyan, 326, 365, 519; Whiteley, 277; Butterfield, *HMC*, 26.
5. Trevelyan, 326. In some such village schools, the "dames" still did not teach reading and writing but only practical skills. Cf. Whiteley, 287f.
6. Until the last third of the nineteenth century this work continued to be left almost entirely to such charitable organizations. After a financial subsidy by the government which began in 1833, it was not until 1870 that a law was enacted guaranteeing an elementary education for all children. Kluxen, 579; Whiteley, 291; Trevelyan, 518.
7. Armytage, 45, tells of more than twenty thousand children who were taught in fifteen years and another ten thousand for whom an apprenticeship had been secured. Another study indicates for the year 1722 that some thirty-two thousand pupils had found a place in 1,400 schools (Whiteley, 286). The main efforts of the SPCK were concentrated on the London area (E. Beyreuther, "Erweckung I," *RGG* 2:621). Gradually, however, the SPCK spread its program to cover all of England, in attempting also to arouse the interest of local authorities and supporters (Trevelyan, 325ff.; Loofs, *RPTK* 12:751).
8. Cole and Postgate, 39.
9. Whiteley, 286. The author even places the beginning of declining interest in the charity schools in the year 1727.
10. Trevelyan, 327, 363f.; Armytage, 53.
11. In many schools rich children even arrived with their own servants and enjoyed a number of other privileges; even the charity schools were concerned to emphasize the necessity of subordination of the lower classes. Trevelyan, 364; Whiteley, 270.

155

12. Body, 40. Even toward the end of the eighteenth century there were still "many misgivings about the dangers of teaching poor people ideas above their station" (Cole and Postgate, 39). The same tendency is shown by Mandeville: "Charity-Schools, and every thing else that promotes Idleness and Keeps the Poor from Working, are more Accessory to the Growth of Villainy, than the want of Reading and Writing, or even the grossest Ignorance and Stupidity" (quoted by Armytage, 47).
13. A detailed description of this is found in Schmidt, *John Wesley* 1:64-90.
14. In his account of "The Condition of the Working-Class in England" in 1844, Friedrich Engels laments the deficiencies in intellectual development "in neglected regions" of the coal-mining districts. "The day schools are not within their reach, the evening and Sunday schools mere shams, the teachers worthless. Hence, few can read, and still fewer write." Engels, *Die Lage der arbeitenden Klasse in England* (Munich, 1932), 250.
15. Kluxen, 579.
16. Warner, 226; Prince, 90. The parallels drawn here between Kingswood School and the contemporary charity schools can be extended also to include other Methodist schools. The instructional projects of individual Methodists also fit into the series of other similarly formed "schools" that had emerged earlier. Cf. chapter IV, section 1.
17. Warner, 226; *Journal* 1.
18. *Journal* 2:183 and note 2: 2:228 and note 1; *Letters* 1:302; Hubery 253. This school for miners' children should not be confused with the boarding school, also established at Kingswood in 1748, for a higher level of instruction.
19. Warner, 227; Edwards, *John Wesley*, 130f.; Body, 77ff. Wesley's detailed report on the Foundery School in London is found within the "Plain Account of the People Called Methodists," *Letters* 2:308ff. On other Methodist schools, cf., inter alia, *Journal* 6:315, 336, 451; 7:331f.; *Letters* 5:153, 181f.; 6:324, 358f.; Body, 146ff.
20. *Letters* 2:309.
21. *Letters* 2:308f.
22. Mary Bosanquet, the later Mrs. Fletcher, whom Wesley so highly esteemed, formulated this self-posed task thus: "We continually impressed on the minds of the children that the only way to be happy was to be like God; to love what he loved, and to hate what he hated" (quoted from North, 100).
23. This is expressed not only in the quotation from Wesley cited above, but also in the care that was devoted to the pupils' participation in religious exercises as well as to the observation of their personal religious development. Cf. *Letters* 2:309; *Journal* 1:359; 6:181; 7:23.
24. Above all, the SPCK and the directors of the foundation (see pp. 50 above). Cf. Whiteley, 268ff.
25. Among the sermons on problems of education, the following are available in written form: "On Family Religion" (*Works* 7:76ff.); "On the Education of Children" (*Works* 7:86ff.); and "On Obedience to Parents" (*Works* 7:98ff.).

Other sermons also refer to this subject, for example *Works* 7:267; *Sermons* 2:322. Notes in his journal about such sermons (*Journal* 4:176; 5:189, 193, 253, 452; 7:99) and an abundance of references testify to Wesley's intense preoccupation with these matters.

26. *Journal* 3:125, 422; 6:334, 482; 7:143, 190, 247, 329, 360.
27. *Journal* 3:125, 357, 424; 4:416; 5:149, 159, 430, 485; 6:181; 7:23; J. S. Simon, *John Wesley and the Advance of Methodism* (London, 1925), 138.
28. *Journal* 1:134; 3:393; 4:157, 416.
29. *Journal* 1:136, 297; 3:530; Whiteley, 279; Body, 99f.
30. *Journal* 3:496ff.; *Works* 13:283f.; *AM* 4:486; Simon, *Advance*, 93.
31. Body, 81.
32. *Journal* 1:467; *Letters* 2:309; 7:361; Prince, 89; Body, 122, 130.
33. *Journal* 2:458; 3:422, 487, 530f.; 4:80; *Letters* 5:123, 137, 165.
34. *Letters* 2:309; *Journal* 3:422, 457, 531; Body, 81, 114.
35. Hubery, 253.
36. *Journal* 4:186, 80; 3:356, note 4; Body, 113f.
37. North, 99; Warner, 227ff.
38. Body (40) rightly characterizes the English Sunday schools that emerged in the second half of the eighteenth century as "chiefly the outcome of the Methodist movement." Simon (*Master Builder*, 267) says that Robert Raikes "commenced his school on the advice and with the assistance of a Methodist lady."
39. Robert Raikes (1735-1811) did not establish his Sunday school in London, as W. Thiel suggests in his article on "Sonntagsschule I. In Europa und Amerika" (*RGG* 6:144f.), nor did his work find "wide distribution in England" only after 1803, as the same article indicates. Cf. Body, 40; Bready, 353f. Armytage, 74, reports 750,000 Sunday school pupils as early as 1795. On July 18, 1784, Wesley noted: "I find these [Sunday] schools springing up wherever I go" (*Journal* 7:3), and on January 12, 1787, he wrote that the Sunday schools "spread wider and wider, and are likely to reach every part of the kingdom" (*Letters* 7:265).
40. Armytage, 74; Bready, 353; Warner, 233.
41. Edwards, *HMC*, 67; North, 105; Thiel, 145; Warner, 234.
42. Bready, 353; North, 103; Thiel, 144; Warner, 233. John Wesley, who had a profound knowledge of church history, wrote about the Sunday schools as "one of the noblest specimens of charity which have been set on foot in England since the time of William the Conqueror" (*Letters* 8:34; cf. 8:208, and Hubery, 254!).
43. *Letters* 7:265, 363f.; 8:23f., 34, 69, 208.
44. The Methodist Conference, the highest governing body of the church, decided in its annual meeting in 1814 that (on the basis of a legalistic interpretation of the commandment to keep the Sabbath day holy) only religious content, not reading and writing, might be included in their congregations' Sunday schools. Nevertheless, a considerable number of Methodist Sunday schools did not obey this prohibition. See Warner, 106, note 2.

45. As an example of the opposition from outside, one may note the attacks in the *Gentleman's Magazine*, which in 1797 accused the Sunday schools of "raising discontent and fomenting rebellion" (Armytage, 74).
46. Payment for the school was not demanded of parents. In contrast to other schools, such as those founded by Raikes, in the Methodist Sunday schools the workers with few exceptions did not receive any pay. *Journal* 7:306, 377, note 1; 8:70; *Letters* 8:24; Warner, 234; North, 106, note 2, 108f.; Edwards, *This Methodism*, 106f; Edwards, *HMC*, 67; Cameron, 64.
47. "I really hope the Sunday Schools will be productive of great good to the nation" (*Letters* 7:265). "It seems to me that these will be one great means of reviving religion throughout the nation" (*Letters* 7:364). Cf. *Letters* 8:23f; *Journal* 7:3, 377 (note 1), 378; Warner, 234.
48. *Journal* 2:323; cf. *Letters* 1:340.
49. *Journal* 3:356, note 4; Body, 72-77.
50. Edwards, *This Methodism*, 107.
51. *Works* 13:296.
52. *Journal* 3:284f.; *Works* 13:297ff. Wesley was by no means alone in his critical reservations with respect to the usual university life: "So the evidence of widely differing men like Swift, Defoe, Gray, Johnson, Eldon, Chesterfield all agree on this point, that both universities (namely, Oxford and Cambridge) were neglectful and inefficient in the performance of their duties" (Whiteley, 269f.).
53. "I cannot say I am yet quite clear of that prejudice. I love the very sight of Oxford; I love the manner of life; I love and esteem many of its institutions. But my prejudice in its favour is considerably abated: I do not admire it as I once did" (*Works* 13:296).
54. *Journal* 5:293, and note 1; *Works* 13:296.
55. *Works* 13:295ff.
56. *Works* 13:287-89.
57. *Journal* 5:117 (1730!).
58. Butterfield, *HMC*, 3; Warner, 230.
59. *Works* 12:261f.; 14:199ff.; *Letters* 8:355f.; Body, 99f.; Edwards, *John Wesley*, 136; Hubery, 255; Marsh, 6f.; Warner, 230f.
60. *Letters* 6:208; 7:219. The value that he ascribed to books can be read from the following comment found in a letter to one of his preachers: "It is true most of the Methodists are poor; but what then? Nine in ten of them would be no poorer if they were to lay out an whole penny in buying a book every other week in the year. By this means the work of God is both widened and deepened in every place" (*Letters* 5:161).
61. Body. 99f.
62. *Letters* 4:83, 272; 5:161; 7:139.
63. G. Gisler, "John Wesley's Tätigkeit und Bedeutung als Arzt," *Schweizer Evangelist* 35 (1928):222, 256; Hill, 117.
64. The preliminary labors date back in his Georgia period; *Journal* 1:425; 3:391, note 3.

65. *Letters* 2:151. In a later letter of December 12, 1760, he cited as a motive for the publication of the Christian Library the wish "to assist those who desire to live according to the gospel" (*Letters* 4:121).
66. *Journal* 4:48, 91; *Letters* 2:152; *Works* 14:222.
67. *Works* 10:381ff., 418ff. 13:389f. It is true that through either negligence of the typesetter or Wesley's haste in working through the material, some one hundred pages were left standing, contrary to his intention (*Works* 10:418f.) and were thus taken along with other passages as Wesley's own affirmations, which brought down upon him many attacks. His tolerance appeared to many to be unbelievable.
68. *Works* 14:222.
69. Cf. Gerdes, 13.
70. *Journal* 4:94; *Works* 13:314; *Letters* 4:208; 7:144, 294; Edwards, *John Wesley*, 136; Edwards, *HMC*, 67; J. Orcibal, *HMC*, 93; F. Sigg, "John Wesley und 'Die Christliche Bibliothek': Einblicke in die verlegerische Tätigkeit des Methodismus im 18. Jahrhundert," *Schweizer Evangelist* 60 (1953):381-85.
71. *AM* 1 (1778):iv-vi (John Wesley's Preface "To the Reader").
72. *Letters* 3:153; 6:9; 7:49, 138, 143; *Works* 13:254; establishment of a book committee: *Journal* 7:441; Armytage, 52; Warner, 230.
73. *Letters* 6:208; 7:144, 219; *Journal* 4:94. Books were to be taken along also on visits to homes (*Works* 8:315). In 1782 a society was formed for the dissemination of religious writings among the poor: Warner, 232. We are not able to determine to what extent the colportage service directed by the S.P.C.K. prompted Wesley in this. Cf. Armytage, 51.
74. "You must not give an exhortation to the bands, but encourage them to speak" (*Letters* 7:94).
75. "Every one here has an equal liberty of speaking, there being none greater or less than another" (*Works* 8:261).
76. Cameron, 39; Hubery, 254; Warner, 230.
77. J. Telford declares that "no man in the eighteenth century did so much to create a taste for good reading, and to supply it with books at the lowest price" (*Encyclopedia Britannica*, 11th ed., 28:530). ". . . one is partly inclined to forget his defects [i.e., in Wesley's views of education] in remembering the tremendous impulse he gave to popular education. No one in Georgian England did more than Wesley to foster its growth" (Edwards, *John Wesley*, 135). Cf. Armytage, 52; Body, 55; Warner, 232.
78. Wesley to one who reads nothing but the Bible: "Then you ought to teach others to read only the Bible, and, by parity of reason, to hear only the Bible: But if so, you need to preach no more. . . . This is rank enthusiasm. If you need no book but the Bible, you are got above St. Paul. He wanted others too" (*Works* 8:315).
79. *Works* 8:315.
80. *Letters* 5:359f.; 7:82, 228; *Works* 7:35, 315, 319; 12:261f.; Edwards, *HMC*, 67; Hubery, 255; Warner, 230f.
81. For more particulars, see section 3 of this chapter. This view has little to do

with the utilitarianism of Bentham, Adam Smith, and John Stuart Mill, though it probably has some connection with the sober strictness of Puritanism, which had influenced Wesley since his early youth.

82. His comments about *Emile*, which he had read with great expectations: "But how was I disappointed! Surely a more consummate coxcomb never saw the sun! ... he is a mere misanthrope; a cynic all over" (*Journal* 5:352f.). "... the most empty, silly, injudicious thing, that ever a self-conceited infidel wrote. But I knew it was quite contrary to the judgment of the wisest and best men I have known" (*AM* 6 (1783):380). "Such discoveries I always expect from those who are too wise to believe their Bibles" (*Journal* 5:353; cf. *Journal* 6:23).

It can hardly be determined to what extent Wesley, who greatly esteemed Samuel Johnson, was affected here by the latter (whose influence also brought about the fateful change in Wesley's attitude toward the American independence movement). Johnson said of Rousseau: "He always appeared to me a bad man. That he was mad I never doubted" (*Journal* 6:23, note 1). Cf. *Journal* 5:352, note 2; and Body, 19.

83. Cf. the extensive correspondence: *Letters* 1:4-249; 8:268f., and 6:47; *Journal* 5:189-253; Edwards, *John Wesley*, 129f.

84. *Journal* 1:116, 121, 124, 301-3, 307; 2:16f.; 3:347; Schmidt, *John Wesley* 2/2:179ff.; Cameron, 63.

85. *Letters* 2:314; 7:82, 228; *Journal* 4:192; *Works* 13:455ff.; Body, 34, 43; Edwards, *John Wesley*, 129.

86. Body, 40; Whiteley, 268: "Eighteenth-century poor parents were quite untroubled about their children's education; they looked upon their offspring as possible wage-earners from the age of four. Wealthier parents then looked upon infancy and adolescence as a kind of mental, moral and physical disease rendering the victims unfit occupants of a civilized home."

87. *Works* 7:79f.; *Journal* 5:285; *Letters* 7:115, 127, 143; 6:362.

88. Vester, 95f., is far too simplistic in his sweeping accusations.

89. *Letters* 5:110; *Journal* 6:329, 347; 5:463, note 1.

90. *AM* 4:382f.; *Works* 13:476f.

91. Original sin is indeed washed away by baptism, but the corrupt nature is not at the same time cured. *Works* 10:193; 13476; 7:87.

92. Wesley also shared this view with Luther: "When Luther . . . holds it to be necessary that 'the child's own will be consistently broken,' this appears, when measured by the educational ideals of the Enlightenment's classicists in pedagogy, to be irrational and barbaric. But by the term 'own will' Luther means the opposite of sensitivity to others. . . . The child's self-will that resists the authority of the parents is the preliminary stage to the anti-social attitude of the adult, and therefore it must be subjugated by skillful, or in extreme cases, even by strict discipline" (Elert, 97).

93. Apart from the consequence that follows for him in this direction from his point of departure, Wesley consistently followed the strict rules of

contemporary pedagogy (Whiteley, 293; Edwards, *John Wesley*, 132) and the counsel of his mother, who had written to him: "The first thing with children is to conquer their wills, and to bring them to an obedient temper" (quoted from Edwards, *John Wesley*, 129f. Cf. *Works* 7:103). Edwards (*John Wesley*, 133f.) expressed the view that "It would be wrong, however, to suppose that he was narrower in his views and more repressive in his system than contemporary educationalists."

94. *Works* 7:87.
95. *Works* 7:88; *Journal* 6:73, 329.
96. *Works* 7:88, 90.
97. *Journal* 3:422; 4:80; 5:149, 159, 430; 6:334, 437.
98. *Journal* 5:353; *Works* 7:271.
99. Whiteley (273) puts it pointedly: "The two men were poles apart; the one based his educational system on what he thought the child-mind was like, whilst Wesley based his practice on what the child-mind ought to be like."
100. *Journal* 5:159.
101. *Works* 7:93f.
102. Cf. articles 9 and 11 of the Thirty-nine Articles; *Works* 10:190, 193; Weissbach, 48.
103. "But it is equally true that 'by the righteousness of one, the free gift came upon all men' (all born into the world, infant or adult), 'unto justification.' Therefore no infant ever was or ever will be 'sent to hell for the guilt of Adam's sin,' seeing it is cancelled by the righteousness of Christ as soon as they are sent into the world" (*Letters* 6:239f.).
104. *Journal* 5:352f.; *Works* 7:80, 98; *Letters* 5:110: ". . . an ounce of love is worth a pound of knowledge." Edwards, *John Wesley*, 137f.; Edwards, *After Wesley*, 102; F. C. Gill, *The Romantic Movement and Methodism: A Study of English Romanticism and the Evangelical Revival* (London, 1937), 46f.
105. Playing was strictly forbidden; instead of play, there was garden work or walking. Holidays were not observed. The children were under constant supervision. Instruction and religious services claimed most of the time during the day. *Journal* 3:530; *Letters* 2:309; *Works* 13284f.; Body, 88, 92f.; Whiteley, 278-80.

   The parallels to the strict discipline of the German Pietist institutions—such as the orphanage in Halle (*Journal* 2:17 and note 1) and the school of J. E. Stolte in Jena (*Journal* 2:58-61; Schmidt, *John Wesley*, 2/2:180ff.)—which strongly influenced Wesley will be immediately evident to the informed observer; Wesley regarded his theory of education as confirmed and strengthened by their example. *AM* 4:434f.; North, 100.
106. *Works* 7:95-97.
107. *Letters* 2:309; *Journal* 5:485; 6:102; *Works* 7:81f.
108. An especially splendid example of how this could happen is found in his sermon, "The Unity of the Divine Being" (*Works* 7:266f.): "He made all things to be happy. He made man to be happy in Himself." Therefore Augustine was right when he said, "Fecisti nos ad te it irrequietum est cor

nostrum, donec requiescat in te." Wesley continued: "Now, is not this the very principle that should be inculcated upon every human creature . . . as soon as ever reason dawns?" In the light and warmth of the sun, and with other similar examples, it should be said repeatedly to even the little children: "He made you; and he made you to be happy in him; and nothing else can make you happy."

109. *Works* 7:267.
110. *Journal* 1:359; 2:540; 6:102, 273; 7:68, 352.
111. On this point, of course, Wesley was only a man of his century. To what extent a lifelong mother fixation determined his pedagogical principles perhaps would deserve a thoroughgoing expert investigation.
112. On this cf. Whiteley, 23f., 63-69.
113. Schmidt provided particulars on this in the second volume of his *John Wesley* (2/2:122ff.). Cf. also Davies, 70f.; Body, 30; Ronald Knox, *Enthusiasm: A Chapter in the History of Religion with Special Reference to the 17th and 18th Centuries* (Oxford, 1950).
114. A thoroughgoing analysis is to be found in Body, 125ff. Cf. *Journal* 3:150, 236f., 244, 266, 474f.; 4:27, 110f., 270, 279f., 311; 5:49f., 371.
115. For example, Kluxen, 526f.
116. *Journal* 3:540; 5:258f., 389ff.; 6:4, 273; 7:68, 377f.
117. *Journal* 3:244; 6:39; *Works* 13:354f.
118. *Journal* 3:244.
119. *Letters* 2:314; 7:82, 288; *Journal* 5:89, note 2; *Works* 13:455ff. He defended Aristotle against Locke (*Works* 13:456, 460) and corrected many specific statements of Locke, especially those concerning the personal identity of man, which according to Locke only emerges through consciousness but according to Wesley is already given before and is independent of consciousness (358). It is characteristic that Locke's "Some Thoughts concerning Education," which influenced Rousseau, found no acceptance in Wesley's pedagogy.
120. *Works* 6:337ff.; 7:89.
121. *Works* 7:88f.; 6:338ff.
122. *Works* 13:456.
123. *Works* 6:337.
124. *Works* 7:81ff.; 13:283f., 289ff.; 7:337.; *Letters* 4:247; 5:359f.
125. Schmidt's assertion that the instruction in Kingswood ". . . conformed to the educational standards generally accepted in Britain at the time" (*John Wesley* 2/2:183) therefore is only conditionally correct. Cf. Hubery, 255; Body, 141f.
126. In the context of the present work it is not possible to discuss other influences of lesser effect, such as those of Milton, Comenius, Fleury, and Poiret.
127. *Works* 7:459.
128. The motto for Kingswood that John Wesley sought out reads: "In gloriam Dei Optimi Maximi in usum Ecclesiae et Rei Publicae." Charles Wesley cast

it in poetic form on the occasion of the opening of the first school in Kingswood: "Unite the pair so long disjoined, Knowledge and Vital piety; Learning and Holiness combined, And truth and Love. . . ." (quoted by Body, 89, and Simon, *Advance*, 93).

129. *Works* 7:127; *Letters* 1:339; 2:309; *AM* 6:381f.; Body, 47; Schmidt, *John Wesley*, 2/2:182; Prince, 87.

CHAPTER V
JOHN WESLEY'S BATTLE AGAINST SLAVERY

1. R. Pfaff-Giesberg, *Geschichte der Sklaverei* (Meisenheim/Glan, 1955), 69f.
2. Lean, 128f.; Kluxen, 388ff.; Pfaff-Giesberg, 70f.
3. Kluxen, 397; Lean, 129.
4. Lean, 129. Cf. Trevelyan, 388f.
5. Up until 1778, fourteen to fifteen thousand (O. Sherwin, *John Wesley, Friend of the People* (New York, 1961), 172.
6. Kluxen, 466, 529.
7. The distinction between slaveholding and the slave trade is understandable because the protest was first directed against the latter and its accompanying cruelties, and only later against slavery as such.
8. William Warburton (1698-1779), from 1759 onward Bishop of Gloucester.
9. Quoted by Cameron, 94, note 33.
10. Cf. G. Bornkamm, *Paul*, trans. D. M. Stalker (New York, 1971), 196ff.; H. Conzelmann, *Commentary on First Corinthians*, trans. James W. Leitch, *Hermeneia* series (Philadelphia, 1975), 225-26; S. Schulz, *Gott ist kein Sklavenhalter: Die Geschichte einer verspäteten Revolution* (Hamburg/Zürich, 1972), 159ff., esp. 184, 190.
11. Schrage, 84.
12. Schulz, 189; A. Lotz, *Sklaverei, Staatskirche und Freikirche. Die englischen Bekenntnisse um Kampf und die Aufhebung von Sklavenhandel und Sklaverei*, vol. 10 of *Kölner Anglistische Arbeiten* (Leipzig, 1929), 85; Whiteley, 28; Cameron, 94.
13. See page 69 above, note 9, quote in text.
14. Whiteley, 28; Lotz, 23; Cameron, 94; Edwards, *John Wesley*, 115.
15. Edwards, *After Wesley*, 63; Warner, 41f.; H. D. Wendland, "Sklaverei und Christentum," *RGG* 6:103; Cameron, 95.
16. These exceptions were—besides the already mentioned Anglican Bishop Warburton—above all, Richard Baxter and some other clergymen (Edwards, *John Wesley*, 113ff.), as well as the governor of the Georgia colony, General Oglethorpe, who was important for an earlier influence on Wesley (Warner, 41).
17. Edwards, *John Wesley*, 113; Warner, 42; Nicolson, 254f.; Cameron, 95.
18. *Journal* 1:181, note 2.

19. *Journal* 1:181, note 2; 260.
20. *Journal* 1:244, note 1.
21. Warner, 41.
22. Lotz, 23.
23. *Journal* 1:350f., 352f., 413, 415.
24. *Journal* 2:362; 4:125, 149f., 194f.
25. *Journal* 3:247f.; 4:292; 6:277f.; 7:144.
26. *Journal* 4:149f., 292; 7:144.
27. Simon, *Master-Builder*, 44, 261.
28. *Journal* 1:350f., 415; 3:247f.; 4:292; 6:277f. Cf. his later remark on the possibility of a successful missionary work among the "Indians": "I am throughly persuaded that true, genuine religion is capable of working all those happy effects which are said to be wrought there; and that, in the most ignorant and savage of the human kind." *Letters* 5:121.
29. *Journal* 4:292.
30. We do not hear of a protest when Wesley baptized a slave owner and two slaves in 1760 (Warner, 240).
31. Warner, 43.
32. Quoted in Cameron, 97. Cf. Warner, 245; Wendland, "Sklaverei und Christentum," *RGG* 6:103; T. W. Madron, "John Wesley on Race: A Christian View of Equality," *Methodist History* 2/4 (1963-64):26.
33. Cameron, 97f., 99; Schulz, 230; Warner, 244; Madron, "John Wesley on Slavery," 26; Lotz, 32.
34. Schulz, 231f.
35. Cameron, 97, 99f.; Schulz, 233; Warner, 245. Whitefield, Wesley's close co-worker in earlier years, condemned cruelties against slaves, but he himself was a slave owner. He pleaded for the establishment of slavery in Georgia and left at his death fifty slaves of his own (Warner, 240; Lotz, 32; Sherwin, 171f.).
36. Kluxen, 466.
37. *Works* 11:59-79.
38. A. Bezenet (1713-1784) descended from a rich Huguenot family. He received his education in London, joined the Quakers and emigrated with his parents to America where he worked as a teacher and wrote books about pedagogical questions. Between 1762 and 1771, he wrote three works against slavery. (*Journal* 5:445f., note 5; Edwards, *After Wesley*, 64; Edwards, *HMC*, 65.)
39. Later writings of other authors of the anti-slavery movement likewise tried "to set into the best light the negro, his character, and his cultural situation and to remove the prejudice which regards the negro hardly as a human being" (Lotz, 19f. Cf. Schmidt, *John Wesley* 2/2:113-14).
40. *Letters* 7:225.
41. The summary of this paragraph reads as follows: "Upon the whole,

therefore, the Negroes who inhabit the coast of Africa . . . are so far from being the stupid, senseless, brutish, lazy barbarians, the fierce, cruel perfidious savages they have been described, that on the contrary, they are represented, by them who have no motive to flatter them, as remarkably sensible, considering the few advantages they have for improving their understanding; as industrious to the highest degree, perhaps more than any other natives of so warm a climate; as fair, just, and honest in all their dealings, unless, where white men have taught them to be other wise; and as far more mild, friendly, and kind to strangers, than any of our forefathers were" (*Works* 11:64f.).

42. *Works* 11:68.
43. *Works* 11:69.
44. Part IV in Wesley's division.
45. "I would now inquire, whether these things can be defended, on the principles of even heathen honestry, whether they can be reconciled (setting the Bible out of the question) with any degree of either justice or mercy" (*Works* 11:70).
46. Ernst Wolf, "Naturrecht II. Christliches Naturrecht," *RGG* 4:1363.
47. "Not-withstanding ten thousand laws, right is right, and wrong is wrong still" (*Works* 11:70).
48. Lotz, 25.
49. *Works* 11:74.
50. It is noteworthy that the "Golden Rule," frequently quoted in other anti-slavery publications (see the resolution of the American Methodist Conference in Schulz, 229), is here not used by Wesley, though he uses it widely in other places. It is likely that Wesley holds that the "Golden Rule," like biblical directions, is too little binding for the debate that is to be conducted here with the supporters of slavery, or Wesley is aware of the fact that the Bible yields unequivocal references for preserving slavery and that the ambivalence is bypassed most easily by avoiding biblicist argumentation.
51. *Letters* 6:126f.; 7:201.
52. Even in Bristol, the main slavery market in England, he was not afraid to preach against slavery (*Journal* 7:359f.).
53. *Journal* 7:360.
54. *Journal* 7:471; *Letters* 8:6f., 23, 265, 275f.; *AM* 11 (1788):208f.; Madron, "John Wesley on Slavery," 24ff.; Kluxen, 528f.
55. *Letters* 8:7, 265, 276.
56. Warner, 244f.; Cameron, 96.
57. *Letters* 8:275.
58. However, for the sake of historical accuracy, one should not speak of Wesley as "the pioneer of this movement," as Schneeberger does (156); Edwards (*HMC*, 65) says only "a pioneer"!

CHAPTER VI
CONCERN FOR PRISONERS AND PRISON REFORM

1. See above pp. 24. *Letters* 1:65, 125ff.; J. L. Nuelsen, *Geschichte des Methodismus,* 29f.; Simon, *Advance,* 65; Simon, *Master-Builder,* 92f.; Schmidt, *John Wesley* 1:99; Telford, *The Life of John Wesley* (London, 1899), 60.

2. General Oglethorpe, by means of a parliamentary investigation that was arranged already in 1729, called the attention of the general public to the scandalous conditions in the prisons for debtors, and he took along many debtors and impoverished people into the Georgia colony that was founded and governed by him.

3. Kluxen, 376f.; Trevelyan, 350f.

4. Trevelyan, 348; Nicolson, 369, lists 253 types of "capital crimes"; Mertner, 326, says "about 200 types."

5. Nicolson, 368f. Cf. Bready, 127; Lean, 130f; Simon, *Advance,* 66.

6. Wearmouth, 131.

7. Wearmouth, 100ff., gives for the years 1764 to 1789 some figures for sentences of death. In 1764, i.e. about 42 sentences of death were pronounced in Old Bailey and about 160 of these sentences were pronounced by the County Assizes. Taken together, in 1785, nearly 500 death sentences were pronounced, a number of which were changed to deportations.

8. Trevelyan, 349. Places for spectators for such "Hanging Shows" were even offered for money in Tyburn (London) (Brady, 127).

9. Even John's father Samuel Wesley, vicar in Epworth and an industrious man, had to spend some months in prison because of debts.

10. Trevelyan, 348.

11. Wearmouth, 112, 132.

12. Trevelyan, 348; Whiteley, 29; Kluxen, 258, 608f.

13. Wearmouth, 163; Whiteley, 29.

14. Wearmouth, 166.

15. Bready, 132.

16. Trevelyan, 348.

17. *Appeal of the Bishops, State Papers, George II, Domestic,* 36:153, quoted in Wearmouth, 97.

18. Kluxen, 375.

19. Wesley describes a great number of that kind of alarming breaches of the law (i.e. *Journal* 3:98-104, 117-119, 409-414). Wearmouth characterizes the attitude that was shown frequently by the justice as follows: "The quiescence, not to say indifference and unconcern, of the local magistrates in regard to the disturbances contrasted suspiciously with the judicial vengeance, including death sentences, inflicted on those accused of offences much less serious in degree and extent. And the contrast with the energetic

action taken by magistrates to suppress mob agitations for increases in wages is cynically remarkable. One law for the poor, another for the rich: it was more than that; if the poor in mob fashion sought to sweep the Methodists and their homes and hearths and businesses away, smashing down everything, then the destructive passion was welcomed tacitly, it would seem, but if the masses agitated angrily and openly for social, economic betterment, then so-called laws were used like a slave-driver's whip" (Wearmouth, 163).

20. Trevelyan, 346.
21. Bready, 367, 132; Trevelyan, 346; K. H. Voigt, "Aus der Geschichte der Gefängnisreform in England," in *Der Methodismus*, ed. C. E. Sommer, 376; Wearmouth, 132.
22. Bready, 367.
23. When in 1750 at a trial before Old Bailey judges, the jury, attorneys and some spectators caught such a sickness, the prisons were cleansed and equipped with fans. A more far-reaching reform did not occur (Simon, *Advance*, 132).
24. Trevelyan, 346, note 3.
25. *Letters* 1:294, 303; *Journal* 2:100, 174ff., 184ff., 336.
26. *Journal* 4:478; 6:79; 2:521, 340f.; 3:29.
27. *Journal* 2:188, 200.
28. *Journal* 2:340f.
29. *Journal* 2:377f. Cf. *Journal* 2:521, 440.
30. *Journal* 7:230.
31. Interpretation of the Gospel of John in several sermons (*Journal* 2:173); sermon about "The Friend of Sinners" (*Journal* 3:43); about the criminal at the cross (*Journal* 5:239); about the joy in heaven over the one sinner who repents (*Journal* 7:41); he offers them "free salvation" (*Journal* 2:70f.).
32. *Works* 8:271; Warner, 237.
33. *Journal* 3:382ff.; 7:230; *Letters* 8:13f.; Simon, *Advance*, 65; Voigt, 378.
34. *Journal* 4:75, 355f., 417; *Letters* 4:78, 84; *Journal* 6:250, 256, 453.
35. *Journal* 4:355f.; *Letters* 4:73f, 84.
36. *Journal* 2:173, note 1. Dagge had looked in an examplary way after the imprisoned poet Savage who was a prisoner in Newgate because of debts. (Cf. *Letters* 4:127f.)
37. *Journal* 4:416f.
38. Voigt, 378; Warner, 237.
39. Warner, 236.
40. Voigt, 374ff., gives some information about that silence and its reasons.
41. *Letters* 4:127; *Works* 8:173.
42. *Works* 8:173 (1745).
43. *Works* 8:173.
44. *Works* 8:166f.
45. *Works* 8:165.
46. *Works* 8:166f.

47. *Journal* 4:355f., 417; 6:256; *Letters* 4:78.
48. Exod. 23:9, KJV; *Journal* 4:355f.
49. *Journal* 4:356 and note 1; 5:256; *Letters* 4:73f., 78, 84.
50. *Letters* 4:74. The possessive pronoun is applied to the helpers.
51. "And how much more noble a satisfaction must result from this to the generous benefactor (even supposing there were no other world, supposing man to die as a beast dieth) than he could receive from an embroidered suit of clothes or a piece of plate made in the newest fashion! Men of reason, judge!" *Letters* 4:84.
52. Cf. Warner, 238. More about Howard in Bready, 130ff, 365ff.
53. "I visited one in the Marshalsea Prison—a nursery of all manner of wickedness. Oh shame to man that there should be such a place, such a picture of hell upon earth! And shame to those who bear the name of Christ that there should need any prison at all in Christendom!" *(Journal* 4:52). The nation is here taken by its claim to be a Christian one.

PART B
THE PRINCIPLES OF WESLEY'S SOCIAL ETHICS

CHAPTER VII
PRESUPPOSITIONS OF WESLEY'S SOCIAL ETHICS

1. See Introduction.
2. Comprehensive expositions of Wesley's dogmatics and examinations of single theological fields, exist, as the bibliography shows, in sufficient number, so that for those who look for further reading information there is fitting material available.
3. Cf. chapter IV.
4. *Sermons* 1:37f.
5. *Works* 7:337 (for Jer. 17:9), Sermon 123, "The Deceitfulness of Man's Heart."
6. *Works* 7:337.
7. For Wesley's doctrine of the *imago Dei*, cf. Warner, 61ff.; Lindström, 24ff.; Williams, 48ff.; and Weissbach, 4ff.
8. *Sermons* 1:143. Infant baptism is necessary, too, because of the depravity and the sinfulness of all men that already are existing ahead of each actual sin *(Works* 10:190, 193ff.).
9. Wesley, *Primitive Physic: or, An Easy and Natural Method of Curing Most Diseases*, ed. A. Hill (London, 1960), 23.
10. *Works* 7:89f.
11. *Works* 6:412.

12. Schmidt, *John Wesley* 2/1:60, pointed already to the fact that Wesley, of course frightened by the quietism of the Moravians, had misunderstood Luther's doctrine of grace, but Schmidt also pointed to the fact that Wesley was on Luther's side in his concern for the irrefutability and the inseparability of justification and sanctification (184). In chapter VII, section 2, we will deal in more detail with the subject of *gratia iustificans et salvificans*.
13. *Sermons* 2:222f.; *Works* 7:338f.; 4:286.
14. *Works* 7:352f.; 271.
15. "Such is the freedom of his will; free only to evil" (*Sermons* 1:188).
16. Cf. *Survey* 1:90ff.; 2:218f.; *Works* 7:350.
17. *Sermons* 1:343f.; 54f.
18. *Works* 7:353; cf. *Sermons* 1:123.
19. *Works* 8:361.
20. *Sermons* 1:308.
21. *Sermons* 1:124.
22. *Works* 7:89.
23. Cf. *Works* 7:338.
24. *Letters* 1:46.
25. Cf. Eph. 5:14; I Thess. 5:6; Rom. 13:11.
26. *Sermons* 1:181 (sermon 9, *The Spirit of Bondage and of Adoption*).
27. "Our Senses are the only Source of those Ideas upon which all our knowledge is founded. Without Ideas of some Sort or other we could have no knowledge, and without our Senses we could have no Ideas" (*Survey* 2:204).
28. *Sermons* 1:182. (Cf. Heb. 12:14; Col. 3:3.) The possibility of a natural knowledge of God *via negationis*, of which Wesley gives hint in his *Compendium of Natural Philosophy* (*Survey*, 2:206f.), cannot be examined closer here. This subject will be treated briefly in the next section in chapter VII. However, a comprehensive discussion of Wesley's doctrine of God would be, in our eyes, an ingenious enterprise.
29. *Sermons* 1:182f.
30. *Sermons* 1:185.
31. Cf. Rom. 6:15; I Pet. 2:16.
32. Minutes of August 2, 1745, *Works* 8:283. Wesley here obviously rejects the position of the Moravians.
33. Wesley writes (following Fletcher's *Checks to Antinomianism*): ". . . by the righteousness of one, the free gift came upon all men (all born into the world, infant or adult) 'unto justification.' Therefore no infant ever was or ever will be 'sent to hell for the guilt of Adam's sin,' seeing it is cancelled by the righteousness of Christ as soon as they are sent into the world" (*Letters* 6:239f.). I have attempted to give more details about this problem in my essay "John Wesley's 'Synergismus'" in *Die Einheit der Kirche: Dimension ihrer Heiligkeit, Katholizität und Apostolizität. Festgabe Peter Meinhold zum 70. Geburtstag*, ed. L. Hein (Wiesbaden, 1977), 96-102.

34. *Works* 7:338.
35. *Works* 7:345.
36. Whether this is a direct allusion to Flacius' *truncus et lapis* is not recognizable; but it is likely that Moravian views have supplied the background material against which Wesley is polemicizing.
37. *Works* 7:345.
38. *Works* 7:345.
39. *Survey* 1:91. *Sermons* 1:55: The "heathen honesty" teaches man "that they ought not to be unjust; not to take away their neighbour's goods, either by robbery or theft; not to oppress the poor, neither to use extortion toward any; not to cheat or overreach either the poor or rich, in whatsoever commerce they had with them; to defraud no man of his right; and, if it were possible, to owe no man anything."
40. "It is far better to leave them to Him that made them . . . who is the God of the Heathens as well as the Christians, and who hateth nothing that he has made" (*Works* 7:353).
41. Ibid.
42. ". . . No man living is without some preventing grace" (*Letters* 6:239).
43. E. von Eicken, "Rechtfertigung und Heiligung bei Wesley, dargestellt unter Vergleichung mit den Anschauungen Luthers und des Luthertums" (Ph.D. diss., Heidelberg, 1934), 14.
44. "Men usually feel desires to please God before they know how to please him" (*Letters* 4:348).
45. ". . . there may be a degree of long suffering, of gentleness, of fidelity, meekness, temperance (not a shadow thereof, but a real degree by the preventing grace of God), before we 'are accepted in the Beloved'. . . ." (*Sermons* 2:359; Cf. *Works* 6:415).
46. *Works* 7:345 (Sermon 124, 1790).
47. ". . . there is no man in a state of mere nature . . . that is wholly void of the grace of God" (*Works* 6:512; 9:273).
48. *Survey* 2:229.
49. *Works* 6:509. A great degree of self-knowledge brings "convincing grace," which is according to its effects nothing but an intensified "preventing grace," which is usually not distinguished from "preventing grace."
50. ". . . the first wish to please God, the first dawn of light concerning his will, and the first slight transient conviction of having sinned against him" (*Works* 6:509).
51. *Works* 8:6f.
52. *Works* 8:7.
53. *Sermons* 1:222f.
54. *Sermons* 1:224. Cf. *Works* 7:187ff.
55. Cf. *Sermons* 2:445: ". . . 'natural conscience', but more properly, 'preventing grace'; all the drawings of the Father. . . all the convictions which His Spirit,

from time to time, works in every child of man. . . ." In order to emphasize the gift-characteristic of the conscience Wesley sometimes even explicitly insists that preventing grace is the author of natural conscience (*Works* 7:188, against F. Hutcheson).

56. ". . . occasioning a degree of complacency in him that does well, and a degree of uneasiness in him that does evil" (*Works* 7:188).

57. *Works* 7:188f.

58. *Works* 7:190.

59. *Works* 7:191f. Thus A. Outler's assertion ("Theologische Akzente," in *Der Methodismus*, ed. C. E. Sommer, 95) that "The *imago Dei* stays and with it stay conscience, reason and freedom as inalienable human properties" is not quite correct.

60. ". . . Wherefore we have no power to do good works, pleasant and acceptable to God, without the grace of God by Christ preventing us, that we may have a good-will, and working with us when we have the good-will" (*Works* 8:53). See the text of Article 10 in *Creeds* 3:493-94. Cf. *The Augsburg Confession*, Article 18, *Creeds* 3:18-19.

61. "Natural freewill, in the present state of mankind, I do not understand: I only assert, that there is a measure of freewill supernaturally restored to every man. . . ." (*Works* 10:229f.).

62. More details about the freedom of the will in Wesley's view in Gerdes, 154ff.

63. "But these I cannot as yet term good works because they do not spring from faith and the love of God" (*Works* 8:47).

64. *Works* 7:353.

65. *Works* 6:511. Cf. Phil. 2:12f.

66. More details about the problem of synergism in Weissbach, 70ff., and in the author's essay mentioned above in note 33.

67. E.g., *Sermons* 1:159; cf. *Works* 8:47; 6:510.

68. *Sermons* 2:359.

69. For this reason, L. M. Starkey's remark in *The Work of the Holy Spirit: A Study in Wesleyan Theology* (New York/Nashville, 1962), 41, that prevenient grace is "redemptive grace in its eventual purpose" is at least ambiguous and his conclusion that "The possibility of an extrascriptural redemption is implicit in several of these Wesleyan statements" (43) is, in spite of the cited quotations, incorrect.

70. Prevenient grace thus gives Wesley not merely "the possibility to be thankfully glad about all the good which he sees in those who dissent and even in heathen" (Eicken, 16).

71. Among the more recent works in German (translation) are Lindström, 55ff.; Schmidt, *John Wesley* 1:231ff.; Weissbach, 98ff.; Williams, 58ff.

72. ". . . the Spirit of the Almighty . . . breaks the hardness of his heart, and creates all things new" (*Works* 7:351). Cf. *Sermons* 1:186f.

73. "To be renewed in the image of God, in righteousness and true holiness" (*Works* 8:279). For the renewal of the *imago Dei* cf. Weissbach, 92ff.
74. The total renewal of the *imago Dei*, a renewal which cannot be completely reached during this earthly life, is hampered by the depraved instrument of man's soul, body, and spirit (*Works* 7:346f.).
75. *Works* 7:346.
76. "All experience, as well as Scripture, show this salvation to be both instantaneous and gradual. It begins at the moment we are justified. . . . It gradually increases from the moment . . . till, in another instant, the heart is cleansed from all sin, and filled with pure love to God and man. But even that love increases more and more . . . till we attain 'the measure of the stature of the fulness of Christ'" (*Works* 6:509).
77. Outler, 97. The contention that Wesley assumes as a rule that conversion can be chronologically fixed (W. Elert, *Das christliche Ethos*, Tübingen, 1949, 288) or that Wesley makes it virtually to a dogma (Lang, 344) cannot be held in such a form.
78. Since his "evangelical conversion" (1738), Wesley had recognized and preached clearer and clearer the fact of the absolute priority of justification for the Christian existence (*Works* 8:111f.). Before that time, faith, for Wesley, was "an assent upon rational grounds, because I hold divine testimony to be the most reasonable of all evidence whatever. Faith must necessarily at length be resolved into reason" (*Letters* 1:23; cf. *Letters* 1:22, 25; 1725). This understanding of faith, derived from Hume and Fiddes (Schmidt, "England und der Deutsche Pietismus," 221), but also held by Jeremy Taylor (Lang, 279f.), was transformed nearly completely and filled with biblical-reformed content in the encounter with the Moravians by texts of Luther and by deepened studies in Paul: "Christian faith is . . . not only an assent to the whole gospel of Christ, but also a full reliance on the blood of Christ; a trust in the merits of His life, death, and resurrection; a recumbency upon Him as our atonement and our life, as given for us, and living in us. It is a sure confidence which a man hath in God, that through the merits of Christ, his sins are forgiven, and he is reconciled to the favour of God. . . ." (*Sermons* 1:40f.).
79. Loofs, *RPTK* 12:799.
80. *Works* 8:5: Faith is "a new creation; and none can create a soul anew, but He who first created the heavens and the earth." Cf. *Works* 8:277f.
81. *Works* 8:49.
82. *Works* 7:352.
83. *Works* 9:453.
84. *Letters* 5:203.
85. *Works* 6:509. Likewise, this does not happen instantaneously: ". . . the believer gradually dies to sin, and grows in grace. Yet sin remains in him; yea the seed of all sin, till he is sanctified throughout in spirit, soul and body" (*Sermons* 1:44, note 6; Minutes, 1745).

86. *Sermons* 1:207. Cf. p. 98f. above.
87. *Works* 10:203.
88. *Sermons* 1:207.
89. *Sermons* 1:192-194.
90. *Works* 10:367. Wesley includes psychological categories, too, in the description of the renewal: *Works* 8:10.
91. Eicken (9) already pointed to the fact that Wesley in his teaching on the renewing effect of grace is in large agreement with Luther. "Faith . . . is something that God effects in us. It changes us and we are reborn from God, John 1:13. Faith puts the old Adam to death and makes us quite different men in heart, in mind, and in all our powers; and it is accompanied by the Holy Spirit." Luther, "Preface to Romans," in *Martin Luther: Selections from His Writings*, ed. J. Dillenberger (Chicago, 1961), 23-24. See below page 100 and note 119.
92. It is clear, says Wesley, "That a man may be saved who cannot express himself properly concerning Imputed Righteousness. Therefore, to do this is not necessary to salvation. That a man may be saved who has not clear conceptions of it. (Yea, that never heard the phrase.) Therefore, clear conceptions are not necessary to salvation. Yea, it is not necessary to salvation to use the phrase at all" (*Journal* 5:243f.). For this reason, mystics (*Journal* 5:244) and Catholics (*Sermons* 2:435) also may be saved. Cf. *Works* 7:354, where the judgment that clear conceptions are not necesary for salvation is justified as follows: "I believe [God] respects the goodness of the heart, rather than the clearness of the head. . . ."
93. *Works* 5:205; cf. *Letters* 2:382.
94. *Works* 5:205; cf. *Letters* 2:381f.
95. *Letters* 2:381.
96. *Works* 8:12; *Letters* 2:383.
97. *Sermons* 1:312.
98. *Sermons* 1:144.
99. *Works* 8:47.
100. *Works* 8:47.
101. Cf. *Sermons* 1:46, notes to §III.1; Edwards, *HMC*, 51; North, 12; Outler, 86; Vulliamy, 51, 56f. Already in chapter I (pages 23-25 above), it has been pointed out that the view which denotes the Holy Club of Oxford as the first form of later Methodism is incorrect. Wesley himself explicitly has postulated the later agreement with the reformed teaching on justification: "I think on Justification just as I have done any time these seven-and-twenty years, and just as Mr. Calvin does. In this respect I do not differ from him an hair's breadth" (*Journal* 5:116; May 14, 1765).
102. *Works* 8:361.
103. *Works* 8:53, 276.
104. *Sermons* 2:66; *Works* 7:363; cf. James 2:17-20.
105. *Sermons* 1:37; Cf. Augustine, who, however, here is not mentioned explicitly.

106. *Works* 7:202.
107. *Sermons* 1:166; 2:358.
108. *Works* 8:53.
109. *Sermons* 2:358.
110. *Sermons* 2:453f.
111. *Works* 8:277.
112. "The more we exert our faith, the more it is increased" (*Works* 8:277). If, however, time and opportunity are missing, a person is sanctified, as well, but a person is not sanctified without faith. (*Sermons* 2:456).
113. P. Scott, *John Wesleys Lehre von der Heiligung, verglichen mit einem lutherisch-pietistischen Beispiel* (Berlin, 1939), 96, says it well: "The doing of the good works is not merely an expression of the new life, it is, as well, essential for the maintenance and the growth of this new life."
114. This danger, however, is kept within limits by the fact that faith alone—and not the works—remains the condition *sine qua non* of justification and sanctification.
115. More details about Wesley's relation to the Moravians and the mystics in: C. W. Towlson, *Moravian and Methodist: Relationships and Influences in the Eighteenth Century* (London, 1957); J. Orcibal, "The Theological Originality of John Wesley and Continental Spirituality," *HMC*, 81ff.; Schmidt, *John Wesley* 2/1:9ff.
116. *Sermons* 1:450.
117. *Sermons* 2:66.
118. *Journal* 2:467.
119. Luther, "Preface to Romans," in *Martin Luther*, ed. Dillenberger, 24. See P. Althaus, *The Theology of Martin Luther*, trans. R. C. Schultz (Philadelphia, 1966), 245ff. Cf. *The Augsburg Confession*, Article 6, *Creeds* 3:11; *The Formula of Concord*, Article 4, *Creeds* 3:121-26; Melanchthon, *Loci Communes* XI, in *Melanchthon on Christian Doctrine*, trans. and ed. C. L. Manschreck (New York, 1965), 158-59.
120. Althaus, 246.
121. We are well aware of the fact that Luther and Wesley, insofar as it is at all possible to establish systematic-theological parallels, do not always agree (see chapter VIII, below, on the question on the evaluation of the Law). In this point, however, they are in the main in agreement. Therefore, M. Piette's statement in *John Wesley and the Evolution of Protestantism* (London, 1939), 421f., that Wesley "threw Luther overboard" in connection with the argument on solafideism, remains superficial because it is solely oriented at the wording of Wesley's utterances.
122. *Sermons* 2:438. Bonhoeffer's expression of "cheap grace," despite the historical distance, would be quite right.
123. *Sermons* 2:66.
124. "Faith is the condition, and the only condition, of sanctification exactly as it is of justification" (*Sermons* 2:453). "In strictness, therefore, neither our faith nor our works justify us. . . . But God himself justifies us" (*Works* 8:362).

125. Schneeberger, 120f.
126. Minutes of the conference, quoted by Simon, *Master-Builder*, 277f. See *Works* 8:337.
127. ". . . we abhor the doctrine of justification by Works as a most perilous and abominable doctrine. . . . We hereby solemnly declare, in the sight of God, that we have no trust or confidence but in the merits of our Lord and Saviour Jesus Christ, for Justification or Salvation . . . and though no one is a real Christian believer (and consequently cannot be saved) who doth not good works, where there is time and opportunity, yet our works have no part in meriting or purchasing our salvation from first to last, either in whole or in part." Quoted by Simon, *Master-Builder*, 296.
128. Cf. *Letters* 6:175; but also Orcibal, *HMC*, 91.
129. Weissbach, 91.
130. "Undoubtedly faith is the work of God; and yet it is the duty of man to believe" (*Letters* 7:202).
131. *Works* 6:511-13.
132. II Cor. 6:1, KJV; Matt. 13:12, I Thess. 1:3 and others.
133. "Qui fecit nos sine nobis, non salvabit nos sine nobis" (*Works* 6:513).
134. *Works* 8:277; Schneeberger, 123f.

CHAPTER VIII: STANDARDS FOR SOCIAL ETHICS

1. The first part of this section which deals with God's love to man could have been included already in the previous chapter in that God's gracious acting with man is grounded in and determined by love. Since, however, a division of the subject in two chapters inevitably would have impaired the lucidity and the unity of the representation, and since, for Wesley, among the standards of social ethics, love is, in a word, of fundamental importance, the treatment within the scope of this chapter seemed to be the more convincing solution.
2. Cf. Gerdes, 15, and Weissbach, 193.
3. *Works* 7:457.
4. Gerdes, 27, has made clear this connection; cf. Weissbach, 192f.
5. *Letters* 1:238ff.; Gerdes, 27; Green, 51ff.; Schmidt, *John Wesley* 1:218ff.
6. Wesley even believed that he adhered more consistently than Law himself to the view that love is the content of true religion. Cf. *Letters* 3:332.
7. *Works* 8:5.
8. *Works* 5:205.
9. *Works* 8:4f.
10. Schneeberger, 138f., gives more details about the nature of this problem.
11. *Works* 7:269.
12. *Journal* 2:496. The similarity with Abaelard's soteriology is obvious. However, there is nothing known to us about a direct influence of

Abaelard on Wesley. Cf. R. Peppermüller, "Abaelards Auslegung des Römerbriefs," *Beiträge zur Geschichte der Philosophie und Theologie des Mittelalters. Texte und Untersuchungen*, New Series, vol. 10 (Münster, 1972).

13. *Works* 7:269.
14. *Works* 8:22.
15. *Works* 7:272.
16. *Works* 7:376ff.
17. *Works* 7:378ff.
18. See G. Hoffmann, "Seinsharmonie und Heilsgeschichte bei Jonathan Edwards" (Ph.D. diss., Göttingen, 1956), 35f.
19. Against the view, some persons would be determined for hell already before their birth, he writes to James Harvey: "I could sooner be a Turk, a Deist, yea an Atheist, than I could believe this. It is less absurd to deny the very being of God than to make Him an almighty tyrant" (*Letters* 3:387; *Journal* 5:116).
20. Since Wesley's reasons for his reflection of predestination are unequivocal and sufficient, the connection with Deism, Latitudinarianism, and Arminianism which is established by Lang (34) appears to be incorrect and too artificially constructed. E. G. Rupp has convincingly shown that Wesley's "Arminianism," despite the use of the word, is rather a term for his teaching of universal grace than a renewal of a tradition that is connected with Arminius (*HMC*, xxiv-xxv); cf. A. H. Pask, "The Influence of Arminius on John Wesley," *LQHR* 185 (1960):260ff.
21. Cell, 326.
22. Cf. Schmidt, "Universalismus," *RGG* 6:1157f; Schneeberger, 104ff.
23. The rejection of the *gemina praedestinatio* is found already in Wesley's early utterances: *Letters* 1:19f., 22 (1725).
24. *Letters* 6:297f.
25. *Journal* 1:292f.; *Works* 8:343, 352. Cf. above (p. 32f.).
26. *Works* 7:272, 377.
27. *Works* 8:229.
28. Schneeberger, 104.
29. *Works* 7:271.
30. "Real disinterested benevolence to all mankind foremost develops out of the God-given love" (*Works* 7:271f.).
31. *Works* 8:8f.
32. *Works* 8:352 ("Advice to the People Called Methodists").
33. Cf. E. G. Rupp, *Principalities and Powers* (London, 1952), 82.
34. More details to this point in chapters IX and X below. Rupp, *Principalities and Powers*, 82f., explicitly and correctly emphasizes that Wesley's teaching on sanctification, which is based on the connection outlined here between faith and love, must not be identified with the nineteenth-century Methodist teaching on sanctification.
35. *Works* 8:5; 7:199, 346; 10:155; 9:292.
36. *Works* 8:204. Cf. *Works* 6:115; 7:47, 269; 8:513.

37. "You cannot love God, because you do not love your neighbour. For he that loves God loves his brother also" (*Letters* 3:237). Weissbach's interpretation (196); "But this social relatedness to the teaching of sanctification, as well, [is] . . . only a means for the salvation of the individual soul. . . ." is ambiguous and contradictory to Wesley's demand for a charity that is unselfish and "a matter of course." ". . . let all men know that you desire both their temporal and eternal happiness, as sincerely as you do your own" (*Works* 7:144). Cf. *Works* 7:272; *Sermons* 1:96f., 293.

38. "That a man is not personally known to him is no bar to his love; no, nor that he is known to be such as he approves not, that he repays hatred for his good-will" (*Works* 8:343). Cf. *Works* 7:47.

39. "Charity is . . . the love of God, and of man for God's sake; no more and no less" (*Letters* 3:237). Cf. *Works* 8:474.

40. *Works* 10:156; 6:298.

41. *Works* 6:298.

42. *Works* 7:144. Cf. *Sermons* 1:293; *Works* 8:3; 6:298; 10:155f.

43. *Works* 8:8f., 343, 352.

44. For more details on the influence of the Enlightenment on Wesley's theology, see W. R. Cannon, *The Theology of John Wesley, With Special Reference to the Doctrine of Justification* (New York/Nashville, 1946), 163ff.

45. *Journal* 5:353 (against Rousseau).

46. *Letters* 2:377.

47. *Works* 7:269. Cf. Schmidt, "Die Bedeutung Luthers für John Wesleys Bekehrung," *Luther-Jahrbuch* 20 (1938):130.

48. Schmidt, "John Wesleys Bekehrung," 130.

49. *Works* 5:205.

50. *Works* 7:199.

51. *Works* 7:353, 198f.; *Works* 8:364; *Letters* 5:208; *Sermons* 2:393; cf. J. Sellers, *Theological Ethics* (New York/London, 1961), 189.

52. *Works* 13:260f.; 7:215.

53. *Works* 6:412.

54. *Sermons* 2:202f.

55. *Works* 7:330f.

56. *Sermons* 2:455f.; 1:298ff.; *Letters* 2:303; *Works* 6:526f.

57. *Works* 6:526f; *Letters* 2:303; *Sermons* 2:455.

58. *Letters* 5:223; *Sermons* 2:448; *Works* 11:442; *Letters* 4:299; *Notes*, Gal. 5:14.

59. *Sermons* 1:116; Weissbach, 202.

60. *Works* 6:412; 11:417; 7:332f.: After the death of the person also, the souls of the believers grow in sanctification. "Entire Sanctification" was effected by God's grace in some while they were still alive (*Journal* 6:213; 8:49), however, it is likely that Wesley speaks in these rare places of a relative degree of perfection, as far as it can be attained at all in this (earthly) life. Cf. P. Watson, "Wesley and Luther on Christian Perfection," *The Ecumenical Review* 15 (1961-61):301. In any case, it is not a sinless perfection (in

agreement with Watson, 290; Schmidt, "John Wesleys Bekehrung," 73—and despite the objection of Lang, 347, which has its origin in an isolating manner of looking at the problem). R. W. Burtner and R. E. Chiles, *A Compend of Wesley's Theology* (New York/Nashville, 1954), 139, contend that "In his terminology the distinction between entire sanctification and the consequent life (Christian perfection) is never clear. The former is considered here as the second work of salvation through faith; the latter as an ideal of the ethical life." This replaces one inaccuracy by another.

61. *Works* 11:417; Weissbach, 209.
62. Weissbach's assertion (197) that Wesley's conception on this point is "entirely different" from Luther's overlooks an important part of the Lutheran doctrine of justification; cf. Althaus, 242ff.
63. *Works* 7:202.
64. In agreement with Edwards, *HMC*, 61, against Warner, 65.
65. *Sermons* 2:377, 393, 453f.; *Works* 10:231.
66. *Works* 8:19.
67. *Letters* 5:349.
68. *Letters* 4:197.
69. "Therefore, that we are justified by faith, even by faith without works, is no ground for making void the law through faith; or for imagining that faith is a dispensation from any kind or degree of holiness" (*Sermons* 2:66f.). Antinomian opponents were found as well among the Moravians (*Works* 10:201ff.), as among his own friends and communities (*Sermons* 2:37, 284) and in the Anglican Church (George Bell); cf. *Works* 10:364ff.; 8:349ff.; A. Outler, *John Wesley* (New York, 1964), 377; Loofs, *RPTK* 12:774.
70. "At the request of several of my friends, I wrote a letter to a Gentleman of Bristol, in order to guard them from seeking salvation by works on one hand, and Antinomianism on the other" (*Journal* 4:247). Moreover, Wesley defends at the same time his own position. Cf. *Sermons* 2:284; *Works* 8:215; *Sermons* 1:236.
71. Discussions that are more detailed can be found in the general works on Wesley's theology, especially in Outler and Williams.
72. *Sermons* 2:42-48.
73. *Sermons* 2:44; 1:400; *Works* 8:343.
74. *Sermons* 2:43; 1:224, 400; cf. what has been said above on prevenient grace!
75. *Sermons* 2:46. Wesley answers the well-known question whether it is just because it is God's will, or whether God wills it because it is just, by rejecting the distinction between God and his will. But he concedes that one could as well say that God wills something because it is just, namely that it corresponds with the essential relation that exist between the things which God has actually created (*Sermons* 2:49f.). Thereby, Wesley avoids the danger to teach a God of arbitrariness, and he emphasizes the ontological unity of God, of the will of God, and of justice.
76. *Sermons* 1:400.
77. *Sermons* 2:73.

78. *Sermons* 1:399f.; *Works* 6:296.
79. *Works* 7:316f.; *Letters* 4:155; *Works* 8:343.
80. *Sermons* 2:77; *Letters* 4:79, 155; *Works* 7:317.
81. *Works* 6:296; *Sermons* 1:399f.
82. Wesley finds the biblical vindication for that first of all in Matt. 5:17ff., Rom. 3:31 and 7:12 (*Works* 10:292; *Sermons* 1:400; 2:38ff., 45, 50, 58ff., 400).
83. *Works* 10:203.
84. *Works* 8:278. For Wesley, there are no biblical proofs for the Moravian view that a believer is free from the law of God in the sense of a dispensation; see *Works* 10:203.
85. *Works* 8:278.
86. *Works* 8:318.
87. *Sermons* 2:285ff.; *Works* 3:20; 7:337ff.
88. The Sermon on the Mount is the sole longer complex of texts on which Wesley preached a connected series of sermons (sermons 16-28 in *Sermons*).
89. *Works* 8:360, 415; *Sermons* 2:319.
90. These include, for example: smuggling as theft on king and nation, obedience to parents, prohibition of slavery and of the collecting of treasures, the commandment of social welfare work and others (see below chapter VIII, section 4). For Wesley, above all, the "Golden Rule" (Matt. 7:12) helps to apply the commandment of love in concrete situations (*Works* 8:360, 415; *Journal* 3:301).
91. Only by way of intimation can it be pointed out that Wesley and Luther agree in some points (i.e., in the obligation over against the will of God), but, as well, differ essentially in others (i.e., in their judgment whether the Law can be fulfilled). For this cf. Schmidt, "John Wesleys Bekehrung," 69f.; Schmidt, "England und der deutsche Pietismus," 222; F. Hildebrandt, *From Luther to Wesley* (London, 1951), 14f.; Piette, 421f. On Wesley's attitude to Luther's Commentary on Galatians see: *Journal* 2:467; *Works* 7:204 and my essay "John Wesley's 'Synergismus'" in *Die Einheit der Kirche*, ed. Hein, 96-102.
92. *Works* 11:415.
93. Ibid.
94. Ibid. The term "law" here is not used in its literal sense but is formed here analogically in the same way as Paul speaks of the "law of the Spirit" (Rom. 8:2) and of the "law of Christ" (1 Cor. 9:21), or as the letter of James speaks of the "law of liberty." Watson, 295f., and Weissbach, 203f., apparently have not recognized this (analogical) use of the term, otherwise (i.e.) Weissbach could not draw the following conclusion: "For the new man, therefore, sin is merely the transgression of the 'law of love' and can bring condemnation to the new man, because the other transgressions of the perfect law for him are forgiven through Christ" (204). Starkey (108) articulates correctly the relation of the moral law and the law of love: "The Wesleyan ethic has for its

179

standard the evangelical law. This includes the moral law of Moses, the prophets, the Sermon on the Mount and culminates in love to God and neighbor. Indeed, he who lives by the law of love fulfills the whole moral law of God." More details on this point are to be found in the following explanations on the function of the law. Cf. also *Letters* 3:79f.; *Sermons* 2:55, 66f.; 1:33; *Works* 11:416; Lang, 338f.

95. In the following, the term "law" used without further addition always designates the moral law.

96. *Works* 7:338.

97. *Sermons* 2:52, 61; *Letters* 3:80. Here, Wesley agrees with Luther; cf. Elert, 26.

98. *Sermons* 2:52. Concerning the perception of good and evil before justification compare the section on prevenient grace. In Wesley's doctrine of the law, the *usus politicus* is of subordinate importance; cf. chapter IX, section 2, below.

99. *Sermons* 2:48; cf. Rom. 7:13.

100. *Works* 7:187; *Sermons* 1:223. Occasionally, the gospel leads to perception of sin, as well, but, as a rule, God uses the law for this purpose (*Sermons* 2:61).

101. *Sermons* 2:53.

102. *Letters* 3:80.

103. *Sermons* 2:53; in this way, Wesley interprets Gal. 3:24.

104. *Sermons* 2:53, 60. Cf. Rupp, *Principalities and Powers*, 84. Hoffmann's contention (176) that for Wesley the preaching of the law has "ultimately but a pedagogical purpose," does not represent Wesley's entire view, but its main intentions.

105. *Sermons* 2:53.

106. See above, 114ff.

107. *Sermons* 2:69.

108. *Sermons* 2:66f.

109. In the rank, which Wesley attaches to the law for the believer, he differs from Luther, but not in the assumption of a *tertius usus legis* on principle. Yet, Wesley differs less from Calvin or Melanchthon; cf. Elert, 26f.; Althaus, 266ff.; O. Weber, *Grundlagen der Dogmatik*, rev. ed., 2 vols. (Neukirchen-Vluyn, 1962-64), 2:427ff. The main difference to Wesley's early views (before 1738), as well, is to be found in placing the doctrine of justification before Christian ethics. Cf. *Letters* 1:138; *Journal* 1:465; Schmidt, *John Wesley* 1:106ff., 123.

110. *Sermons* 2:53f.

111. *Sermons* 2:54. Thereby, Wesley refuses any enthusiastic perfectionism that can develop either by a mistaken doctrine of justification or by an overestimation of human natural abilities, and that has not always been avoided in the later history of Methodism.

112. *Works* 7:189; 11:417.

113. *Sermons* 1:298ff. "The holiest men still need Christ . . . to make atonement

for their holy things. Even perfect holiness is acceptable to God only through Jesus Christ" (*Works* 11:417).

114. *Sermons* 2:54.
115. *Works* 8:15f.
116. *Sermons* 2:67f., 77; *Works* 7:15f.
117. *Letters* 3:80.
118. *Sermons* 2:54.
119. *Sermons* 1:227f.
120. *Works* 8:188, 344.
121. *Sermons* 1:228, 232.
122. *Works* 7:189, 190f., 317; *Sermons* 1:222ff.; *Letters* 3:80; 4:19.
123. Schneeberger, 162. Cf. *Works* 7:192; 8:343.
124. *Works* 11:416 (cf. Rom. 13:9f.).
125. *Sermons* 2:51, 465; *Works* 8:199, 343; *Sermons* 1:232f.
126. *Works* 8:344, 352.
127. *Letters* 4:79; 5:349; *Sermons* 2:77.
128. Therefore, Schmidt is right when he says ("John Wesleys Bekehrung," 70) that "God is not so much the demanding God and Lord, but he is the creator who leads everything to completion." Wesley's view maintains a great seriousness, as well, by the fact that he holds fast on the expectation of the Last Judgment in which everyone, the one who has been justified, as well, will have to render account of all his deeds (*Sermons* 2:326, 474; *Letters* 3:122; *Journal* 4:419; 6:136; *Works* 6:238; 7:37). As for the rest, eschatology plays a very little role in Wesley's ethics (as also Schneeberger, 153ff.). Cf. *Works* 6:237; *Letters* 2:306; *Sermons* 1:429, 473f.
129. *Sermons* 1:314ff. By the Sermon on the Mount, Christ has not brought a new religion into the world, but, as Wesley formulates with an allusion to Matthew Tindal, such a religion "the substance of which is, without question, as old as the creation," but never "so fully explained, nor so thoroughly understood. . . ." (*Sermons* 1:401). Cf. *Sermons* 1:316ff.
130. *Works* 8:364.
131. "The (whole) mind that was in Christ (Jesus)," "to walk as Christ (your Master, He) walked": *Works* 7:215, 272, 353; 8:20, 244, 364; *Letters* 5:54, 208; 6:207 and others; similar: "tread in His steps" (*Sermons* 1:97), "to resemble or imitate Him" (*Sermons* 1:499).
132. Weissbach, 182, even speaks of an "*imitatio* piety." This, however, in view of the finding described in the following, can be called appropriate only to a very limited degree.
133. *Works* 8:365; cf. *Sermons* 1:499, where God is the prototype! But Wesley, at this point, seems to have in view Jesus, as well, when he describes the details of a mind of love.
134. "Kind, benevolent, compassionate, tender-hearted," "real disinterested benevolence" (*Sermons* 1:499; *Works* 7:272).
135. *Works* 8:244.
136. *Works* 11:417; see above (124f.).

137. Williams, 81. Only subsequently, Wesley realized that it was actually this for which he had been searching in vain during his time in Oxford (Schmidt, *John Wesley* 1:123).
138. One of the few texts that gives more details is to be found in Wesley's sermon on "Scriptural Christianity" (*Sermons* 1:97), in which Wesley, paraphrasing Matt. 25:35ff., describes the one who is following in the footsteps of Jesus. In a letter, Wesley advises a young lady, not to associate solely with noble or fashionable people, since he does not find any example for doing so in the life of Jesus or his apostles (*Letters* 6:207).
139. Wesley receives even the nickname "Primitive Christianity" for that (*Letters* 1:50).
140. Piette, 420f.; Schmidt, *The Young Wesley*, 19.
141. Schmidt, *The Young Wesley*, 21-22.
142. Outler, *John Wesley*, viii-viv; Schmidt, *The Young Wesley*, 19; Schmidt, "England und der deutsche Pietismus," 205-9; Schmidt, "England," *RGG* 2:483. Ancient Christian ideals indeed have played a role, as well, in German Pietism (cf. Schmidt, "Pietismus," *RGG* 5:373).
143. *Works* 8:346.
144. *Works* 6:256ff.
145. *Works* 6:256.
146. *Letters* 2:303.
147. *Letters* 2:306ff.; *Works* 7:126.
148. *Letters* 2:308, 299.
149. *Works* 7:126; *Letters* 2:306.
150. *Letters* 2:294, 300. Wesley refers to the "practice of the ancient Christians," as well, when he pleads for the keeping of the "Watchnights" (*Letters* 2:299).
151. This restriction not only must be made for reasons generally to be found in the historical distance, but also because the passivity in questions as slavery—a passivity that is motivated by an impending apocalyptic expectation—as well as that impending expectation itself, was obviously not numbered among the essential stock of ancient Christianity by Wesley.
152. *Letters* 4:121f.; *Works* 14:220-233.
153. *Journal* 1:175; 6:98; *Letters* 5:338; 6:292. Cf. also chapter III above.
154. See chapter III, section 3, above; *Journal* 3:245.
155. E. Troeltsch, *The Social Teaching of the Christian Churches*, trans. Olive Wyon, 2 vols. (New York/London, 1931), 2:721.
156. *Works* 8:513; cf. *Works* 8:9.
157. *Journal* 2:475f.; *Sermons* 1:203; 2:84ff.; *Works* 6:351.
158. Two of Wesley's most extensive writings bear the titles: "An Earnest Appeal to Men of Reason and Religion" and "A Farther Appeal to Men of Reason and Religion" (*Works* 8:3-247).
159. *Works* 8:13; 6:350f., 355; *Letters* 3:27; 6:50; 8:112.
160. Occasionally, it is contended that these writings contradict Scripture and experience: *Letters* 3:332 (against W. Law); *Journal* 4:298 (against F. C.

Oetinger); *Journal* 3:17f.; 5:46, 521 (against J. Böhme); *Journal* 5:353 (against Rousseau); *Works* 13:414ff. (against Montesquieu); the nuisances in the legal proceedings before the civil court, as well, are "contrary to all sense, reason, justice and equity" (*Works* 8:167).

161. *Letters* 6:60; cf. *Letters* 3:26f.; *Works* 13:476.
162. Schmidt, "England," *RGG* 2:65. It is true, the reproach of enthusiasm frequently has been raised against Methodism, a reproach to which Lang (344) remarks correctly: "In many cases, Christianity itself, the effect of the Holy Spirit who produces living faith, assurance of salvation, peace and joy, were considered as enthusiasm."
163. *Letters* 5:217; Davies, 97.
164. *Works* 8:12f.; *Letters* 2:302.
165. On Locke, cf. *Works* 13:455ff.; *Letters* 2:314; 7:82, 228; *Journal* 5:89, note 2. Wesley did not follow the eudemonistic ethics and utilitarianism.
166. Cf. chapter V and chapter X, section 2; Cameron, 95ff.
167. Mainly Wesley's "Natural Philosophy," his medical activity and his conception of sensual perception as the sole natural source of knowledge (*Works* 8:13f, 456; 6:336ff.; *Survey* 1:90ff.) bear witness of that fact. On Aristotle cf. *Works* 13:459f.; in the controversy which Hutchinson has erected by setting a biblicist-speculative system against Newton's law of gravitation, Wesley sides with Newton (Gerdes, 47).
168. *Works* 6:351ff.; Schneeberger, 40 (further references are to be found there).
169. *Works* 8:11ff.; 7:82; 6:337ff.; *Letters* 6:49, 60.
170. ". . . continually reasoning with their opposers" (*Works* 8:12).
171. *Works* 8:248; 12:476f.
172. *Survey* 2:226f.; *Letters* 5:364.
173. *Survey* 2:227.
174. *Survey* 2:227.
175. *Works* 11:429.
176. *Works* 6:395; *Works* 8:407, 448.
177. *Works* 14:249; S. B. Frost, *Die Autoritätslehre in den Werken John Wesleys* (Munich, 1938), 72.
178. *Works* 11:429.
179. Emendations of texts, discussion on the question of authorship (cf. G. E. Lacy, "Authority in John Wesley," *LQHR* 189 (1964):117); reflection of predestination and of slavery against positive biblical references (*Works* 7:383; Lotz, 85f.); the New Testament as canon for the Old Testament (*Works* 5:193); superiority of some biblical books over against others (*Works* 7:45f.); instruction for a correct understanding of Scripture (*Works* 10:142); refusal of the transferability of scriptural utterances on all corresponding situations (*Sermons* 2:270f.); cf. *Works* 5:3, 113; 8:340; *Journal* 3:217; *Letters* 3:117; 6:60.

180. *Works* 8:8f.
181. *Letters* 2:292, 302; *Sermons* 2:315, 97f.; *Works* 7:273.
182. *Works* 8:188.
183. *Sermons* 2:97f.
184. *Sermons* 2:815. Indeed, God teaches through experience, as well (*Letters* 6:292). If, however, subjective experiences are clearly contradictory to the Scriptures, the latter is to be given priority because it teaches God's will (*Works* 11:177). For this reason, Scripture and experience are not of the same rank as principles of knowledge, as Cell (72) apparently sees it.

CHAPTER IX
AIMS OF WESLEY'S SOCIAL ETHICS

1. By this, not the immediate purposes of an action, as for example, to give someone who starves to eat in order that he is freed out of a depressing plight, are meant, but the goals of social acting on the whole, which exceed the momentary effects and envisage the whole of ethics.
2. ". . . Christianity is essentially a social religion; and . . . to turn it into a solitary one is to destroy it" (*Sermons* 1:381f.).
3. Frost (96) attempts to place Wesley into a wider context of intellectual history by writing: "The connecting link between Rousseau, John Wesley, Schleiermacher and the English Romanticism is a rediscovery of the value of the individual." Cf. S. G. Dimond, *The Psychology of the Methodist Revival* (London, 1932), 113f., who attributes the emphasis on individuality to the influence of Hobbes.
4. That should be imprinted already on the minds of children, as soon as they are able to grasp it: "You are made to be happy in God" (*Works* 7:267).
5. Cf. Lerch, 179.
6. *Works* 8:203.
7. Renewal of the prisons by converting the prison directors (*Journal* 2:173, note 1; Voigt, 378); social welfare work of the mayor of Cork (*Journal* 7:275); improvement of the desolate condition of the working houses (*Journal* 5:401; cf. MacArthur, 134); directions to the visitors of hospital patients to teach "industry and cleanliness" (*Works* 7:123); assistance until self-help was possible (*Journal* 5:247).
8. Troeltsch, 2:724.
9. For the mentioned schools of thinking see A. Schweitzer, *The Philosophy of Civilization*, trans. C. T. Campion (New York, 1949), 150ff.
10. Schulz, 239.
11. Wendland, *Sozialethik*, 22; "The individualistic and the social conceptions of Christianity are not in antagonism: they are complementary" (Dimond, 114).
12. In this also lies the element that carries on Wesley's social ethics beyond the

older Pietism and a broad strand of Puritanism. Cf. Renkewitz, *EStL*, 1128; Marlowe, 30.

13. *Letters* 6:127f.; *Works* 1:382, 426. The occasional use of the metaphor "Christ's soldiers" also points in that direction (*Letters* 2:128; Schmidt, *John Wesley* 2/1:396). ". . . the spiritual was always passing into the ethical; life in God meant life for God; and life for God meant life for the sake of others" T. F. Lockyer, *Paul: Luther: Wesley: A Study in Religious Experience as Illustrative of the Ethic of Christianity* (London, 1922), 262; cf. Schneeberger, 144; R. C. Monk, *John Wesley, His Puritan Heritage: A Study of the Christian Life* (Nashville, 1966), 243.

14. *Works* 7:118f., 123f.; 8:3f., 270f., 346; *Letters* 2:297; *Sermons* 2:463ff. and others.

15. *Works* 8:7.

16. *Works* 8:3.

17. Bett, 143, points to the fact that it was not Wesley, but Burke who said "that the deserts of the poor would be adjusted in 'the final proportions of eternal justice.'" That Wesley also admonishes to exercise patience and to be ready to suffer (i.e, *Works* 6:233, 236) is not contradictory to the fact that there actually are unalterable evils as well. Yet, faith in the power of God is for Wesley no reason for the renunciation of vigorous personal activity, but its enablement. In a sermon on Luke 16:19ff., we find a consolation for the poor in view of eternal bliss; this motive, however, is pretensed by the text, and it is very seldom found in Wesley. For Wesley's eschatology and its meaning for ethics, cf. Schneeberger, 139ff.

18. *Works* 8:7; *Sermons* 1:32, note 5; 426.

19. *Letters* 1:15. Cf. Schmidt, "John Wesleys Bekehrung," 127.

20. The demand for social involvement was even laid down in the "General Rules," so that one can say with Wearmouth (230): "It was impossible to be a good Methodist without engaging in social activities." Cf. *Works* 8:270f.

21. *Works* 8:7; 7:23; cf. *Letters* 2:297; *Works* 8:254; 11:74.

22. That was valid including the hated French soldiers who were captives in England, and other foreigners; *Letters* 6:73f.; 7:308; 8:261; *Journal* 8:79 and note 1. Cf. Engels, 302f.

23. *Works* 8:309f., 346; *Sermons* 2:293, 300.

24. *Works* 8:3.

25. Finally, Kluxen (528): "For Wesley, it was decisive, that England through his activity again became a religious country. In 1760, when George III ascended the throne, Christianity was dried up to a feeble, conventional matter; in 1820, when he died, England had become a Christian country."

26. *Letters* 7:305: A Tory is "one that believes God, not the people, to be the origin of all civil power. In this sense he (i.e., his elder brother Samuel) was a Tory; so was my father; so am I. But I am no more a Jacobite that I am a Turk; neither was my brother."

27. Kluxen, 424f., 499, 57ff; G. M. Trevelyan, *The History of England, Vol. 2: From 1603 to 1918* (London and Colchester, 1956), 501.

185

28. *Journal* 8:325; *Letters* 6:156, 161.
29. *Works* 11:48, 52.
30. *Works* 11:47f.
31. *Works* 11:48ff.
32. *Works* 11:52; Thomas Aniello, Naples, seventeenth century.
33. Ibid.
34. *Works* 11:46.
35. With Rom. 13:1ff.; *Works* 11:48.
36. *Works* 11:37ff.
37. Wesley shared with such illustrious contemporaries as Voltaire and Montesquieu the high esteem for civil liberty in England, as well as the rejection of a rule of the people. (Nicolson, 76, 83f.; Lean, 14; Thompson, 80). The French encyclopedists, as well, trusted less in democracy than in philanthropic absolute monarchs (Nicolson, xixf.). The theories of Locke and Rousseau of a contract are rejected without being mentioned explicitly.
38. Cf. K. Kluxen, *Das Problem der politischen Opposition. Entwicklung und Wesen der englischen Zweiparteienpolitik im 18. Jahrhundert* (Freiburg/Munich, 1956), 16f.
39. Trevelyan, *History of England*, 2:501.
40. I Pet. 2:17; Acts 23:5; Exod. 22:27; *Letters* 6:267; *Journal* 3:123f.; *Letters* 2:41; *Works* 11:154f.
41. Frost, 63.
42. *Works* 11:14ff.; *AM* 5:151f.; *Works* 8:161.
43. *Letters* 5:371ff.; *Works* 8:161; *AM* 5:152.
44. *Letters* 5:374ff.
45. *Letters* 5:373.
46. *Letters* 5:376ff.
47. First of all, the Wilkes riots, but not solely them: *Works* 8:161; 11:1ff., 155; *Letters* 5:376ff. On Wilkes, cf. Kluxen, *Geschichte Englands*, 468ff.; Edwards, *John Wesley*, 61ff.
48. *AM* 5:151ff.; *Works* 11:154f.
49. "Accordingly, there is most liberty of all, civil and religious, under a limited monarchy; there is usually less under an aristocracy, and least of all under a democracy" (*Works* 11:105; cf. *Works* 11:45f.).
50. Thompson, 79f.; Edwards, *John Wesley*, 29. 68; Kluxen, *Geschichte Englands*, 410.
51. In 1741, George II by an official declaration condemned persecution for religious reasons. By this, he contributed essentially to the termination of the outrages against the Methodists. Cf. Simon, *Advance*, 186; Simon, *Master-Builder*, 95.
52. *Letters* 8:231; complaint about lacking freedom for Methodists; *Letters* 5:376ff.; *Works* 11:14ff.; MacArthur, 24ff.; Edwards, *John Wesley*, 13f.
53. *Letters* 8:196: "We are no republicans, and never intended to be."
54. *Works* 8:7; cf. *Works* 8:204.

55. In the 1740s, the Methodists had suffered the negative consequences of public riots. Cf. Edwards, *HMC*, 64.
56. *Journal* 3:300.
57. *Letters* 8:196.
58. Ibid.
59. *Works* 8:120f., 113f.
60. Thompson, 375, states that, for this reason, Methodism could become both the religion of the oppressors, as well as that of the oppressed.
61. W. E. Sangster, *Methodism: Her Unfinished Task* (London, 1947), 54ff.; M. S. Edwards, "Methodism and the Chartist Movement," *LQHR* 191 (1966):304ff.; M. Edwards, *This Methodism*, 47ff.; MacArthur, 183f.; Vester, 93f.; Thompson, 41, 354f. Therefore, it is incomprehensible how, despite Wesley's positive influences on the development of democratic patterns of behavior which are yet to be examined, an otherwise meritorious Wesley scholar as J. W. Bready is able to assert: "Wesley was the [!] father of British and American Democracy." See Bready, *Wesley and Democracy* (Toronto, 1939), x. This work also contains other risky statements as, for example, the historically not verifiable speculation that, without Wesley, England would have "perished through moral decay" (5; cf. 7f., and others, which by numerous superlatives, resemble more a Methodist founder legend than a historically correct representation).
62. *Letters* 6:156; cf. *Letters* 6:161. It is also not correct to contend with Schneeberger (15) that Wesley "never could win a positive understanding for the struggle for independence of the American colonies in the 1770s."
63. One cannot speak here of a developed doctrine of natural law, since Wesley's explanations lack the closeness, the inner systematic cohesion, and the completeness that are necessary for a developed doctrine.
64. *Works* 11:70.
65. *Works* 11:37f.
66. So also in Calvinism; cf. J. Weerda, *EStL*, 1120.
67. *Letters* 8:231. For this reason, W. A. Gifford, *John Wesley: Patriot and Statesman* (Toronto, 1922), 21, is not right in contending: "That there were fundamental human rights, . . . to which indeed the law must be adjusted, was a question he [Wesley] did not consider."
68. *Works* 11:34. Wesley, of course, did not hold the rationalistic thesis that the natural law is valid *etsi deus non daretur*. Rather, in his conception Augustinian and Platonic influences stand out. In this question Wesley separates, as well, from Locke, who ultimately does not trace back the natural law to God, but, as we still shall see, he follows Locke in the determination of the content.
69. *Works* 11:92.
70. *Works* 11:41, 92; 8:7; *Letters* 5:22.
71. *Works* 11:34, 37f., 70, 92; *Letters* 8:207, 231, 265, 275; *AM* 11 (1788):208.

72. Cf. H. Gollwitzer, "Krieg und Christentum," *RGG* 4:66ff.; M. Edwards, *This Methodism*, 67, 87.
73. Nicolson, 2f.
74. When the Stuart Pretender threatened to attack England, Wesley offered to organize and to finance a company of volunteers, if the king needed it and made available to him weapons and instructors. An official reaction to this offer has not become known (*Letters* 3:165; *Journal* 4:151 note 1; W. H. Hutton, *John Wesley* (London, 1927), 142; Simon, *Advance*, 307f.). In 1745, in a similar situation, Wesley already had publicly and repeatedly summoned to the support of the king by fulfilling one's duty and by prayer (*Letters* 2:41; M. Edwards, *John Wesley*, 59).
75. *Works* 11:128.
76. Cameron, 54; Simon, *Master-Builder*, 19; the Methodist conscientious objector John Nelson, therefore, was the exception rather than the rule (cf. Cameron, 55).
77. *Works* 9:221.
78. *Works* 9:221f.
79. *Works* 9:123ff.
80. A short quote from Wesley's appeal to his fellow-countrymen may serve as an example (*Works* 11:120f.): "Who knows, when the sword is once drawn, where it may stop? . . . If the sword should be drawn, upon whom may it light? This we know not. But supposing it should be on yourself, or a beloved wife, an aged parent, a tender child, a dear relative, what recompence can be found for such a loss? . . . But, suppose you escape with your life, and the lives of those that are near and dear to you, there is yet another dreadful evil to fear, and which has been the case; plunder, lawless plunder, may deprive you of your little all. . . . [Describing two groups of armed men moving toward each other]: what are they going to do? to shoot each other through the head or heart; to stab and butcher each other. . . . Why so? What harm have they done to one another? Why, none at all. Most of them are entire strangers to each other. But a matter is in dispute. . . . So these countrymen . . . are to murder each other with all possible haste, to prove who is in the right. Now, what an argument is this! What a method of proof! What an amazing way of deciding controversies! . . . At what a price is the decision made! By the blood and wounds of thousands; the burning cities, ravaging and laying waste the country." Cf. *Letters* 6:156ff.; 160ff.; *Works* 9:222f.
81. *Works* 11:122; 9:223.
82. *Letters* 6:156, 161.
83. *Letters* 6:157f.
84. *Letters* 6:156, 161.
85. *Works* 11:123.
86. So already in 1757: *Works* 9:223.
87. *Works* 11:123-128.

88. *Journal* 6:66f., note 3; *Works* 11:80; M. Edwards, *John Wesley*, 71; Bett, 51; M. Wallace, "John Wesley and the American Revolution," in *Essays in Honor of Conyers Read*, ed. N. Downs (Chicago, 1953), 53ff.
89. Wallace, 55f.
90. *Works* 11:81ff.
91. Wallace, 59.
92. *Works* 9:235; *Sermons* 2:490.
93. *Works* 7:407f.
94. *Works* 11:183ff.; 9:235; 8:148, 155ff., 470f.; *Journal* 8:327f.; *Letters* 6:159.
95. *Letters* 2:297.
96. *Works* 8:151ff.
97. *Works* 11:235.
98. M. Edwards, *After Wesley*, 118f.; W. M. Wallace, 61.
99. Against bribery at elections: *Works* 8:157ff., 308; 11:196-198.
100. Against slavery: *Letters* 8:275; criticism at the House of Lords: *Journal* 7:46; general criticism: *Letters* 5:376ff.
101. Fiscal policy: *Letters* 7:234f.; economical interventions: *Journal* 8:327f., 334f.; *Letters* 6:159, 366.
102. M. Edwards, *This Methodism*, 41f.: "Half of the seats in the Commons could be bought or were in the hands of great landowners. Birmingham and Manchester, Leeds and Sheffield had no representatives. Yorkshire had one member, but Cornwall had forty-two members. The new industrial areas had no voice in the Commons." Cf. Wearmouth, 129, 220f.; Nicolson, 365f. Kluxen, *Geschichte Englands*, 427ff.
103. Cf. Whiteley, 270f.

CHAPTER X
CONCLUDING OBSERVATIONS

1. Beginning with insignificant incorrect decisions, such as the prohibition by the Conference of 1814 to teach literacy in Sunday schools (Warner, 235), going on to Wesley's uncritical support of king and Parliament (Thompson, 350; M. Edwards, *This Methodism*, 19f.) to the expulsion of politically active members and the religious proscription of all reform movements (M. Edwards, *After Wesley*, 87ff.; M. S. Edwards, "Methodism and the Chartist Movement," 304f.; W. E. Sangster, 55ff.).
2. On October 25, 1760, Wesley writes in his Journal: "King George (II) was gathered to his fathers. When will England have a better Prince?" *Journal* 4:417. Simon (*Master-Builder*, 95) remarks to this: "We know that Wesley was distinguished for his Loyalty to the reigning monarch; but if the word 'better' refers to the King's moral character, and his devotion to the interests of England, we wonder at the question." Cf. also the case John Wilkes: Kluxen, *Geschichte Englands*, 468ff.; M. Edwards, *John Wesley*, 63f.

3. Cf. MacArthur, J. W. E. Sommer, and W. A. Gifford.
4. Walsh, *HMC*, 307; Vester, 96; W. E. Sangster, *Methodism*, 52f. 59; M. S. Edwards, "Methodism and the Chartist Movement," 306f.; Thompson, 391.
5. For this reason, Williams' statement (30f) that Wesley draws his ethics "entirely from Revelation" is one-sided and incorrect.
6. Cf. to this the gross distortion in C. E. Luthardt, *Geschichte der christlichen Ethik*, Part 2: *Geschichte der christlichen Ethik seit der Reformation* (Leipzig, 1893), 338f., which is satisfied with secondary quotes as proofs!
7. ". . . the time will come when Christianity will prevail overall, and cover the earth . . . a Christian world," a world of peace and love (*Sermons* 1:102f.). Cf. *Letters* 4:294.
8. Schmidt, *RGG* 4:915; M. Edwards, *HMC*, 59; Cameron, 74f.
9. Nicolson, 385f; Kluxen, *Geschichte Englands*, 528f.
10. For this reason, as well, Wesley rejected the doctrine of predestination, which, in the social area, appears to be static.

BIBLIOGRAPHY

JOHN WESLEY'S WRITINGS

Arminian Magazine. 1778-97.
Explanatory Notes upon the New Testament. London, 1831.
The Journal of John Wesley. Edited by N. Curnock. 8 vols. London, 1938.
The Letters of John Wesley. Edited by J. Telford. 8 vols. London, 1931.
Primitive Physic: or, An Easy and Natural Method of Curing Most Diseases. Ed.
 A. W. Hill. London, 1960.
*A Survey of the Wisdom of God in the Creation: or, A Compendium of Natural
 Philosophy.* 2 vols. Bristol, 1770.
Wesley's Standard Sermons. Ed. E. H. Sugden. 2 vols. London, 1921.
The Works of John Wesley. Ed. T. Jackson. 3rd ed. 14 vols. London, 1872.
 Reprinted Grand Rapids, 1958-59.
The Works of John Wesley. Begun as "The Oxford Edition of the Works of
 John Wesley." Oxford, 1975-83. Continued as "The Bicentennial
 Edition of the Works of John Wesley." Nashville, 1984—. 34 vols.
 planned. 13 vols. published to date.

REFERENCE WORKS

The Creeds of Christendom, with a History and Critical Notes. Ed. P. Schaff. 3
 vols. New York, 1877.
Evangelisches Staatslexikon. H. Kunst and S. Grundmann. 2nd ed. Ed. H.
 Kunst, R. Herzog, and W. Schneemelcher. Stuttgart, 1975.
A History of the Methodist Church in Great Britain. Vol. 1. Ed. R. Davies and
 G. Rupp. London, 1965.

New Cambridge Modern History. 14 vols. Cambridge, 1964-74.
Realencyclopaedie für Protestantische Theologie und Kirche. Ed. J. J. Herzog. 3rd edition. Ed. D. Albert Hauck. Leipzig, 1896–1913.
Die Religion in Geschichte und Gegenwart. 3rd ed. 6 vols. plus index vol. Ed. K. Galling, Tübingen, 1957-1965.

SECONDARY LITERATURE

Althaus, P. "Die Bekehrung in reformatorischer und pietistischer Sicht." *Um die Wahrheit des Evangeliums.* Stuttgart, 1962.
_____. *The Theology of Martin Luther.* Trans. Robert C. Schultz. Philadelphia, 1966.
Armytage, W. H. G. *Four Hundred Years of English Education.* 2nd ed. Cambridge, 1970.
_____. *Heaven Below: Utopian Experiments in England, 1560-1960.* London, 1961.
Baker, F. "Methodism and the '45 Rebellion," *LQHR* 172 (1947):325-333.
Barclay, R. *The Inner Life of the Religious Societies of the Commonwealth.* 3rd ed. London, 1879.
Bett, H. *The Spirit of Methodism.* London, 1943.
Beyreuther, E. "Quietismus." *RGG* 5:736-738.
_____. *Zinzendorf und die Christenheit, 1732-1760.* Marburg, 1961.
_____. "Zinzendorf und Luther." *Luther-Jahrbuch* 42 (1961):1-12.
Blaser, Klauspeter. *Wenn Gott schwarz ware. . . Das Problem des Rassismus in Theologie und christlicher Praxis.* Zürich/Freiburg, 1972.
Body, A. H. *John Wesley and Education.* London, 1936.
Bornkamm, G. *Paul.* Trans. D. M. Stalker. New York, 1971.
Bready, J. W. *England Before and After Wesley.* 3rd ed. London, 1939.
_____. *Wesley and Democracy.* Toronto, 1939.
Burtner, R. W. and R. E. Chiles. *A Compend of Wesley's Theology.* New York/Nashville, 1954.
Butterfield, H. "England in the Eighteenth Century." *HMC*, 1-33.
Cameron, R. M. *Methodism and Society in Historical Perspective.* New York, 1961.
Cannon, W. R. *The Theology of John Wesley, With Special Reference to the Doctrine of Justification.* New York/Nashville, 1946.
Carpenter, S. C. *Church and People, 1789-1889.* London, 1959.

Carter, H. *Das Erbe Johannes Wesleys und die Oekumene.* Zürich, 1951.

Cave, S. *The Christian Way. A Study of New Testament Ethics in Relation to Present Problems.* London, 1949.

Cell, G. C. *The Rediscovery of John Wesley.* New York, 1935.

Clarkson, L. A. *The Pre-Industrial Economy in England, 1500-1750.* London, 1971.

Cole, G. D. and Postgate, R. *The Common People, 1746-1946.* Bristol, 1963.

Conzelmann, H. *Commentary on First Corinthians.* Trans. James W. Leitch. *Hermeneia* series. Philadelphia, 1975.

Cragg, G. R. "The Churchman." *Man Versus Society in Eighteenth Century Britain,* ed. J. L. Clifford. Cambridge, 1968.

Cross, W. C. "Wesley and Medicine." *The Magazine for the Wesleyan Methodist Church* 137 (1914):613-18.

Davies, R. E. *Methodism.* London, 1963.

Dibelius, M. "Das soziale Motiv im Neuen Testament." *Botschaft und Geschichte* 1:178-203. Tübingen, 1953.

Dimond, S. G. *The Psychology of the Methodist Revival.* London, 1932.

Edwards, M. *After Wesley: A Study of the Social and Political Influence of Methodism in the Middle Period (1791-1849).* London, 1948.

_____. *John Wesley and the Eighteenth Century: A Study of His Social and Political Influence.* London, 1955.

_____. *This Methodism.* London, 1939.

Edwards, M. S. "Methodism and the Chartist Movement." *LQHR* 191 (1966):301-10.

Eicken, E. von. "Rechtfertigung und Heiligung bei Wesley, dargestellt unter Vergleichung mit den Anschauungen Luthers und des Luthertums." Ph.D. diss., Heidelberg, 1934.

Elert, W. *Morphologie des Luthertums,* vol. 2: *Soziallehren und Sozialwirkungen des Luthertums.* Munich, 1932.

Engels, F. *Die Lage der arbeitenden Klasse in England.* Munich, 1973.

Faulkner, J. A. *Wesley as Sociologist, Theologian, and Churchman.* New York, 1918.

Fischoff, E. "Die protestantische Ethik und der Geist des Kapitalismus." *Social Research.* Vol. 11 (1944), 53-77; reprinted in M. Weber, *Die protestantische Ethik. II. Kritiken und Antikritiken,* ed. J. Winckelmann, 346-379. Munich/Hamburg, 1969.

Flachsmeier, H. R. "John Wesley als Sozialhygieniker und Arzt." M.D. diss., Hamburg, 1957.

Frost, S. B. *Die Autoritätslehre in den Werken John Wesleys.* Munich, 1938.

Geissler, H. "Comenius." *RGG* 1:1853f.

Gerdes, E. W. "John Wesleys Lehre von der Gottesebenbildichkeit des Menschen." Ph.D. diss., Kiel, 1958.

Gifford, W. A. *John Wesley: Patriot and Statesman.* Toronto, 1922.

Gill, F. C. *The Romantic Movement and Methodism: A Study of English Romanticism and the Evangelical Revival.* London, 1937.

Gisler, G. "John Wesleys Tätigkeit und Bedeutung als Arzt." *Schweizer Evangelist* 35 (1928):221-23, 240f., 255-57, 270-73, 284f., 306f., 318f.

Gollwitzer, H. "Krieg und Christentum." *RGG* 4:66-73.

Green, J. B. *John Wesley and William Law.* London, 1945.

Green, V. H. H. *The Young Mister Wesley: A Study of John Wesley and Oxford.* London, 1961.

Gulzow, H. "Kirche und Sklaverei in den zwei Jahrhunderten. Unter besonderer Berücksichtigung der romischen Gemeinde." Ph.D. diss., Kiel, 1966.

Halévy, E. *The Birth of Methodism in England.* Trans. and ed. B. Semmel. Chicago, 1971.

Harding, F. A. J. *The Social Impact of the Evangelical Revival.* London, 1947.

Heussi, K. *Kompendium der Kirchengeschichte.* 13th ed. Tübingen, 1971.

Hildebrandt, F. *Christianity According to the Wesleys.* London, 1956.

_____. *From Luther to Wesley.* London, 1951.

Hill, A. W. *John Wesley among the Physicians. A Study of 18th-century Medicine.* London, 1958.

Hobsbawm, E. J. *Labouring Men.* London, 1968.

Hoffman, G. "Seinsharmonie und Heilsgeschichte bei Jonathan Edwards." Ph.D. diss., Göttingen, 1956.

Hubery, D. S. "Unterweisung und Erziehung." *Der Methodismus,* ed. C. E. Sommer. Stuttgart, 1968.

Hulley, L. D. *To Be and To Do: Exploring Wesley's Thought on Ethical Behaviour.* Pretoria, 1988.

Hutton, W. H. *John Wesley.* London, 1927.

Hynson, L. O. *To Reform the Nation: Theological Foundations of Wesley's Ethics.* Grand Rapids, 1984.

Karrenberg, F. "Sozialethik." *EStL,* 1109-19.

Kawerau, P. "Kirchengeschichte Nordamerikas." *Die Kirche in ihrer Geschichte. Ein Handbuch.* Ed. K.D. Schmidt and E. Wolf. Vol. 4, 1-22.

Kingdon, R. M. "Laissez-faire or Government Control: A Problem for John Wesley." *Church History* 26 (1957):342-54.

Kluxen, K. *Geschichte Englands. Von den Anfängen bis zur Gegenwart.* Stuttgart, 1968.

_____. *Das Problem der politischen Opposition. Entwicklung und Wesen der englischen Zweiparteienpolitik im 18. Jahrhundert.* Freiburg/Munich, 1956.

Knox, Ronald A. *Enthusiasm. A Chapter in the History of Religion with Special Reference to the 17th and 18th Centuries.* Oxford, 1950.

Knudson, A. *The Principles of Christian Ethics.* New York/Nashville, 1943.

Kuczynski, J. *Die Geschichte der Lage der Arbeiter unter dem Kapitalismus.* Vols. 22 and 23. Berlin, 1961-62.

Lacy, H. E. "Authority in John Wesley." *LQHR* 189 (1964):114-19.

Lang, A. *Puritanismus und Pietismus. Studien zu ihrer Entwicklung von M. Butzer bis zum Methodismus.* Vol. 6 in *Beitrage zur Geschichte und Lehre der Reformierten Kirche.* Neukirchen, 1941.

Lean, G. *John Wesley, Anglican.* London, 1964.

Leger, A. *La jeunesse de Wesley.* Paris, 1910.

Lerch, D. *Heil und Heiligung bei John Wesley, dargestellt unter besonderer Berücksichtigung seiner Anmerkungen zum Neuen Testament.* Zürich, 1941.

Lincoln, A. *Some Political and Social Ideas of English Dissent, 1763-1800.* Cambridge, 1938.

Lockyer, T. F. *Paul: Luther: Wesley: A Study in Religious Experience as Illustrative of the Ethic of Christianity.* London, 1922.

Lohse, E. *Commentary on Colossians and Philemon.* Trans. by William R. Poehlmann and Robert J. Karis. *Hermeneia* series. Philadelphia, 1971.

Loofs, F. "Methodismus." *RPTK* 12:747-801.

Lotz, A. *Sklaverei, Staatskirche und Freikirche. Die englischen Bekenntnisse im Kampf um die Aufhebung von Sklavenhandel und Sklaverei.* Vol. 9 in *Kölner Anglistische Arbeiten.* Leipzig, 1929.

Luthardt, C. E. *Geschichte der christlichen Ethik.* Part 2 *Geschichte der christlichen Ethik seit der Reformation.* Leipzig, 1893.

MacArthur, K. W. *The Economic Ethics of John Wesley.* New York/Cincinnati/Chicago, 1936.

Madron, T. W. "John Wesley on Race: A Christian View of Equality." *Methodist History* 2/4 (1963-64):24-34.

_____. "Some Economic Aspects of John Wesley's Thought Revisited." *Methodist History* 4/1 (1965-66):33-43.

Marlowe, J. *The Puritan Tradition in English Life.* London, 1956.

Marsh, D. L. "Methodism and Early Methodist Theological Education." *Methodist History* 1/1 (1963-64):3-13.

Mathews, H. F. *Methodism and the Education of the People, 1791-1851.* London, 1949.

Michael, W. *Englische Geschichte im achtzehnten Jahrhundert.* Vols. 1-5. Hamburg/Leipzig/Basel, 1896-1955.

Monk, R. C. *John Wesley, His Puritan Heritage: A Study of the Christian Life.* Nashville, 1966.

Muelder, W. G. "Methodism's Contribution to Social Reform." *Methodism,* ed. W. K. Anderson. Cincinnati, 1947.

Newton, J. A. *Methodism and the Puritans.* London, 1964.

Nicolson, H. *The Age of Reason.* London, 1960.

Niebuhr, H. R. "Individual- und Sozialethik." *RGG* 3:715-20.

North, E. M. *Early Methodist Philanthropy.* New York/Cincinnati, 1914.

Nuelsen, J. L. "John Wesley als Bahnbrecher der inneren Mission und der sozialen Reform." *Deutsch-Amerikanische Zeitschrift für Theologie und Kirche* 24 (1903-04):1-14.

_____. *Kurzgefasste Geschichte des Methodismus von seinen Anfängen bis zur Gegenwart.* 2nd ed. Bremen, 1929.

Orcibal, J. "The Theological Originality of John Wesley and Continental Spirituality." *HMC,* 81-111.

Outler, A. C. *John Wesley.* New York, 1964.

_____. "Theologische Akzente." *Der Methodismus,* ed. C. E. Sommer. Stuttgart, 1968.

Pask, A. H. "The Influence of Arminius on John Wesley." *LQHR* 185 (1960):58-263.

Peppermüller, R. "Abaelards Auslegung des Romerbriefes." *Beiträge zur Geschichte der Philosophie und Theologie des Mittelalters. Texte und Untersuchungen.* New Series, vol. 10. Munster, 1972.

Pfaff-Giesberg, R. *Geschichte der Sklaverei.* Meisenheim/Glan, 1955.

Piette, Maximin. *John Wesley in the Evolution of Protestantism.* London, 1937.

Plumb, J. H. *England in the Eighteenth Century.* Harmondsworth, 1950.

Prince, J. W. *Wesley on Religious Education. A Study of John Wesley's Theories and Methods of the Education of Children in Religion.* New York/Cincinnati, 1926.

Purifoy, L. M. "The Methodist Anti-Slavery Tradition, 1784-1844." *Methodist History* 1/4 (1965-66):3-16.

Rattenbury, J. E. *Wesley's Legacy to the World: Six Studies in the Permanent Values of the Evangelical Revival.* 3rd ed. London, 1938.

Renkewitz, H. "Sozialethik des Pietismus." *EStL,* 1127-30.

Rupp, E. G. "Luther in der englischen Theologie." *Lutherische Rundschau* 5 (1955):12-24.

_____. *Methodism in Relation to Protestant Tradition.* London, 1954.

_____. *Principalities and Powers.* London, 1952.

Sangster, W. E. *Methodism: Her Unfinished Task.* London, 1947.

Schempp, J. *Seelsorge und Seelenführung bei John Wesley.* Stuttgart, 1949.

Schilling, S. P. *Methodism and Society in Theological Perspective.* New York, 1960.

Schmidt, M. "Die Bedeutung Luthers für John Wesleys Bekehrung," *Luther-Jahrbuch* 20 (1938):130

_____. "England und der deutsche Pietismus." *Evangelische Theologie* 13 (1953):205-44.

_____. "Englischer Deismus." *RGG* 2:59-69.

_____. "Methodismus." *RGG* 4:913-19.

_____. "Die ökumenische Bedeutung John Wesleys." *Theologische Literaturzeitung* 78 (1953):449-60.

_____. "Pietismus." *RGG* 5:370-81.

_____. "Universalismus." *RGG* 6:1157f.

_____. *The Young Wesley: Missionary and Theologian of Missions.* Trans. L. A. Fletcher. London, 1958.

Schmidt, Martin. *John Wesley: A Theological Biography.* 2 Vols. in 3. Trans. Norman P. Goldhawk. New York/Nashville, 1962-73.

Schneeberger, V. *Theologische Wurzeln des sozialen Akzents bei John Wesley.* Zürich, 1974.

Schrage, W. *Ethik des Neuen Testaments.* Göttingen, 1974.

Schrey, H. H. *Einführung in die Ethik.* Darmstadt, 1972.

Schulz, S. *Gott ist kein Sklavenhalter. Die Geschichte einer verspäteten Revolution.* Hamburg/Zürich, 1972.

Schweitzer, A. *The Philosophy of Civilization.* Trans. C. T. Campion. New York, 1949.

Scott, P. *John Wesleys Lehre von der Heiligung, verglichen mit einem lutherische-pietistischen Beispiel.* Vol. 17 in *Studien zur Geschichte des neueren Protestantismus.* Berlin, 1939.

Sellers, J. *Theological Ethics.* New York/London, 1968.

Sherwin, O. *John Wesley: Friend of the People.* New York, 1961.

Sigg, F. "John Wesley und 'Die Christliche Bibliothek,' Einblicke in die verlegerische Tätigkeit des Methodismus im 18. Jahrhundert." *Schweizer Evangelist* 60 (1953):381-85.

Simon, J. S. *John Wesley and the Religious Societies.* London, 1921.

_____. *John Wesley and the Methodist Societies.* London, 1923.

_____. *John Wesley and the Advance of Methodism.* London, 1925.

_____. *John Wesley: The Master-Builder.* London, 1927.

_____. *John Wesley: The Last Phase.* London, 1934.

Sommer, C. E. "John Wesley und die Mystik." *Mitteilungen der Studiengemeinschaft für Geschichte des Methodismus.* Vol. 3, parts 1/2, 6-22. Frankfurt, 1965.

_____. "John William Fletcher (1729-1785): Mann der Mitte. Prolegomena zu seinem Verständnis." *Basileia. Walter Freytag zum 60. Geburtstag.* Ed. J. Hermelink and H.J. Margull. Stuttgart, 1959.

Sommer, C.E., ed. *Der Methodismus.* Stuttgart, 1968.

Sommer, E. F. "John Wesley, eine bibliographische Skizze." *Mitteilungen der Studiengemeinschaft für Geschichte des Methodismus* 4 (1966-67):4-47.

Sommer, J. W. E. *John Wesley und die soziale Frage.* Vol. 1 in *Beiträge zur Geschichte des Methodismus.* Bremen, 1930.

Southey, R. *The Life of Wesley and the Rise and Progress of Methodism.* 2 vols. London, 1925.

Spector, R. D. *English Literary Periodicals and the Climate of Opinion During the Seven Years' War.* The Hague, 1966.

Stadtland, T. *Rechtfertigung und Heiligung bei Calvin.* Vol. 32 in *Beiträge zur Geschichte und Lehre der Reformierten Kirche.* Neukirchen-Vluyn, 1972.

Staehelin, E. *Die Verkündigung des Reiches Gottes in der Kirche Jesu Christi. Zeugnisse aus allen Jahrhunderten und allen Konfessionen.* Vol. 6 in *Von der Mitte des 18. bis zur Mitte des 19. Jahrhunderts.* Basel, 1963.

Standop, E. and E. Mertner. *Englische Literaturgeschichte.* Heidelberg, 1971.

Starkey, L. M., Jr. *The Work of the Holy Spirit: A Study in Wesleyan Theology.* New York/Nashville, 1962.

Telford, J. *The Life of John Wesley.* London, 1899.

_____. "John Wesley." *Encyclopaedia Britannica,* 11th ed., 28:1157f.

Thiel, W. "Sonntagsschule I. In Europa und Amerika." *RGG* 6:144f.

Thomas, W. *Heiligung im Neuen Testaments und bei Wesley.* Zürich, 1965.

Thompson, E. P. *The Making of the English Working Class.* London, 1963.

Todd, J. M. *John Wesley and the Catholic Church.* London, 1958.

Towlson, C. W. *Moravian and Methodist: Relationships and Influences in the Eighteenth Century.* London, 1957.

Trevelyan, G. M. *History of England,* Vol. 2: *From 1603 to 1918.* London and Colchester, 1956.

_____. *English Social History: A Survey of Six Centuries, Chaucer to Queen Victoria.* London: 1946.

Trillhaas, W. *Ethik.* 3rd ed. Berlin, 1970.

_____. "Natur und Christentum." *RGG* 4:1326-29.

Troeltsch, E. *The Social Teaching of the Christian Churches*. Trans. Olive Wyon. 2 vols. New York/London, 1931.

_____. *Die Sozialphilosophie des Christentums*. Gotha, 1922.

Tyerman, L. *Life and Times of the Rev. John Wesley, M.A.* 3rd ed. 3 vols. London, 1876.

Urwin, E. C. and D. Wollen. *John Wesley—Christian Citizen. Selections from his Social Teaching*. London, 1937.

Vester, M. *Die Entstehung des Proletariats als Lernprozess. Die Entstehung antikapitalistischer Theorie und Praxis in England 1792-1848. Veröffentlichungen des Psychologischen Seminars der Technischen Universität Hannover*. Frankfurt, 1970.

Voigt, K. H. "Aus der Geschichte der Gefängnisreform in England." *Die Innere Mission* 58 (1968):374-81.

_____. "Diakonia: Der Christ in der Gesellschaft." *Der Methodismus*, ed. C. E. Sommer. Stuttgart, 1968.

Voll, D. *Hochkirchlicher Pietismus. Die Aufnahme der evangelikalen Traditionen durch die Oxford-Bewegung in der zweiten Hälfte des neunzehnten Jahrhunderts. Ein Beitrag zum Verständnis des neueren Anglikanismus*. Vol. 19 in *Forschungen zur Geschichte und Lehre des Protestantismus*. Series 10. Munich, 1960.

Vulliamy, C. E. *John Wesley*. 3rd ed. London. 1954.

Wallace, W. M. "John Wesley and the American Revolution." *Essays in Honor of Conyers Read*, ed. N. Downs. Chicago, 1953.

Walsh, J. "Methodism at the End of the Eighteenth Century." *HMC*, 275-315.

Warner, W. J. *The Wesleyan Movement in the Industrial Revolution*. 2nd ed. New York, 1967.

Watkin-Jones, H. *The Holy Spirit from Arminius to Wesley: A Study of Christian Teaching Concerning the Holy Spirit and His Place in the Trinity in the Seventeenth and Eighteenth Centuries*. London, 1929.

Watson, D. L. *The Early Methodist Class Meeting: Its Origins and Significance*. Nashville, 1985.

Watson, P. "Wesley and Luther on Christian Perfection." *The Ecumenical Review* 15 (1962-63):291-302.

Wearmouth, R. F. *Methodism and the Common People of the Eighteenth Century*. London, 1945.

Weber, H. "Wirtschaftsethik." *RGG* 6:1740-47.

Weber, M. *Gesammelte Aufsätze zur Religionssoziologie*. 4th ed. Vol. 1. Tübingen, 1947.

_____. *Die protestantische Ethik.* 2 vols. I. *Eine Aufsatzsammlung.* II. *Kritiken und Antikritiken.* 2nd ed. Ed. J. Winckelmann. Munich/Hamburg, 1969.

_____. *The Protestant Ethic and the Spirit of Capitalism.* Trans. Talcott Parsons. New York, 1958.

Weber, O. *Grundlagen der Dogmatik.* 2 vols. Neukirchen-Vluyn: Neukirchener Verlag, 1955. Vol. 1 rev. 1964; vol. 2 rev. 1962.

Weerda, J. "Sozialethik des Calvinismus." *EStL*, 1119-23.

Wehr, G. *Jakob Böhme in Selbstzeugnissen und Bilddokumenten.* Reinbek: Rowohlt, 1971.

Weissbach, J. *Der neue Mensch im theologischen Denken John Wesleys. Beiträge zur Geschichte des Methodismus.* 2nd supplement. Stuttgart, 1970.

Wendland, H. D. *Einführung in die Sozialethik.* Berlin, 1971.

_____. *Ethik des Neuen Testaments.* Vol. 4 in *Das Neue Testament Deutsch, Ergänzungsreihe: Grundrisse zum Neuen Testament.* Ed. G. Friedrich. Göttingen, 1970.

_____. "Sklaverei und Christentum." *RGG* 6:101-4.

Whiteley, J. H. *Wesley's England. A Survey of 18th Century Social and Cultural Conditions.* London, 1945.

Williams, C. W. *John Wesley's Theology Today.* Nashville, 1960.

Wolf, Ernst. "Naturrecht I. Profanes Naturrecht." *RGG* 4:1353-59.

_____. "Naturrecht II. Christliches Naturrecht." *RGG* 4:1359-65.

_____. "Sozialethik des Luthertums." *EStL*, 1124-27.

Wölfel, E. "Naturrecht." *EStL*, 1360-64.

INDEX

A Word to a Smuggler, 45
Abolition (anti-slavery movement), 67, 70-72, 75, 85, 134
Ad absurdum, 124
Adoption, 90
Adult education, 55-60, 62
Adultery, 120
Africa, 67-68, 73
Alcohol, 28, 36, 46, 80, 131
America, 22, 67, 71, 75, 127, 130
Anglican (Church of England), 22-23, 27, 46, 49-50, 54, 58, 68, 71, 79, 95, 99, 101, 115, 123, 133
Anthropology, 60-62
Antiquity, 120
Apologetics, 125
Apprenticeship, 20, 50
Aristocracy, 123
Arminian, 58
Arminian Magazine, 54, 58
Asceticism, 26, 41, 115, 122
Asiento clause, 68
Atheist, 62, 65, 105-6
Atonement, 91, 110
Augustine, 95, 101, 103
Augustinian, 90
Authority, 21, 46, 48, 61-62, 64, 79-80, 85, 115, 118, 123-25

Baas, E., 13
Ball, Hannah, 54

Bank of England, 36
Baptism, 63, 69, 71
Baptists, 50, 73
Begging, 20
Benezet, Anthony, 73
Bible, 25, 54, 74, 82, 118, 125
Birkner, H. J., 13
Bockmühl, K., 13
Book of Common Prayer, 22, 25
Boston Tea Party, 127
Bowmer, John, 13
Breweries, 44-45
Bristol, 51-52, 81
Brutality, 21, 79-80, 84, 121
Burke, Edmund, 47

Calvin(ist), 58, 74, 101, 105
Cambridge, 56
Capitalism, 42
Capitalist spirit, 39, 41-43
Catechism, 22, 54, 63
Catholic(ism), 54, 69, 72, 99, 135
Ceremonial law, 110
Charitable work, 27-28, 32-33, 84, 122
Charity Schools, 50, 53
Charterhouse, 51
Christian Library, 58, 116
Christology, 108
Civil officials, 24
Clarkson, Thomas, 75
Class leader, 28

Class meeting, 15, 28
Clemency, 82
Comenius, 61
Colonies, 67, 75, 127, 129
Commandment(s), 26, 32-33, 37, 39, 45, 48, 62, 109, 110-14, 116, 118, 121, 124, 136
Community(ies), 33, 38, 115-16, 122, 126
Condemnation, 112
Congregational schools, 53
Conscience, 93-94, 112-13, 124, 128, 134, 136
Conservative(ism), 21, 32, 72, 85, 133
Conversion, 104, 119
Corruption, 39
Creation, 33, 92, 122
Creator, 33, 37-38, 48, 74, 90-91, 97, 104, 106-8
Crime, 80, 84

Dagge, Abel, 83
Dahn, K., 13
Davin, D. M., 13
Debt(ors), 77-78, 80, 83
Decalogue, 110
Deism, 65, 117, 120
Democracy, 123-25, 127
Descartes, R., 65
Devil, 61, 91, 98-99
Dictatorship, 123
Diderot, 70
Dissent(ers), 22
Dissenting academies, 50
Divine punishment, 30
Doctrine, 24, 95, 113, 115
Dreams, 117
Drunk(ard), 83, 120

Ecclesiastical officials, 24, 79, 82, 126
Economics ethics, 35, 41
Economy(ics), 21, 42, 44, 47-48, 67
Education, 24, 29, 49-66, 71, 128
Eicken, E. von, 93
Election, 43, 58
Elizabethan era, 20
Emancipation, 75
England, 19, 21, 30, 34, 45, 49, 57, 67-68, 75, 124-25
English Africa Company, 68
Enlightenment, 65, 70, 74, 90, 116-17, 120, 136
Epworth, 26, 51
Eschatology, 38, 69, 72

Essay on Human Understanding (John Locke), 60, 65
Ethical norm, 25
Ethics, 32, 41, 74, 94, 118, 135-36
Evangelism, 22, 27, 49, 71, 77, 81, 128
Evil, 32, 36, 43-44, 47, 64, 70, 90, 94, 97, 103, 120, 122-23, 128
Execution, 78
Extortion, 80

Factories, 28
Faith, 64, 95-101, 103-4, 107-8, 111-14, 118, 135
Fall, the, 90-93, 95, 109
Farmers, 20, 134
Fasting, 24, 47, 75
Fatalism, 44, 120
Fideism, 100
Fornication, 120
Fox, George, 70
Francke, A. H., 61, 116
Fraud, 37, 45
Free will, 90
Freedom, 45, 68, 97, 110, 113, 125, 128-29
Fruit of the Spirit, 98, 112

Gebhardt, R., 13
General Conference, 72, 83, 92
Georgia, 23, 25, 28, 51, 71-72, 77, 114
German(y), 11-13, 83, 99, 116
Ghosts, 117
Gibson, Edmund, 68
Gloucester Journal, 54
Golden Rule, 111
Good(ness), 36, 94-95, 97, 103, 122, 128
Governmental groups, 46
Grace, 28, 61, 64-65, 81-82, 90-91, 93-97, 100-1, 105, 108, 113, 135
Gruneke, K. H., 13

Halle, 51, 116
Happiness, 26, 48, 62, 64, 91, 105, 108, 122
Harle, W., 13
Herms, E., 13
Herrnhut(ters), 51, 61, 96, 97, 99
High Wycombe, 54
Holiness, 91, 98, 108
Holy Communion, 22, 71
Holy Spirit, 64-65, 94, 96-99, 101, 105, 108, 112, 118
Honesty, 36
Horneck, Anton, 22

Hospitals, 22, 28
House of Commons, 68
Household of faith, 37
Howard, John, 80, 83
Human rights, 74, 136
Humanist(ic), 49, 105-6
Humanitarian(ism), 21, 48, 82-83, 134
Hume, David, 106

Imago Dei (image of God), 92-94
Imitation of Christ (Thomas à Kempis), 57
Indians (Native Americans), 25, 72
Industrial Revolution, 19, 41, 43, 134
Industrialization, 20, 67
Injustice, 79

Johnson, Samuel, 130
Judge, 37
Justice, 48, 69, 74, 78, 128
Justification, 26, 33, 41, 82, 90, 93-101,
    103-4, 108, 110-12, 114, 119, 136

King of England, 46-47, 68, 77, 85,
    124-25, 127, 130, 133-34
Kingswood, 51, 53, 55-57, 62
Kumm, K., 13
Kuczynski, Jürgen, 19

Labor unions, 136-37
Latin schools, 49
Law, William, 22-23, 104, 116
Legal(ism), 101, 104, 107
Life of Savage (Samuel Johnson), 83
Liverpool, 68
Loan fund, 29
Locke, John, 60-61, 65, 117, 131
London Society for the Establishment of
    Sunday Schools, 54
London, 29, 34, 51-52, 58-59, 68, 81
Loofs, F., 97
Lord Herbert of Cherbury, 65
Lower classes, 19, 28, 32, 36, 42, 50, 53, 55,
    57, 78, 121
Luther, Martin, 26, 40, 100, 135
Lutheran, 40, 58, 99-100

Medical care, 20, 28-29
Medicine, 24, 28, 122
Mennonites, 70, 73
Methodism, 11, 15-16, 34, 37, 39, 41-42,
    46, 53-54, 58, 81, 107, 115-17, 119-20,
    122, 127, 134, 136
Methodist fellowships, 30, 35, 53

Methodist schools, 51-53, 57
Milton, John, 60-61
Mind of Christ, 39, 66, 97, 108-9, 114
Missions, 72
Monarchy, 123-25
Moral law, 110, 136
Moravians, 26, 71, 99-100
Moses, 110-11
Mystics, 99

Natural law, 74, 127
Natural man, 89-92, 98
Negro's Advocate, 71
Neighbor(s), 26, 31-33, 36, 39-41, 43,
    103-9, 114, 120-21
Newcastle upon Tyne, 52
Newgate Prison, 81, 83
Nutrition, 28, 44

Oglethorpe, General, 71, 77
Oligarchy, 123
Outler, Albert, 96
Oxford, circle, 23, 26, 77
Oxford Holy Club, 23-24, 31, 103, 113
Oxford University, 19, 23, 51, 56, 123

Parliament(ary), 20, 46-47, 68, 74-75, 78,
    85, 125, 127, 130-31, 134
Pastoral care, 53, 63, 71, 80, 82-84, 119
Pastors, 68-69, 71, 81-82
Peace, 48, 130-31
Pedagogy(ical), 49, 51, 56, 60-61, 71
Pelagianism, 92
Penal law, 77-78, 131
Penal system, 128, 134
Pharmacies/clinics, 29
Philanthropy, 21-22
Philosophy, 117
Physicians, 28, 58
Physics, 117
Pietism, 22-23, 26, 51, 61, 63, 65-66, 91,
    99, 101, 103-4, 116, 121
Police, 46, 78
Poor house, 20, 34, 134
Poor-laws, 20, 132
Poverty, 21, 27-34, 38, 42-43, 71, 74, 122,
    132
Praxis, 11, 41, 72, 89, 99, 134-35, 137
Prayer, 47, 54, 75
Preaching, 63, 71, 82, 112, 117, 119-20,
    125, 136
Predestination, 105, 120
Prejudice, 131

Presbyterian, 50
Prevenient grace *(gratia praeveniens)*, 89-95, 101, 103
Primitive Christianity, 115-16
Primitive Physic, 29, 57
Prison, 24-25, 28, 77-86, 131, 134
Prison reform, 80, 83
Prisoners of war, 83, 85
Private schools, 49
Professional ethics, 40
Proletariat, 120
Property, 36, 78-79, 124
Property owners, 20, 23, 30, 41, 46
Prophets, 110
Prostitution, 80, 83
Protestant(ism), 42-43, 54, 74, 99, 127
Public schools, 49-50
Punishment, 21, 40, 61, 74, 79, 80-81, 84
Puritan, 41, 105, 124

Quakers, 50, 70, 72-73, 128
Quietism, 99, 101, 105

Raikes, Robert, 54
Reason, 116-18, 136
Reconciliation, 130
Redeemer, 33, 107
Reformers, 40, 89, 91, 96-97
Reformation, 69, 111, 135
Regeneration, 98
Religious societies, 22-23, 27
Repentance, 109, 112
Republican, 125, 127, 133
Revenge, 85, 90
Righteous(ness), 131
Robbe, H., 13
Rousseau, Jean-Jacques, 60, 62, 70, 73

Salvation, 26, 39, 95, 122
Sanctification, 26, 33, 89, 95-99, 107, 109, 111-12, 114, 119, 121, 136
Schneeberger, V., 13, 15
Schools, 22, 24, 49-54, 57, 71, 131
Schultz, Siegfried, 72
Schwabe, B., 13
Science, 27, 50, 65, 90
Scripture, 58, 62, 64-65, 94, 115, 117-18
Sense experience, 65
Sermon on the Mount, 40, 111, 114, 135
Shakespeare, William, 57, 60
Sheeby, E. P., 13
Simul iustus et peccator, 109
Slaveholder, 67, 71-75

Slave merchants, 67, 74
Slavery, 67-75, 127-28, 130-31
Smith, Adam, 131
Smithies, Richard, 22
Smuggling, 45-46, 131
Social agencies, 20
Social groups, 44-46
Social history, 27
Social justice, 32, 38, 121
Social obligation, 39, 44, 46, 121
Social reform, 30
Social work, 19, 22-26, 30, 49, 51, 60, 63, 89, 100, 116, 119-20, 122, 125, 131, 134
Socialism, 19
Society for Promoting Christian Knowledge (SPCK), 22, 50-51, 71
Society for the Propagation of the Gospel, 22
Solafideism, 99-100
Sommer, Bishop Dr. C. E., 13
Soteriology 72, 135
Spain, 67-68
Steckel, K., 13
Stocks, Thomas, 54
Stolte, J. E., 61
Stuart, Charles, 127
Sunday schools, 54-56

Tax(ation), 44-47, 129, 134
Taxation no Tyranny (Samuel Johnson), 130
Taylor, Jeremy, 22-23
Teachers, 24, 50, 52
The State of Prisons in England and Wales (John Howard), 84
Theological ethic, 49
Theologians, 15-16, 26, 32, 73, 82, 85, 89, 94, 96, 99-101, 105, 108, 111, 116-18, 128
Thirty-Nine Articles, 95
Thomas à Kempis, 23, 57
Thoughts on the Present Scarcity of Provisions, 44
Thoughts upon Slavery, 73, 75
Three simple rules, 35, 41
Tories, 46, 123-24, 126-27, 131, 133
Trade union, 127
Troeltsch, Ernst, 116, 121
Tucker, Josiah, 44, 47

Utrecht peace accord, 68

Vester, M., 42
Visions, 117

Voigt, K. H., 13
Voltaire, 106

War, 128-30
Warburton, Bishop Weber, M., 68-69, 93
Weissbach, J., 101
West Indies, 68, 74
Whig, 124-25
Whitefield, George, 26, 51, 71
Wilberforce, W., 68, 75
Will of God, 26, 37, 39, 52, 58, 62, 64-65, 69, 90-92, 95, 98, 109-11, 113, 118

Witches, 64, 117
Wittwer, W., 13
Wölfel, W., 13
Worldly goods, 35-36
Workhouse, 22, 24, 28
Works, 42, 94, 96, 98-101, 103, 105, 110-11, 114, 135
Works-righteousness, 26, 99-100, 104, 135
Wüthrich, P., 13